WHY THE WORLD DOESN'T END

DOESN'T END

Tales of Renewal in Times of Loss

Illustration for Cover

The cosmic egg or world egg is a mythic image of the primal unity that appears in many creation stories. Often the egg is golden and is first found floating on the endless ocean of chaos in the time before time began. Eventually life stirs inside the egg and as the original vitality begins to grow it cracks the egg and creation begins. Some stories say that Eros, the god of love and all connections, was the first to emerge from the primal egg. The breaking of the original oneness leads to the creation of the many, but the origin of everything is shared.

In Sunrise by the Ocean, *the painter Vladimir Kush has captured the ancient sense of the world egg that cracks open to reveal the golden orb of the sun. He sets the primordial images in a modern context that seems to suggest the need to repair the egg of world. At the same time the golden sun rises where the egg has cracked as if to remind us of the myth of the eternal return of dawn from the primal ocean of life.*

The painting appears on the cover of this book about the eternal "world behind the world" that secretly renews life from the ends of time. We are grateful to the artist for his generosity in making the image available.

Sunrise by the Ocean

WHY THE WORLD DOESN'T END

Tales of Renewal in Times of Loss

MICHAEL MEADE

GreenFire Press

An Imprint of Mosaic Multicultural Foundation

GreenFire Press
An Imprint of Mosaic Multicultural Foundation

Contents

I

Holding the Thread of Life

CHAPTER 1

THE STORY OF APOCALYPSE

*The end lies concealed in the beginning; but the opposite is also true.
The beginning is hidden in all that comes to an end.*

Sometimes the only place to begin is at the end. Sometimes it seems that the end could come at any moment and we have to face the darkness in order to find ways to begin again. When culture seems about to unravel and even nature seems to rattle and reel, ideas and images of "the End" can occur to anyone. Periods of great uncertainty and radical change can stir our deepest forebodings and awaken the darkest corners of our souls, where fears of catastrophe and apocalyptic endings reside and have always resided. For fears of the end have been with us from the very beginning. When the balance of the world slips towards chaos, nightmares of apocalypse can rise to the surface and affect even the most rational of people. It has happened many times, for the world often seems on the verge of collapse or complete disaster.

Tales of apocalyptic endings can be found in most cultures; like stories of creation they are part of the human inheritance of myth and imagination. Endings and beginnings are mythic moments par excellence; they are the extremities of existence and the bookends of cosmology. Whereas creation stories tend to gather the potentials of life and establish the elegant orders of nature, end-time dramas feature violent storms and monstrous beasts as the underside of creation erupts and chaos threatens to undermine all levels of order. At the apocalyptic extremes, the basic elements turn against life as waters flood, fire falls from the sky, the earth quakes, and everything that exists is brought to the edge of annihilation.

Apocalypse represents The End written in large letters; the mother of all catastrophes driven forth by a withering wind of destruction, a veritable cosmic blast that threatens to end it all for once and for all. Yet there is more to the story of apocalypse, more to the meaning of the word itself. Even a word that seems to announce the very end of everything has to have a beginning and "apocalypse" begins with ancient Greek terms like *apokalein* and *apokalypsis*. These root words mean "to reveal" and "to uncover;" they can also mean "to disclose" and "to discover." Apocalyptic events and times are revelatory, but in more ways than one. While raw energies of life may become uncovered and the trouble in the world may intensify, there is also a greater possibility that hidden meanings might become revealed and new ways of proceeding become discovered.

Although most often used to proclaim the final, fiery end of everything, another root meaning of *apocalypsis* is "to lift the veil;" to reveal what was concealed, to disclose what was hidden behind closed doors; to uncover what was covered over as well as what has been covered up. When not taken literally or religiously, the archetypal dynamic of apocalypse refers to what happens when the web of life loosens, when the veils lift and the underlying forces of life become more palpable and evident; but also more transparent. Old structures may collapse and once vital systems may fall apart; yet other patterns and barely imagined designs are on the verge of being revealed.

Ends and beginnings may be polar opposites, but like most opposed things, they are secretly connected. Part of the revelation of the end-times is that things do not actually end altogether. In the great drama of the world, the end leads back to the beginning and, from what went before, things begin again. No one can say for sure, but The End that has been feared since the beginning and has been predicted many times before has never quite come.

Words are condensed stories and like a good story, each word carries more than one meaning. The meaning of the word "end" might seem obvious and conclusive; yet root meanings of the word reveal "tailings" and "remnants," and "that which is left over." Even when we come to the very end we find that there are "loose ends" that cannot simply be tied up. For there is always something left over, a remnant or remainder that remains; a residue that persists. This is not simple wordplay, for something mysterious and essential about the world we live in is being hinted at.

The "world as we know it" may come to an end; that has happened many times before. Yet the fiery conclusion of all creation, so greatly feared and seemingly close at hand, never quite arrives. The final judgment keeps being postponed and the literal end of time remains an unfulfilled prediction. When everything goes out of balance and seems about to fall apart, the issue is not the actual end of the world as much as what to do when it seems about to end.

The Apocalypse of John

Common conceptions of apocalypse mostly derive from the use of the word in the opening verse of the fiery text that became the final book of the New Testament. It was natural for the author, writing in ancient Greek, to use the word "apokalypsis" to begin the revelatory vision of hell on earth that had gripped him and compelled him to write. When translated, the burning vision became known as The Book of Revelation, or simply using the first word of the text: The Apocalypse.

Few details are known about the life of the man who became known as John of the Apocalypse or about the events that led him to a solitary life in a cave on the island of Patmos in the Aegean Sea. It was about the year AD 96 and the original audience for the incendiary writings consisted of persecuted Christians and other visionaries living through a time of radical change. Like the current era, it was a period of great upheaval and wild uncertainty. Chaos was in the air, political conflicts were everywhere, and new spiritual visions were battling old religious practices. People were uncertain about the future and anxious about the present.

It is likely that John had been preaching revolution as well as revelations. Prophecy with political implications would likely have been perceived as a threat to the stability of Roman rule as well as a danger to those holding local power. Early in the text the writer refers to himself as, "John, your brother and partner in hardships." A key part of John's hardship involved the fact that Patmos was a prison island at the time and he had been sentenced to permanent exile for rabble rousing and preaching unorthodox and disturbing messages.

John seems to have woven together threads of older apocalyptic stories. And he seems to have taken his end-time vision of horned beasts, false prophets, lakes of fire, and fiery dragons literally; ever since then many others have taken it the same way. Near the end of the book, in true apocalyptic style, the prophet declares to his readers that the ultimate battle between good and evil and all the horrific events he has described will happen soon. He attests that an angel sent by Jesus informed him that the apocalypse was imminent and people should prepare for the end. The sense of immediacy and urgency is part of the core dynamic of apocalypsis. Yet time went on, the year AD 100 came and went. There was great turmoil and trouble of all kinds, but the world persisted and so did the vision of John of Patmos.

The idea and image of a final drama between the forces of good and evil leading to a fiery end of everything is deeply imbedded in the human psyche and so compelling to some that they simply overlook the fact that it never happens the way the prophets predict. Christians in the first century believed that the end of the world would come during their lifetime. When the world-ending cataclysm did not occur the apocalyptic calendar was reset for the year 300AD. When the expected storm of disasters did not arrive, the focus shifted to the year 500. The approach of the first millennium, with its array of zeros, seemed certain to be the ultimate year and final date. Yet time turned over and the terminal predictions again remained unfulfilled.

There has always been a fascination with the concept of zero and a tendency to dramatically countdown to a point of nil that nullifies everything. Even when the date proclaimed for the end of all time does not conclude with a zero point, it will somehow involve notions of a zero date. Modern fascinations with the intricacies of ancient Mayan calendars focus upon the year 2012, which does not end in zero. However, 2012 is considered to mark the last year in the Mayan Long Count calendar, one of the oldest and most accurate of all time keeping devices. Although

Mayan myths consider creation to be ongoing, many have fixed on the zero date of the ancient calendar as the final end of all time. Once the idea of an apocalyptic ending has been taken literally, a final date must be chosen; better yet, it must seem to have been revealed by a divine source. Whenever there is a period of radical uncertainty and cultural disorientation, a date will be found that seems to settle everything by ending it all. As an archetypal condition, the end is always near; as an actual historical event, it never comes.

Beliefs about "the End" tend to be not only predetermined but also over determined. Whenever the end seems near, there is a tendency to literalize as well as to finalize things. The usual problem with predictions of "the End" is that people take it literally and believe in it absolutely. Instead of a period when the veils lift and many things become revealed, people imagine the falling of the final curtain that dramatically concludes all aspects of creation. Instead of seeing the end of an era or a great turning point in time psychologically, people tend to see it historically and literally. Those who insist on an exact date for the beginning of creation tend to require an exact time for the destruction of all that has been created.

In the end however, it seems that the world outlasts the last days and outlives its own demise. Even at the end of a great cycle when things progress faster and faster, the zero date comes and goes. Despite dire predictions, time turns over and the calendar begins to count all over again. "Calendar," of course, has many meanings as well as many days. Ancient Romans counted months by the appearance of the new moon. They termed the first days of each month the *calends*, meaning "the called." What we now think of as a document to be read or a schedule to be followed was originally a verb meaning "to call, to announce; to cry out." One of the oldest phrases associated with calendars is "dawn-calling," as if to remind people that even calendars look forward to the dawn of the next day, the beginning of next period or of the next world. No one can prove it before hand, but so far, at the end of all the counting down, there comes another dawn and a new day and the counting starts up again.

Apocalypsis

The fact that a plethora of dates for the final end have already come and gone does not keep people from thinking that this time the End will actually come. For the archetype of apocalypse describes a psychological condition or state of mind that becomes more activated during times of tragedy and loss and when radical change is predominant. The energies inherent in apocalypse include raw emotions, deep vulnerabilities, wild fantasies and extreme attitudes. When the archetype is activated "the center cannot hold;" there can be wild mood swings and surges of paranoia. There can be fantastical prophecies on one hand and literalizing tendencies on the other with no common ground to be found between. The sense of the end-times pushes everything to the far ends as intense oppositions develop and extreme positions become commonplace. While some use the zero point of the Mayan calendar to predict the final end, others use the same date for the dawning of a new age that has more of the characteristics of Paradise. The paradox of apocalypse continues to express itself in opposing beliefs about a specific date, or symbol, or text.

Often apocalyptic prophecies reveal most about those having the revelatory experience. In the case of John of Patmos it seems no accident that his overwhelming vision came after suffering condemnation, isolation, and a long imprisonment. A literal belief in apocalyptic endings is attractive to those who feel trapped by their life circumstances, often those who have been painfully rejected by the world around them. There is a psychological connection, even an underlying dynamic between extreme feelings of oppression or rejection and notions of worldwide destruction. Often there is an element of fanatic resentment against others for refusing to see the world in the same way. Whether they are actually imprisoned or just feel essentially trapped, they see no practical way out of their oppressive circumstances and no effective way to change the world around them. If a sense of rejection is all this god-forsaken world can offer them, then let the whole thing be destroyed.

John of the Apocalypse states that an angel from god has revealed to him that the end-times were near. He describes how he is drawn to a voice that he hears as coming from behind him. A psychological rather than a religious interpretation would suggest that the voice comes from the unconscious, which can be felt to be within us, but also can be experienced as behind us. The unconscious involves not just the deeper layers of individual memory, but also the collective archaic past of humanity. The compelling vision of John of Patmos can be seen as a breakthrough of archaic material and raw emotions that flood forth with a storm of ancient symbols that overwhelm him and at least temporarily dissolve his personal ego and sense of self. Apocalypse can be a lifting of the veils that reveals a helpful hidden truth or a radical tearing away that leaves a person stripped to the bone and exposed to the raw energies and extremities of the unconscious.

Fundamentalists and "true believers" continually miss the point that the exaggerated imagery refers not simply to facts about the present and the future of the outer world, but to psychic facts and psychological conditions of the inner world. Apocalyptic states involve psychic invasions from above and from below as cosmic images descend upon the psyche at the same time that normally repressed primal emotions erupt from within. Religious fanaticism and political extremism can be seen psychologically as symptoms of a "return of the repressed," as raw emotions and ancient energies erupt and can overwhelm the rational mind. Under the stress and disorientation that accompany troubled times, even highly rational individuals can succumb to unconscious energies. Behind the presentation of seemingly logical positions, exaggerated emotions can be felt; behind seemingly logical arguments, the smoldering fevers of religious conversion can be sensed. Anyone can become an "extremist" at any moment as everyone becomes increasingly exposed to all kinds of irrational influences, raw emotions, archaic energies, and disturbing fantasies. Some people become fixated upon a particular date for "the End," while there seems to be no end to wild fantasies or conspiracy theories.

The dramatic vision of fire and brimstone and worldwide destruction that arrived during the tumultuous beginnings of Christianity has remained a compelling part of the religious context and metaphysical background throughout the development of Western civilization. A horde of apocalyptic prophecies and fearful religious visions have shaped a deep shadow that has accompanied the Western Enlightenment with its dedication to reason and rationality. At times of great uncertainty and collective anxiety, whether the cause comes from a natural disaster or arises from cultural violence and tragedy, the ancient symbolism and archaic feelings of apocalypse rise to the surface and break through the skin of normal life. The more rational a culture seems to be, the more irrational will be its underside when the dark times come, the veils lift, and more is revealed than most want to see.

Apocalypse Now

To be alive at this time means to be exposed to the raw forces of nature as well as the rough edges of culture. Given the radical changes affecting both culture and nature in contemporary life, it is easy to understand how fears of cataclysm and images of apocalyptic nightmares might intensify. The world as we know it is awash with profound problems and puzzling changes and beset with seemingly endless conflicts. It is a time of great uncertainty and surprising changes that include extreme weather patterns as well as religious and political extremists. When the typical "holding institutions" of a culture no longer protect people and fail to hold back the collective fears of disaster, people become more vulnerable to visions of annihilation. Increasingly, it does seem that everything might come to a screaming end, that it could happen at any moment, and that it might happen from a mistake of culture or from a catastrophe of nature.

For many years the possibility of a nuclear holocaust has hung like a threatening cloud over the entire world. At the same time, concerns about global warming and radical climate change have also grown. At the far ends of the earth, polar ice caps are melting, while everywhere else modern "culture wars" develop and ancient animosities rise to the surface and heat up. All the great questions about life and death and all the great fears about dissolution and destruction hang in the polluted air and trouble the waters all around us. To be alive at this time means to be caught between the opposing poles of existence as more and more things polarize and conflicts multiply. We face huge issues, massive threats, and seemingly impossible tasks; there seems to be no end to our problems and time seems to be running out on everyone.

Whether it manifests as a divine fire or a nuclear explosion, global warming or a sudden comet falling from space, we are subject to increasing levels of fear about the health and future of the planet we live on. Even if we are willing to "face the facts," the facts themselves keep changing. Radical change may be the fact that most needs to be faced. It is our shared lot in life to be alive during a time of great upheaval and radical changes that affect culture and nature alike. It is our mutual fate not simply to feel an increasing loss of time, but also to experience a time of increasing loss. We become like a "collective Job," inundated with loss, tested by both god and the devil, and left alone to face various scenarios of impending doom.

Scientific theories and religious beliefs—so often at odds—seem to echo each other as both statistics and scriptures predict apocalyptic scenarios on earth. Science and religion, so long divided and seemingly opposed, finally find agreement with each other at the point of the earth's imminent annihilation. On one level, we are more exposed to the rays of the sun, as the very source of light and life becomes a danger to our skin in the form of cancers; on another level, the skin of the planet is overheating. There is also an increasing danger of being devoured by huge energies and raw emotions that rise from the depths of the collective unconscious that is being churned as time turns over and things turn upside down. Common notions of progress become hard to hold when everything seems about to collapse, when the once great religions spawn fundamentalists and extremists of all kinds, when the waters of creation heat up at the same time that the collective unconscious boils over and a flood of repressed fears and angers are released upon the world.

At this time, it takes very little to tear the skin of civilization and reveal massive, festering, emotional wounds full of fear, rage, resentment, and vengeance. The collective mood darkens as intractable forms of greed and destructive types of creed rise to the surface of life and threaten the very notion of civil society. Amidst increasing uncertainty in financial markets, the failing of social systems, and lack of genuine internal stability, political and religious groups begin to act out growing collective insecurities. For apocalyptic possessions can occur in secular groups whenever rigid ideologies become infused with religious fervor.

Religion has always worked a borderline area of the human psyche where pathology also prowls. Now, religious fanaticism and political terrorism combine in new forms that connect raw emotions with ancient energies for vengeance. The spread of terrorism involves both the broad "shadow" of mass cultures and the increasing eruption of archaic religious inflations. It is as if inner psychological conditions must now be lived out; as if the inner must become the outer and everything must go upside down before things can turn around again.

As tensions in the outer world escalate, anxieties intensify on both collective and individual levels. Normally suppressed feelings of insecurity and dread become heightened as people feel more helpless and unable to control things and everyone becomes more vulnerable to mysterious forces. We share in a collective trauma as the hollowing of institutions and the flood of rapid changes leave everyone not only uncertain, but increasingly disoriented and at a loss; not only more isolated, but also at odds with one another. People say, "Beware, the End is coming," yet it in many ways we have already passed the turning point. Our common fate places us in the winding down of some great cycle that has entered a dramatic turning point and it is not clear where we might end up. Call it the great turning or the great churning; call it the ends of time or the "archetype of apocalypse," when everything seems to happen at once and nothing remains in place for very long.

When seen as an archetypal dynamic, apocalypse describes a dark and troubling period of uncertain duration in which the underlying tensions and oppositions of life become uncovered and rise to the surface. The conflicts between culture and nature become more apparent both in terms of global warming issues and in the intense competition for the basic resources of the earth. As the veil of normality lifts, the growing disparity between the rich and the poor, between those suffering in poverty and those living in luxury, becomes revealed. At the same time, age-old conflicts between ethnic groups rise with a vengeance to the surface and religious factions become willing to destroy the world rather than find ways to heal their theological rifts.

To be alive at this time means to become a witness, willing or unwilling, to the loosening of the web of nature as well as the unraveling of the fabric of culture. It means to be present as accepted patterns dissolve, as institutions become hollow and uncertainty comes to rule. It is not simply that the air has become dangerously polluted and overheated or that the political atmosphere is increasingly poisonous and self-destructive. Seen in mythical terms, the world drifts from cosmos towards chaos, it slips from order to collapse, as everything shifts back towards the original state of chaos that existed before creation. The issue is not the literal "end of the world," but the winding down and speeding up that happens on the downside of a cosmic cycle.

Disconnections

Speed is the romance of the modern world as time seems to be running out and everything moves faster and faster. High speed connections and the World Wide Web rise to prominence even as the underlying web of life and fabric of culture seem more threadbare each day. Despite and because of all the high speed connections there are more and more "disconnects." Through modern technologies the word can move swiftly across great distances, yet language itself becomes diminished and impoverished in the rush to communicate. We can send a text message to anyone, anywhere, yet the context and texture of life seem to diminish before our screen-weary eyes.

Increasingly, we are all interconnected and tuned to the great uncovering and the slow unraveling and fearful of what the next tragedy might be. Everyone is more exposed—whether it is a natural disaster, a suicide bombing, or mass killing—as tragic news spreads instantly. It is not simply that tragedies seem to grow in scale and increase in number, but that they also travel at the speed of cable. Bad news may travel fast, but tragedy now travels at the speed of fiber optics. The modern condition seems to prove the old idea that it is the same to live in a tragic time as to live in a tragic place. Modern technology collapses time and place and often leaves us on the ground of tragedy; as if everyone is wired to the sense of "apocalypse now" and the global acting out of all the deeply repressed and suppressed fears and emotions.

Creation myths suggest that everything must be there at the beginning and correspondingly "everything must come out in the end," as the end-times become when "all is said and done" and everything seems to be happening at the same time. The latest version of the seeming "ends of time" produces a flowering of obsessions and an explosion of compulsions as unconscious energies and collective anxieties flood into the daily world. The felt sense that time is running out "on the planet" causes people to rush about and fill the little time remaining with endless projects as well as mindless details. People seem to fill each moment with as many things as possible. There is never enough time in a day and no one can find the time needed to finish all that has been started. Given the loss of time and the increasing pressure to get more things done, daily life becomes both more manic and more depressive; both more impulsive as well as more compulsive at the same time. Despite the high speed connections and all the social networking, the loose ends of our lives seem to loosen further and radical feelings seem about to erupt and overflow.

Things seem increasingly catastrophic as huge corporations turn out to be hollow; not just bereft of feelings, but empty of real capital. Governments reveal that they cannot pay their debts and it seems that the worldwide markets might all collapse at the same time. As ice caps melt and the holes in the ozone layer grow larger, the sense of catastrophe becomes part of daily life. It is not just the great number of serious problems that we face, but also the size of the issues. The postmodern era is beset with problems that are huge in size and dangers that are massive in scale. Things speed faster and faster towards an uncertain future while the pool of despair nearby darkens and deepens. The final product of globalism may turn out to be global despair.

The catastrophic quality and pressure of insurmountable problems are essential elements of apocalyptic visions and of periods of apocalypse. *Katastrophe* is another old Greek word with meanings that extend from "a downturn" to "an overturning" and "a sudden end." When the sense of catastrophe is in the air, it becomes easier to feel that an economic downturn can lead to a financial collapse that can suddenly bring down the whole financial system. The archetype of apocalypse carries the sense that the current state cannot continue and that it is too late for things to simply be repaired. In order for things to change in a meaningful way, many things must come to an end. As archetype of radical change, apocalypse presents a pattern in which a shattering of forms occurs before the world as we know it can be reconstituted. In the cosmic turnaround, if enough endings can be found, things can begin again.

In ancient Greek theater, *katastrophe* defined the crucial turning point in the last scenes of the drama being played out on the stage. Before the final curtain could fall, the veils would lift to reveal all kinds of plots twists and undercurrents that had been hidden within the action of the play. Even when all the aspects of the plot were pointing to an inevitable tragic conclusion, a reversal could already be underway. Like all things apocalyptic, moments of catastrophe can go either way; either they will lead to a fatal downfall or else to a surprising turn of events in which some saving element becomes revealed. Another root meaning of *katastrophe* includes the idea of a "reversal of what is expected." The idea is not to deny the presence of tragedy and loss, but to realize that the great drama of the world includes twists of fate that cannot be predicted and revelations that only appear when the end seems to be drawing near.

Last Days and Lasting Things

Apocalypse has to do with alternative visions of reality, with reversals of fortune in all directions as things appear and disappear and rise and fall with increasing rapidity. All manner of extreme notions and outlandish beliefs take the worldwide stage at the same time and there is no end to what might be uncovered or be discovered. All manner of gadgets and technologies rise to prominence only to become obsolete and disappear as other innovations suddenly take the stage. Most things turn out to have a short expiration date, yet there are surprising things that last and last. In the same way that the word "end" involves remnants and remainders, the word "last" involves last chances and long-lasting qualities as well as lasting things.

The word "last" can indicate finalities, as when the time has come for the last rites or for someone's last words. Yet, as a verb "last" can mean "lasting;" it can refer to patterns that endure and things that last no matter what else happens. Something that lasts continues on; it persists even after other things have passed. Not only that; but having the last word in art or technology implies being on the cutting edge and introducing the latest innovation or the newest thing. In the end, that which is last can also be first; that which lasts becomes the basis not only for that which sustains life, but also for that which renews it. When the end seems near ancient and lasting things are also close and waiting to be rediscovered.

Just as the end-times tend to come and go, the "last days" turn out to have a lasting quality. When looked at with an eye for apocalypse, what we find at the end are both last things and things that last. The deeper texts of life are full of lasting ideas; postscripts and even post-scriptures that can indicate the ways to salvage time and redeem meaningful aspects of life. From what went on before, things can go on again. Being willing to face all the things that come to an end and taking the sense of "last days" seriously can lead to finding those things that last long enough to begin it all again.

At the mythic level, ends and beginnings are essentially connected and one keeps leading to the other as the eternal drama of life continues to unfold. When the end seems near and everything spins faster and faster, something old and lasting, something deep and meaningful, is trying to catch up to us. Something subtle and enduring about the world is trying to be remembered and be rediscovered, and it seems to take some big trouble to awaken to it. The overwhelming problems and massive threats are real enough, but they also function as a cosmic wake-up call intended to awaken us from the sleep of so-called "reality."

Apocalypse presents the psychic condition of being betwixt and between; especially between the ending of one era and the beginning of another. It is what the ancient Kalahari Bushmen called a *ja-ni*, or a "yes-no," situation. Is the world going to end? Yes, for the world as we know it has already ended in many ways. Is it the end of the world altogether? Not likely, as what we call the "real world" is secretly connected to what people used to call the "world behind the world." The manifest world grows old at times; it suffers varying levels of dissolution and collapse, yet it regenerates again from the eternal world that has been behind it all along.

An apocalyptic period can involve the uncovering of many wounds and revelations of collective and cultural shadows. Yet it can also lead to the discovery of new directions in life as well as a rediscovery of old and valuable ideas that had been forgotten. With the collapse of familiar structures, there can be a loosening of restrictive patterns as well as revelations of the roots of renewal. At the end of an era, fact approaches myth and myth can take on its old meaning of "emergent truth." When all seems lost and logic is of no avail, when everything seems about to unravel, mythic imagination and narrative intelligence can offer surprising ways of not only surviving but also contributing to the renewal waiting to happen.

What literalists and fundamentalists consider to be the final end is, in the big story of creation ongoing, only the "beginning of the end." Most end-of-the-world visions and end-time myths involve images of a regenerated world. Even the vision of John of Patmos included the three stages common to the archetype of apocalypsis: an initial period of destruction, followed by surprising revelations, and a subsequent renewal or regeneration of the world. Disorientation and disorder are essential aspects of apocalypsis, but so are revelation and renewal. For one side of revelation is connected to collapse and destruction, while the other is related to discovery, renewal, and recreation. In the grand story of the world, the ends of time are connected to the roots of eternity that can reveal new patterns of energy and new forms of life waiting to be found and become known.

In mythic terms the world cannot simply come to an end. When time is running out and all seems lost, the saving grace can best be found in the movement from the literal sense of life to the mythic, not the other way around. When the world as we know it comes to its inevitable end, it is helpful to have some mythic imagination and some narrative intelligence that can perceive the threads of renewal amidst the unraveling of the garments of culture and the web of nature. When the world dips into chaos, the two great garments of life seem to unravel at the same time. At that time it is helpful to know that chaos not only describes the way that things fall apart at the end, but also depicts the original state from which all of creation continually arises.

Only for those who remain stubbornly literalistic or dogmatically religious does apocalypse have to mean overwhelming catastrophes that lead to a final end. Apocalypsis describes a state of necessary confusion and disorientation that occurs in the time and space between collapse and renewal. While the rational mind reels from the irrational blows coming from cultural unraveling and natural disasters, a more psychological sense is required if cynicism and despair are to be avoided. For those willing to peek behind the veil, for those who are able to be resilient in the midst of turbulent times, apocalypsis can mean a time of revelation on many levels.

At the mythic level, change is the key element of life and some revelation is always at hand. "Reveal" is another cloth word; as a verb it means "to fold back." It comes from the French *voile*, which gives both "veil" and Voilà! Deep within the world and in the depths of the human soul, old and lasting ways of seeing, being, and imagining wait to be uncovered, rediscovered, and learned from again. The deeper sense of apocalypsis means to see with a revelatory eye, to re-vision and revise the big picture, and to find our place again in the ongoing, metaphorical, metaphysical, and cosmological story. For there are two great and lasting stories in this world: the wondrous and daunting drama of the world unfolding before us and the surprising and unique stories trying to unfold from within each human soul.

A Mythic Inoculation

Once we recognize that we are in a paradoxical, yes-no situation it makes more sense to face the psychological presence of apocalyptic fears and terrors. Denying the sense of a period in which many things come to an end only intensifies the feelings of chaos and disorientation. Accepting that we are caught in the middle of a great turnaround helps make sense of the tumultuous events and feelings all around us. It is in the middle of what seems like the very end of everything that things secretly begin again.

Caught between fears of the bitter end and secret hopes of it all beginning again, we might learn to be truly human again. Despite the contemporary fixation on rational thought and the insistence on facts and measurements, the human soul is mythic by nature and mystical by inclination. To be truly human is to be both psychological and mythological, for we are mythic by nature, each imbued with a living story and each tied to the enduring story of this world that ever teeters on the edge of annihilation.

Modern parlance uses myth to mean something that is patently false, yet what is most true is also most elusive and cannot be captured by logic or arrived at by reason alone. Where reason fails and logic stumbles, myths wait to open paths of imagination and understanding. A mythical story is an installment of eternity that can interrupt the march of time and break the spell of the ordinary world. Myths are not things of the past, but rather the eternal, ongoing stories that point to the underlying truths and essential meanings of creation. Mythic imagination can light the way when the world seems most dark. Entering into the ideas and imagination of what happens at the very end can create a mythic condition that helps to reveal the underlying unity of life and the presence of the eternal world behind the world.

Mythic threads are woven into us from the very beginning, and those who can imagine how things come to an end can also find the threads of imagination for beginning again. For being near the end also means being near the threads of existence and being invited to lend a hand in the great reweaving of the garment of life. In such a time of many endings, it becomes important to have a sense for lasting things, a narrative feel for life, and a reverence for the unseen. In the end, or near it, the real issue is not simply the future of humanity, but the presence of eternity.

When it seems that everything might end, the point is not to believe in one or another final date or end-time scenarios; rather, the point is to recognize the archetypal ground of extremes, the surprising territory where things both end and begin again. Nightmare scenarios of the end may turn out to be a dramatic device intended to awaken people to deeper levels of awareness as the curtain falls on the last act of the preceding era. Seeing apocalypse as metaphor helps to lift the veil on the end-times and reveal more than dire threats and fears of calamity. Life reaches not a final end but a vital edge of revelation rippling with sudden disclosures and pregnant with surprising insights.

With the eye of apocalypse, we learn to see behind the scenes, peek behind the veils, even see beyond the pale. Peeking behind the veil of reality can reveal glimpses of the eternal realm that is the source of life and that can be the source of radical change. Quantum physics reveals this essential otherworld when peeking in at the level where matter and energy play at being each other as they put on a cosmic shape-shifting show. That which seems completely solid when seen with the naked eye suddenly shifts to being mutable and magical as matter becomes energy or vice versa. Each time people think they have found the bottom line or building blocks of reality, some new discovery turns things upside down. Quantum physics may begin as part of positivistic science, but it also approaches a mystery. When seen with an eye for apocalypse and with a feeling for revelation, physics threatens to become metaphysics once again.

The Loom of Eternity

The world around us is a place of mystery and wonder and revelation waiting to happen; it is always more that it seems to be. In mythic terms the issue is not simply the end of the planet, but the loss of the earth as a place of mystery and wonder where the ends of time are secretly connected to the roots of eternity. *Planet* means "wandering star" and what we call the world is a reckless, wondrous story, a wild, star-crossed narration being told through the breathing green garment of Nature and revealing itself continually in both the tragedies and comedies of earthly life. Life always hangs by a thread and all events of history are loosely stitched on the "loom of eternity." The great hubris of creation and the terrible and grand gestures of death, all played out again and again, pulled on by an imperishable tide.

As the endless story of the world reaches another cosmological turning point and the fabric of life loosens, the veil between this world and the otherworld becomes more transparent. Things become both impossible and more possible at the same time. Just as time seems to be running, out the sense of the eternal tries to slip back into awareness. That is what the old stories say, and the old stories have survived the ages and all the previous stages that seemed surely to be the last act of creation. The wonder of creation is that it continues to create; it is the ongoing story that starts over again each time it reaches the End.

The world, despite its disasters, tragedies and villainies, cannot end unless it runs out of stories. This world may be made of atoms, but it is held together by stories and it cannot end unless all the stories come to an end at the same time. Even then, there would be some remnant of some tale from which it could all begin again. Ends and beginnings are secretly connected, but it takes a mythical mind and a metaphorical sense to see how one might lead to the other. Whenever the end seems near, the beginning is also close at hand. The mystics know that, but so do the nuclear physicists. At the mystical, mythical, and metaphysical level of life, the world is ending and beginning every moment. The "next world" is right next to this world and the two intersect in little moments of redemption and re-creation. Most religious visions of the end-times predict a renewal of the world, but only after a divine intervention first destroys the "world as we know it." In many ways, the world as we knew it has already ended and we are already standing on the threshold of the next world.

To be alive at this time means to be in a mythical condition that includes being faced with all the massive problems and impossible tasks that currently plague the modern world. It is an extraordinary time as both nature and culture need all the healing and creative attention that people are capable of giving. There is an increasing sense that time is running out and whatever can be done must happen immediately. There is a need for true agency in dealing with pressing issues and there can be a great urgency for doing everything that might be done right now. Yet old mythical ideas suggest other ways of seeing the situation. When time is running out and no one can find the time anymore, it is not simply time that is missing, but the touch of the eternal. Like everything else, time originates in eternity and when it can no longer be found, that is the place to look for it. The "ends of time" lead back to the roots of eternity, which are also the unending source of genuine inspiration, great ideas, and meaningful visions.

Agents of the Eternal

An old mythic idea suggests that each human soul can be an agent of the eternal, each having a touch of genius and each being born at a time when they can be useful to creation. In this view, each person arrives on the earth with a specific story trying to unfold from within. Each also carries from before birth a unique arrangement of character, talents, and gifts that are needed in this world. The deepest human resources tend to awaken amidst the greatest human disasters. When the troubles are all around us, everyone can find some place where they are needed, where they can help heal all that is wounded and help protect all that is threatened.

During the Renaissance period of Western culture, the sense of individual genius rose into collective awareness along with the revival of the idea that everything is connected to, and through, the Soul of the World. The renewing ideas and artful images of the Renaissance came into prominence during a time of great upheaval and radical change. Amidst all the conflicts and calamities, the atrocities and tragedies of that time, the thread of genius and deep imagination arose amidst the rubble of history. There were many new inventions, and many old and lasting ideas were rediscovered as the hidden resources of life and the resiliency of the human soul emerged from the Dark Ages.

At that time, there was a saying amongst artists and philosophers: *Festina lente*. Or, "make haste slowly." This saying does not deny the pressing issues and tragic problems of the time, or the need for radical transformation, but it does suggest the need to trust the underlying energies of creation. For rushing ahead without touching the eternal; without finding the threads of individual genius and keeping close to the subtleties of creation, can leave us out of touch with the underlying energies of renewal and the hidden coherence that is trying to surface amidst all the chaos around us.

When the issues become huge and massive and the tasks seem impossible, rushing ahead without a genuine vision of where to go indicates a lack of wisdom as well as an excess of fear. No matter how dire things may seem, there is always time for a story. For stories are made of a beginning, middle, and an end, and if people can learn to hold the beginning together with the end, then we may all survive the darkness and live to hear the "dawn calling" that signifies that the story of creation ongoing has turned time over and another day or a new era or another world has begun.

CHAPTER 2

RUN TOWARDS THE ROAR

We will become our opposite if we do not learn to
accommodate the opposition within us.
Carl Jung

One of the roles of myth is to give life meaning. Without the narrative intelligence of stories, life can feel incoherent and seem to be meaningless. A genuine story opens a territory that can give meaningful shape to experiences and feelings that otherwise might seem random. Experience alone cannot give us meaning; only when the story has been told do we begin to see what life-changing and life-enhancing events might truly mean. Myths and stories make sense to us because we are "narrative beings" who find our way by "storying" the world around us. We are natural storytellers who learn about the nature of the world and our own inner nature through the stories we tell ourselves. Stories help teach us who we are and where we fit in life. We find our way by stories and become most lost when we do not have a coherent narrative to live within.

One of the problems with the modern world is that it lacks the kind of shared myths that make it possible for people to feel connected, protected, and meaningful. In what most people now believe to be an "accidental universe," we have lost the cohesive myths and cosmological stories that help make sense of the world and our place in it. The modern world suffers from a lack of the meaningful narratives needed to properly orient life and help reveal the soul's hidden resources at a time when those resources are most needed.

Stories are the oldest school for humankind; a living school where the only entry requirements are an active imagination, some capacity to feel one's own feelings, and a willingness to approach the world as a place of wonder and revelation. Stories are the imaginal, timeless base of the world, the "once upon a time," living literature that underlies and secretly unifies everything. People feel more whole when listening to a story and feel most at odds when there is no myth to make sense of life's intricate and necessary dramas.

Myths cannot be proven to be true, but they can prove to be very valuable when life becomes chaotic and no one seems to know which way to turn. For myths reveal things about the world that cannot be seen with the naked eye, that cannot be grasped by reason alone. Stories deal with those things that cannot simply be measured or reduced to "the facts of the matter." Stories can reveal things that matter more than simple facts can ever tell. You cannot eat stories, but genuine stories can keep people alive when all else seems lost.

Myths and stories used to be an essential part of the education of young people under the understanding that stories help each person make sense of life in general and of the struggles of their life in particular. It is natural for young people to get in trouble and feel at risk, for they must risk themselves in order to learn what story is trying to live through them. Modern youth grow up in a world that is itself at risk, and they increasingly ask whether the world might come to an end in their lifetime. Whether it be educated youth considering the dangers of global warming and climate change, less privileged ones who feel the bite of poverty and the growing disparity between rich and poor, or those exposed to the increased threats of violence and extremism modern youth grow up amidst threats of natural disaster and nightmares of terrorism, and they cannot help but doubt the future of the world. Young people, who are supposed to be the "future of the world," can find themselves fearing that the world has very little future to offer to them. What kind of story are we living in when young people ask those who are older whether the world will continue or not?

There is a deep human instinct to turn to those who are older for guidance when faced with obstacles or danger. Yet part of the problem in modern cultures is that those who are older often feel as lost as young people just starting out on the roads of life. When a culture falls apart it happens in two places at once: where its youth are rejected and not fully invited into life and where its elders are forgotten and forget what is important about life. Modern cultures tend to produce a mass of "olders" who live longer and longer, but a lack of genuine elders who know what to live for.

The problem is that modern cultures try to produce obedient citizens and life-long consumers instead of people who know the meaning and purpose of their own lives. Everyone born grows older, but elders are made, not born. The lack of meaningful elders leaves youth less protected, more isolated, and more exposed to extreme conditions, tragic deaths and wasted lives than they would normally be. Youth are at greater risk when the "olders" fail to act as elders and neglect to risk fully living their own stories. When the world rattles and times become hard, those who become older without growing wiser can become more fearful and disoriented than young people first facing their fears.

This world has always been at risk, and at times the only safety comes when the right risks are taken for the benefit of everyone. The traditional role of elders included remembering what was most important about life and how to hold ends and beginnings together when times become hard. Elders were the guardians of the mysteries and keepers of the stories who helped people make sense of life's inevitable struggles. Having survived the troubles of their own lives and having grown deeper and wiser, they knew both how to survive and how to find genuine vision where others could only see disaster. Being "old enough to know better" they would know that life renews itself in surprising ways and that the greatest dilemmas can serve to awaken the deepest resources of the human soul.

Traditionally, the elders would speak in stories. *Story* also means "storehouse" and what can be found in stories is what keeps being lost and forgotten in the daily world. Sometimes a little story can open an uncommon way of seeing a path forward that otherwise would remain hidden to simple observation or common sense. There is an old African tale that elders would tell the young people when times became dark and the future seemed most uncertain. Like many tribal tales, it draws upon nature and the animal world to illustrate the inevitable dilemmas of life and the need to see and feel more deeply when danger threatens and a wholehearted human response is needed for survival.

The story begins on the ancient savannas of Africa where the hunger of life pours forth in the form of teeming, feeding herds. As the hungry hordes eat their way across the plains, lions wait in the tall grass nearby, anticipating their chance to prey upon the grazing animals. In preparation for their attack, the lions send the oldest and weakest members of the pride away from the rest of the hunting pack. Having lost much of their strength and most of their teeth, the roar of the old ones is far greater than their ability to bite, so they slip away and settle in the grass directly across from where the strong and hungry members of the pride wait for the grazing herds.

As the herd enters the area between the hunting pack and the old lions, the old ones begin to roar with all their might. At the sound of the terrifying roars, most of the herd panics. Blinded by fear and overwhelmed by a sense of imminent danger before them, they turn away from the roaring and flee from the threat of death. They run wildly and desperately in the opposite direction. Of course, they run right to where the strongest lions wait in the tall grass for dinner to arrive.

"Run towards the roar," the old people used to tell the young ones. When faced with great danger and when people panic and seek a false sense of safety, run towards the roaring and go where you fear to go. For only in facing your fears can you find some safety and a way through. When the world rattles and the end seems near, go towards the roar.

The Lions of the Moment

To be alive at this time is to feel the roaring of the world on many sides; both nature and culture are endangered and human life seems to hang in the balance as fierce factions battle all around us. The fury of raw emotions and the punishing rigidity of fixed beliefs seem to mix with each other to produce new forms of terror that threaten to divide the earth into explosive groups continually fueled by winds of fear. At the same time, radical alterations of climate produce storms of change that include life-withering heat waves and massive hurricanes, while expanding holes in the ozone layer leave everyone exposed to the invisible rays of an increasingly unfriendly sun.

These days the roaring of the end of the world seems to have more teeth than usual; amidst the many threats, paths to safety become increasingly difficult to find. Collective anxiety is on the rise, fanaticism and extremism are on the march, fear is in the air, and the tendency to panic can strike anyone at any time. Whether one is young or old, it becomes easier to panic and run away from all that roars and threatens in this world of increasing uncertainty. Old folks fear that they will lose health care and retirement benefits, those in their prime earning years fear that they won't earn enough to survive or might lose their jobs, and young people fear there may be no place for them in this fearful world which could simply end at any moment.

Humanity seems trapped amidst growing disasters, sudden changes, massive problems, and multiplying conflicts that roar at everyone and plague societies worldwide. Like a terrified herd, many seek simple solutions or simply run for a safe way out. Faced with increasing tensions at the level of existence and trying to find a sense of safety or certainty amidst all the confusion, many run right into the array of narrow ideologies and fundamentalist beliefs that claim to provide immediate solutions and offer absolute answers. They turn to fundamentalist doctrines and fixed ideas that offer a false sense of security while further dividing the herd and increasing the danger for everyone.

The problem is that fear and anxiety can cause people to lose common sense as well as the deeper sense that, with the increasing number of worldwide problems, we are all in this together. As more people panic and rush into extreme positions, the hard issues harden and harder and harder attitudes prevail. Driven by fears of loss, many people grab whatever they can and hold on tight. Some try to amass wealth in order to feel more secure amidst the growing insecurities. Many turn to the seeming safety of narrow ideologies and fundamentalist creeds as fear produces one-sided, end-time thinking that polarizes people on either side of almost any issue. Some even seek a "clash of civilizations" as the archetype of apocalypse overwhelms those who already hold extreme political or religious positions. Amidst the rise of extremist religious ideas, the increase of fanatic attitudes, and the mania of single-issue politics, it becomes easier to feel the bite of raw human greed as well as the punishing rigidity of narrow creeds.

Caught in the teeth of huge dilemmas, everything seems to polarize into fundamental oppositions between various religious factions, upper and lower classes, or older and younger generations. The hungry lions of contemporary life include the many forms of literalism and factions of fundamentalism that claim to have all the cures for what ails you in this world, or else provide a complete escape from it and salvation in a higher realm. Those who try to run away from the roaring problems and intractable issues of life during the hard times tend to run straight into the teeth of the many "isms" that promise to deliver either security in this world or salvation in the next.

Fundamentalists staunchly inhabit the narrowest end of the fields of literature, language, and human expression. At the extreme, in the hard ground of fixed dogmas and rigid ideas, things must appear to be absolute. There can be no doubt; people prefer things to be "written in stone." As times become more difficult it can develop that "the best lack all conviction, while the worst are full of passionate intensity." Ideologies intensify when genuine thought is absent, when doubt is not allowed, and when true imagination has been excluded. Ideologies and blind beliefs are narrow forms that promise much but, in the end, lack genuine significance and meaningful solutions. When the chips are down and genuine ideas and true courage are needed, ideologies leave people split inside, radically unstable and unable to respond to necessary changes. As the philosopher Voltaire once said, "Doubt is not a pleasant condition, but certainty is absurd."

They say that those who forget history are doomed to repeat it, yet those who forget that the world is a great mystery can feel altogether doomed. The sense of impending doom increases with the loss of imagination and denial of the living mysteries imbedded in all levels of life. Instead of wonder and awe at the fluidity and continuing surprise of the world, ideologies and fixed beliefs leave people enthralled with a single idea, a literalized theory, a one-sided, single-minded way of viewing everything that happens in the world. Unfortunately and increasingly, our motivating ideas and shared images are not mythical or mystical, not philosophical or even logical, but are simply ideological.

The Tension of the Opposites

The uncertainty principle—which states that the more precisely you measure one quantity, the less precisely you can know another associated quantity—may rule modern sciences, but the rise of absolutism tends to characterize politics, religion, and public discourse. People often emphasize simple statements of opinion by adding, "Absolutely." It is as if the deepening of uncertainty and mind-boggling increase of complexity in most areas of life must be counteracted by statements of absolutism when it comes to preferences or opinions. It is not just the atom that became split in the course of modern discoveries; the world itself has become more divided and essentially polarized. The twin offspring of the modern world and the nuclear age seems to be Uncertainty and Absolutism.

Modern life not only moves faster and faster, but things polarize very quickly and anything can suddenly become an issue through which people experience a radical sense of the tension of opposing forces. An increasing tension of opposites that seems about to tear everything apart is one of the ways that the world roars at everyone at this time. The presence of apocalypse means that any issue can quickly become a polarizing dilemma that irrationally divides people into entrenched oppositions. Back and forth we are thrown as each side of an issue is presented as the only way to go and as the opposing forces intensify, it seems that a choice must be made.

Yet being one-sided about a true dilemma only delays or intensifies the issue at hand. Each time one side of a dilemma is chosen, the other side will resurface with a vengeance as the conflict will only return at a deeper level at some later time. The moment that we predetermine the meaning or the outcome of the issues that life places in our path, we deprive ourselves of the immediacy of the spirit of life and at the same time lose the genuine humility and open-mindedness required for learning and real change.

Moral crises and ethical dilemmas form the crucibles for growth and transformation for societies as well as individuals. Avoiding the teeth of the dilemma by picking one side prematurely produces only a temporary release of stress and most often creates greater conflict as the opposing side comes to be seen as the enemy of one's own safety or security. Ideologies and abstract systems of belief try to predetermine the "right" choices to make; yet genuine ethical challenges begin where either choice can be seen as right or wrong, where both ways can be seen as necessary in some way. In this world, good and bad tend to be mixed. Only by suffering the tension that grows between one thing and another can a person learn what is trying to surface and become known.

The problem is not simply the presence of painful dilemmas and the increase of opposing forces; the problem is that most pick one side and try to prove that side to be right before the tension of the opposites becomes truly creative. A creative tension underlies everything in this world made of darkness and light, left and right, and life and death. Either the opposing energies are aimed at some as yet unseen solution, or the world is a hopelessly divided and unredeemable place. Going towards the roar means facing the increasing tension of dilemmas—involving both nature and culture—as the underlying polarities of life become more revealed. A meaningful dilemma will keep returning at deeper and deeper levels until a creative solution is sought and consequently becomes discovered. It is as if the basic split in the world must be touched before the hidden third and unifying thing can be uncovered.

Many wars begin because those in power fail to hold the tension of opposing interests or needs. Huge projects collapse and turn to dust because those involved lack personal and collective ways of holding the tension long enough for a creative solution to arise. Only when a person can experience both sides simultaneously and hold the tension long enough does a surprising third thing appear that allows a true solution. Genuine change and meaningful transformation are the secret aims of the tension inside life and the dilemmas that constantly arise. Despite notions of an accidental universe, life is not pointless; the tension of the opposites secretly hints at a "hidden third" behind all dichotomies. The purpose of the elemental oppositions in this world is to stimulate life itself; the hidden aim of all oppositions is to keep creation continuing.

The third thing trying to appear and become consciously known not only relieves the tension, but also renews and revitalizes life at another level. Mythically speaking, the third time and the third thing are always the "charm." Charm means "magic spell, incantation, a song or enchantment." When situations become completely polarized, the magic touch, the breath of inspiration, and the song of life that can dispel the sense of disenchantment are lacking. Caught in the trap of literalism and blinded by ideologies, the modern world has lost the enchantment of existence and the touch of the eternal. No amount of reason or dogma or blind belief can substitute for the charm, wonder, and mystery of immediate life. When the enchantment that makes this world beautiful and the meaning of the struggles within it are lost, all that is left is the underlying tension and the raw sense of division without the cloak of beauty.

Life roars at us when it wants or needs us to change. Ultimately, change means trans-formation, a shifting from one form to another that involves the magic of creation. The trouble with entrenched oppositions is that each side becomes increasingly one-sided and single-minded and unable to grow or meaningfully change. In the blindness of fear and the willfulness of abstract beliefs, people forget or reject the unseen yet essential unity that underlies all the oppositions in life. Whereas blind oppositions lead either to explosions or a slow draining of energy, consciously accepting the tension of opposing views can lead to a surprising vitality and hidden qualities trying to be born into the world. For despite all the oppositions and conflicts, all the disasters and betrayals, this world remains a place of small redemptions and ongoing creation. Genuine solutions appear only where the sense and feeling of dissolution has been risked.

Genuine and Undivided

At the human level, when faced with a great obstacle or a true dilemma, there will be one of two outcomes: Either we will become bigger people who understand ourselves and the world better, or we will become smaller souls more narrow in our thinking and ultimately more rejecting of the mystery and wonder of life. We may feel overwhelmed by fear and anxiety as the tension in life becomes greater and problems seem to grow in size as time runs out, but what life wants is meaningful change. Either we face the way that life roars at us and become wiser and more of a friend of the world, or else we run in fear and shrink from life, mystery, and love.

When faced with a difficult choice, a child will run to one side or the other, typically looking for the place of least tension and greatest comfort. Maturity, however, is related to a person's ability to withstand and even understand the tensions that come with growing up and facing up to the issues at hand. To *mature* means "to ripen," not simply to take on responsibilities but to be exposed to the weather of life and become fully grown well-rounded, and finally ripened. In order to withstand the stress of life, a person must become who they truly are at seed and ripen into the unique individual they are intended to be from the very beginning.

In the end, all the troubles we face and the struggles we endure serve the purpose of helping us become true and unique individuals. *Individual* means "un-divided," the one not divided on the inside, thus able to withstand great pressure from the outside world. The genuine individual is a less divided person who has suffered their own inner conflicts enough to know that an underlying unity can at times be found. Those who insist upon choosing one side of an issue and condemning those on the opposite side are themselves split and divided within. Their insistence on certainty in the outside world belies a greater uncertainty and lack of self-knowledge in the inner realm. A *neurotic* is a "divided person," one who suffers inner splits that obstruct meaningful change as well as emotional and spiritual growth. A neurosis forms where honest suffering has been avoided.

Becoming a genuine individual requires learning the oppositions within oneself. Those who deny or refuse to face the oppositions within themselves have no choice but to find enemies to project their inner conflicts upon. *Enemy* simply means a "not-friend;" until a person deals with the not-friend within them, they will find many seeming enemies all around them. There are certainly real conflicts and unfriendly people in the world, but real change has to begin where we each are conflicted within ourselves. The genuine individual or undivided person must be made again and again from creative tensions generated by facing fundamental oppositions within the self.

Whereas literalists and fundamentalists tend to choose one pole of any dilemma or opposition, whereas modern political parties and religious groups tend towards demonizing each other, the creative individual must be born again and again in the crucible created by the tension between opposing instincts, conflicted feelings, and contrasting ideas. The same is true for groups that create unnecessary enemies by refusing to deal with their own shadow elements and inner conflicts.

The actual end of the world seems most possible when the power of imagination becomes diminished and people cannot envision creative ways to handle the inevitable conflicts and dilemmas of life. The emergence of the third thing requires an act of imagination and becomes an act of creation as something that was unknown or unseen becomes manifest and consciously known. The eruption of the third thing coming between opposing poles creates a quantum change that changes everything. From a mythic perspective, it repeats the original process of creation when the sky and earth were separated and the world became visible and life became viable.

For creation does not simply rest quietly back at the beginning of time; fundamentalists as well as modern literalists are wrong about that. Creation is ongoing in this world where cells divide to produce new life and opposites can attract surprising energies as well as pull us apart. This world may be at times a valley of tears, a place of great conflict where the blind lead the blind, the one-eyed man rises to rule, and the single-minded, true believers battle endlessly. But it is also the realm where creation is ongoing and each person is threaded to the eternal, capable of being a vehicle for revelation in some way.

Each moment which is fully entered into becomes momentous in some way; the world offers second chances more than once. In mythic terms, it is rarely "three strikes and you're out," but more the sense that the third time is the charm. The third thing waiting to be found beyond or below any opposition turns a seeming end into the beginning again—not because someone intelligently figures the whole thing out, but because an unseen aspect enters the space between the opposites. When one genuinely suffers the tension of the opposites, something unexpected will occur; something as yet unconscious or unknown will become conscious, and with that awakening there will also come a renewal of vitality and basic life energy.

The notion that the apocalyptic end is literally at hand may motivate some people to change the direction of their lives, but it will fail to produce the kind of sustained attention and greater understanding needed to transform human culture and help heal nature of all its current ills. On the other hand, dismissing the increasing sense of disaster and presence of apocalyptic energies as paranoia or foolishness may cause us to miss the imagination hidden within the growing tension of opposing forces manifesting in the world. The threat of the end of the world can be viewed as an old lion that has roared many times before, yet has never delivered a mortal blow. Yet the sense of being at the end of the world as we know it must be faced in order to find the creative tension and hidden imagination that can open paths of survival as well as threads of renewal. In the end, the issue is not the certainty of earthly annihilation, but the problem of surviving creatively until the cosmic turning turns things around.

Most stories of the end include visions of a regenerated world, as if to say that a willingness to face all that is coming to an end is required for new images and enduring visions to be found. The roaring of a world beset by massive problems threatening to overwhelm culture and dismantle nature can be seen as a cosmic wake-up call that asks each of us to try to recall what the gift of life is truly about. Facing the roaring of the end and acknowledging that some things have lost their purchase in this world may be the first step that leads to the point where things begin again.

The modern world has lost its cosmic connection and its reason for being. Running towards the roar means facing up to the existential crises and all that has already been diminished in the daily world. To be modern is to be lost and caught in the lurch of existence, to be trapped in a sea of facts that cannot add up to anything whole, to be facing the roar of annihilation without a story to explain it all or contain it all. While many fear a sudden collapse or a devastating explosion that signals that the end has finally come, a "slow apocalypse" of lost connections and missing meanings has already been draining life from our lives for a long time.

In fearing that an overwhelming disaster may come sometime soon, people miss the sense that it is already here in the many losses that people feel each day; not simply that people feel a loss of time, but also that it has become a time of great loss. There is a loss of species as well as a lengthening list of endangered traditions that used to hold people together. There is a loss of forests and wilderness preserves as well as a growing sense of a loss of direction, an absence of purpose, and a lack of meaning in human societies. Amidst the spread of materialism and the rise of literalism, there has already been a loss of imagination as well as a seething wound of separation from the subtle levels of life, the loss of tender connections to unseen things, and the lack of a felt sense of the immediacy and beauty of life. The End so greatly feared may come more as a lessening of life rather than a grand and fiery finale.

Modern Means Lost

To be modern means to be lost in many ways, to be losing time all the time, and to be running out of space as overpopulation overwhelms even the most private places. Things move faster and faster as the elements of time become smaller and smaller, each digital bit flashing from a myriad of clocks seemingly timed to a final countdown. Life is reduced to fractions of time and an endless outpouring of details and trivia. Amidst a mania for measuring and counting people collect reams of statistics and compile endless opinion polls as if to arrive at something meaningful by the simple act of piling up facts and figures. Yet all the deconstructed bits and bytes can never add up to produce meaning or restore what has already been lost. No amount of counting or accounting can add back the missing sense of meaning or the lost sense of wholeness. For it is the elusive, unprovable sense of wholeness and the underlying coherence of things that has been lost.

Human events become trapped at the soul-starved surface of life, where brief flashes of fame and narrow forms of egotism pass for accomplishment, and cleverness takes the place of genuine learning and the search for real knowledge. There is a growing insensitivity to human suffering amidst a decreasing aptitude for authenticity. The instinct for finding meaning becomes replaced with a "concentration of cunning" that can only trade in short-term gains while a sea of despair grows just under the flashy, rushing surface of modern life.

Modern economics functions as a secular religion, a fundamentalism based in fixed ideas and abstract laws that seem to justify worldwide pathologies of individual greed and collective consumption. Under the "rule of scarcity," people believe that there can never be enough to go around, which justifies the resolve, "I'm going to get mine." Simplistic notions of winners and losers replace the subtle sense of the dignity of all life as immature urges to power and maniacal devouring of resources become sanctified and raw greed becomes elevated to a virtue.

Meanwhile, the massive imbalances of mass societies lead to greater and greater gaps between the rich and the poor, and the increasing disparity actually diminishes the dignity of all involved. The consumer society begins to consume itself as infantile greed and adolescent fantasies of wealth and power replace healthy notions of managing resources and helping those in need. It is not just that modern life has lost its way—not simply that mass societies suffer with ideas of mass destruction—but also the loss of the ancient sense of each life as meaningful and each death as significant. An increasing tension pits mass culture against the natural practice and life-long work of becoming a genuine individual.

Soul in Exile

One way to view the condition of loss that permeates modern life is an increasing loss of the soul connections that make life meaningful, beautiful, and truly rich. When we lose our way, it is the soul's way of being in touch with the world that has been lost, for soul is the connective tissue of life. The human soul can feel increasingly isolated and exiled in a world of intensifying oppositions, ideological blindness, and technological dominance. It is the soul in us that feels the losses around us that can sense that the loss of species means something, that the loss of authenticity lessens the presence of the world, and that the loss of imagination reduces the possibilities of life. The loss of the soul connection leaves humans in the lurch of existence, falling into a sullen void, the increasing despair only barely disguised by busyness and virtual realities. Under current conditions, the feeling of exile makes great sense. Going towards the roar means accepting the sense that the modern world has lost the soul connection that would keep culture and nature essentially related, and would also protect the inner nature and unique value of the individual soul.

For the great crises of the world do not take place outside the human soul; history is made in the struggle of the soul to survive and make meaning of the world around it. The inner-seeded story of the individual soul is secretly tied to the great drama of the world and to the surprising ways in which it changes, renews, and recreates itself. Acknowledgment of what has been lost and acceptance of feelings of exile are not symptoms to be treated as much as a requirement for finding genuine ways to proceed. As both myth and literature constantly assert, it is the awakened exiles who know that something essential has been lost and must be sought for again and can only be found where others fear to go.

The issue is not simply one of needing to save the world, but also of needing to solve the problem of the loss of soul throughout the modern world. Part of what has been lost in the reckless rushing of modernity is the sense that each life has an authentic interior that shelters important emotions as well as inherent purpose, and that the dignity of existence includes a necessary instinct to unfold the unique story woven inside each living soul. The soul's way of being is unique to each person; it was seeded and sewn within each of us from before the beginning and it tries to ripen throughout our lives. What exiles us more than anything is the separation from our own instinctive, intuitive way of being. We are most lost and truly in exile when we have lost touch with our own soul, with our unique, inward style and way of being in this world.

Amidst all the disconnections of the modern world, it becomes more important than ever to find the inner connection and deepening presence of one's own soulful way of being present in life. Soul adds "psychic reality" to common experience; it adds depth and meaning to whatever we attempt in life. Spirit may connect us to higher things, but it is soul that holds spirit and matter, heaven and earth, together and is the hidden thread and vital vein that holds things together within each of us. Soul holds body and mind, individual and collective together, and when all seems about to polarize and fall apart, it is the soul connection that is missing and must be found.

We are in danger of becoming empty and being overwhelmed by fear and anxiety whenever there is a loss of soul. Yet soul can be grown during times of loss. Great crises and impossible demands often provoke the inner wisdom and hidden resources of the awakened soul. Thus, the threat of collapse and utter loss can also provoke a deeper sense of wholeness when nothing but total involvement and whole-heartedness will work. The point of "apocalypse now" may be a deeper initiation of the creative self and unifying soul within each person. In this darker revelation, things become both impossible and more possible at the same time.

When the structures of life loosen and everything seems about to fall apart, the hidden unity inside life may be closer to the surface and calling for attention. Modern cultures, so dedicated to the outer world, may find more solace through revelations of the deep soul and creative self within and the underlying, in-dwelling sense of a unifying principle and guiding force in each life. In the midst of radical changes in nature and the rattling of cultural institutions, the point may be to turn again to the inner realm where old practices and deep awareness can produce moments of wholeness. When the whole thing seems about to fall apart, revelations of the deep self and "old soul" within may be closer than ever. Rather than the need to save the whole world, the real work of humanity may begin with finding greater wholeness within.

Three Kinds of People

There is an old idea that suggests that when it comes to facing trouble or dealing with the real dilemmas of life, there are three kinds of people in this world. The first sort of people are those that are preoccupied with themselves; they are simply out to satisfy their own needs and immediate desires. They tend to refer everything back to "I, me, and mine." At this basic and limited level of literal self-awareness and thorough self-involvement, life is limited to self-interest and ruled by fixed attitudes and simple self-assertion. At this level, everything can seem simple and language can become simplistic; these types of people use single-syllable words. They say, "I am what I am," or "What you see is what you get," or "A man has to do what a man has to do."

This level of life is the arena of "survival of the fittest," where many feel strongly that "what's mine is mine, and what's yours may be mine too." As the first and most basic level, it is often the place to which people regress when they feel threatened or challenged. Although a sense of self-assertion and instinctive drives are necessary for survival, a person can become blind and dangerous when no greater sense of awareness develops.

This primal level includes the sense of flight or fight and it can manifest as collective aggression as in fanaticism and mob mentality. "We are Number One" is an instinctive manifestation of the first level of life and the basic drive to survive, to belong somewhere and feel secure. Of course, this first level and lowest common denominator can easily be manipulated through forms of "patriotic" exaggeration as well as ideological systems that depend upon a sense of entitlement and false superiority.

At this basic level, aggression and greed are self-justified and often only restrained by fear of some kind of punishment by authorities or retaliation on the part of others. The exaggerated sense of entitlement and self-interest can be contained by social rules with penalties for excess aggression or uncontrolled greed. The other method for reducing personal greed, raw power, and delaying immediate satisfaction involves moral systems that often include the idea of a final judgment and severe punishments that occur after death. Immediate penalties and punishment at the end of life tend to be the ways of containing the instinctive urges toward self-indulgence and self-aggrandizement.

The second types of people are those whose awareness includes a greater sense of self as well as a deeper sense of the needs and the value of others.

At this level, people develop greater self-discipline and more tempered ambitions. A sense of being connected to a community of souls develops here, and people aspire to be more noble as well as more tolerant and generous when it comes to the needs and desires of others. This second level involves a greater awareness of differing views among people and the value of diverse communities. The suffering of others becomes more evident as a sense of sympathy and even empathy expands personal awareness. There is a greater maturity and an increased willingness to serve the "greater good."

This second level includes an increased ability to seek solutions that work for all parties and involves attempts to forge "win-win" agreements. Through such agreements, blind competition can be reduced and the exploitation of poor and vulnerable people may be minimized. It is in this greater sense of understanding that genuine justice develops and protective institutions are formed. Charity organizations and not-for-profit groups develop, as well as noble experiments that seek peace, equality, and justice for all.

In addition to greater cultural awareness, this second level involves a greater awareness of the importance of natural environments and ecological systems. At this level of human culture, nature is respected and protected and long-term issues of sustainability replace short-term exploitation of resources. There are considerations for the continuance of other species, for the health of forests, and the purity of rivers. The sense of nobility extends to notions of culture and nature working in partnership for the benefit of future generations as well as planetary wholesomeness.

The second level of awareness supports the possibility of equal opportunities, civil societies, and the sense of sustainability for both culture and nature. However, when faced with great pressure, enduring threats, persistent dilemmas, or unusual hardships, those on the second level tend to fall back to the first level of life. When the obstacles seem overwhelming, when the threats are dire, or when there is simply not enough to go around, the sense of fairness, mutual benefit, and justice becomes more difficult to sustain. When the times get hard and stay that way, those on the second level tend to revert to the attitudes of simple survival and the self-involvement that characterize basic self-interest and self-justification.

History is marred and stained with the collapse of principles and loss of integrity among great societies and noble institutions, among religious groups and revolutionary parties that espoused good intentions and expressed lofty spiritual goals. Many a great project and noble effort has come to a sudden end once the times become truly hard and the greater dilemmas of life must be faced. Out of confusion and fear and the eruption of unconscious aggressive energies, institutions of all kinds have found themselves caught in their own shadows and mired in the blood of innocents.

Good intentions can only go so far and collective beliefs can only withstand so much. Tragedies and great troubles can only be withstood where there are enduring visions that do not collapse under pressure from outer circumstances. The enduring visions that become indelible and can withstand any amount of external pressure primarily develop from the awakening of inborn qualities found in the depths of the individual soul. The only thing capable of withstanding the pressures of collective fear and the rise of hate that often accompanies it is the unique visions that can awaken at the deepest levels of the soul, where a person can draw upon a consistent source of integrity that does not collapse when faced with outer threat or troubled by inner fears.

The old idea is that each soul is born with an indelible inner pattern that can shape a unique and enduring vision for that life. Each person has an inner design that can make life meaningful and make genuine integrity possible. The problem is that in order to find this deeper sense of self—and thus reach the third level of individual coherence and enduring vision—a person must first undergo and survive a period of loss and descent into darkness. The greatest resources and inner gifts of the soul are the aim of all the struggles in life, yet they can only be found after the troubles of life strip away most everything but the uniqueness hidden in the soul.

The third kind of person is forged from life experiences that involve both the darkest moments of human existence as well as the brightest moments of human vision and conscious awareness. The problem in this world is not that people lack genuine vision or true nobility of soul, the problem is that a person must suffer disillusionment and a thorough loss of hope before the hidden vision and natural destiny seeded within them can be found and raised to consciousness.

Safety and Risk

An old African proverb says: "I do not trust those who have never fallen, for one day they will fall like everyone else." A "dark night of the soul" seems to be required in order for the inner light of life and enduring flame of imagination to be found and be confirmed. How else do we understand that everyone suffers in this world? If the suffering itself has no redeeming quality, then survival of the fittest and despair of any higher purpose would make the most sense. On the road of life, everyone must fall and, in falling, learn what carries them inside all along. Soul would have us face the lions of fate in order to find the threads of destiny that allow us to discover and participate in the continuing creation of this world, one that ever slips into darkness only to return when a new dawn breaks and dispels all the shadows, terrors, and fears.

The first adventure in this world involves growing up and making a place for ourselves in the sun; establishing ourselves in the ground of common things and basic needs. The second adventure—and deeper aim of all—which makes a person unique and meaningful involves a deepening and growing down in order to learn who we are in our essence and at our core. The deeper and greater adventure of one's life involves a necessary descent; for each must die a "little death" in order to find a greater life. Whether it comes from a tragic loss or a debilitating illness, an extended period of poverty or a devastating experience of battle, we all find ourselves descending into darkness at some point.

Secretly, the soul would lead us to places of renewal, but only after some descent and loss occurs; soul would have us understand who we truly are at our core and in our depths. Spirit might wish us to depart for a higher realm, but soul would have us each find our part in the ongoing story of the earthly world. Soul is the source of authenticity and the root of spontaneity; both the most ancient presence of life and its most immediate, spontaneous manifestation. Soul is the light found in the darkness; not a reflection of light in the outer world but an inner flame that burns with emotional heat and flickers with inborn intelligence. Soul is the resilient and resourceful aspect of our being that can deal with great loss and handle even despair. And soul can often be found at the rough edges of life, in the dark margins where things are more mysterious and where meaningful change becomes more possible.

It is part of the mystery of life on earth that the human soul can awaken, grow greater, and reveal inner gifts when everything turns dark and seems about to fall apart. Soul does not fear a downturn or seek to avoid a period of darkness. Soul carries a deeper wisdom and darker knowledge born of descent and loss and renewal. Soul would have us go where we fear to go in order to learn who we are intended to be. When we are willing to accept the fate of the exile, we become more able to find a true path and join the great company of awakened exiles and the long line of seekers who go towards the roar when most people run the other away. Then, the alchemy of the awakening soul becomes a source of meaningful change and a living root of remedies for what ails both culture and nature.

The times are dark and the roar of the world keeps getting louder; it is no time to be grazing in the fields of denial or seeking safety among the rocks of false certainty. As the outer world loosens, slips, and seems about to unravel, the inner archetype of apocalypse rises closer to the surface. It brings with it a greater tension of opposing extremes, an increase of both hard attitudes and paranoid fears. The tendency to panic can strike at any time. At certain times, fear itself is the issue; not just the uncertainty of change or the threat of loss, but simply the presence of fear itself can erase the sense of imagination and vision needed for both survival and renewal.

Fear, the Awakener

What we usually think of as fear is actually our response to the presence of fear; an increased heartbeat, growing anxiety, and panic are all effects of fear, not fear itself. Fear can cause hesitancy, loss of confidence, and fragmentation, but those are results of fear that has not been fully faced. *Fear* is an old word that derives from the same roots that give us "fare," as in "thoroughfare." Although it often causes people to run away from troubling situations, at a deeper level, *fear* means "to go through it." The hidden purpose of fear involves bringing us closer to natural instincts for survival, but also for awakening inner resources and sharpening our intelligence when faced with true danger and the basic need to change.

Fear used to be called "the awakener," for healthy fear intends to awaken us to our inner nature and the meaning and purpose embedded in our souls. When faced with danger or disintegration fear would have us respond from the depths of our soul, where the core pattern of life tries to grow and guide our way. The problem is that modern people doubt that there is a core pattern and inherent purpose in their life. Lacking that intuitive sense that trouble can lead to greater knowledge, people begin to fear trouble and even develop a fear of fear. From the thing to be undergone in order to awaken, our sense of fear has shifted to the dread of undergoing it. To be modern can mean to have a fear of going through what we fear, even to have a habit of avoiding the full experience of fear by trying to insure everything and deny the necessity of loss and radical change.

Many people believe that eliminating the apparent causes of fear will eliminate it, but fear, like beauty, is part of the world. The fear of fear results in the growth of terror as well as a loss of the beauty and wonder of the world. By fearing fear, we create the room for terror and panic to grow. People become blinded by fear, driven by anxieties, and increasingly ruled by phobias and obsessions. When we fail to recognize how fear works in the world, we become ruled by it. The point is not to become paralyzed with foreboding or be caught in the panic that can grip the collective and cause people to run blindly in the wrong direction. The point is to willingly go where most fear to go, to follow where the fear might lead and face the ways that the world roars at us.

Recognizing fear can be the beginning of finding the inner wisdom and hidden imagination in a situation. Fear can be a guide that clarifies what needs to be risked for a greater life to be found. The conditions in which we find ourselves are the conditions through which we must find our true selves and our genuine way of being in this world. Making and growing soul includes passing through the places we fear; risking the feeling of being afraid in order to become awestruck by the great otherness of the world we live in.

In the end, what we fear will not go away, for it indicates what we must go through in order to awaken, become more genuine, and live more fully. The problem is that we tend to be most afraid of what our own souls require of us. Often our deepest fear is that we might become who we are intended to be, who we already are at our core. For becoming who we truly are requires the greatest amount of change. As many old teachings suggest, bringing forth that which is in our nature will save us, while failing to bring forth our genuine nature will doom us. The real risk in this life has always been that of becoming oneself amidst the uncertainties of existence. As an Irish poet once said, a false sense of security is the only kind there is.

The modern world has lost the soul connection and thereby misses the thread of revelation that can be found at the edge of trouble and in the shadows of uncertainty. Sometimes, the greatest safety can be found in taking the right risk. Whether it be an individual, a community, or a country, when faced with tragedy or fearful uncertainty, we either become bigger and enter life more fully, or else we accept a diminished life and resign ourselves to a smaller way of being. That is the way of this world; safety is found where meaningful ways of living have been fully risked. Just when everything seems headed for disaster, facing fears of the end of the world as we know it can begin to open ways of surviving and being creative.

In the end, all we can offer the world is the life we came here to live and the gifts our souls would have us give. When the end seems near, genuine security can only be found in taking the kind of risks that lead to a greater sense of life and a more encompassing way of being in the world. When the world roars at us continually, it is time to go where we fear to go. When the enemy is fear itself, only boldness and imagination can save us from it. In story terms, the end always involves a loose thread or last chance that turns everything around. When it seems that the end is near, the best way to help the world involves learning the threads of story that are woven into our souls to begin with. All the rest is the roaring and wailing of unlived energies. In living the life the soul came to earth to live, a person automatically contributes to the meaning and continuance of life on earth.

CHAPTER 3

HOLDING THE THREAD OF LIFE

The new paradigm is an old archetype stirred up from the depths of creation; refashioned for the current times and come round again.

The essential meaning of the word *planet* involves old roots like "wanderer" and "stray;" the earthly realm that we call home is also a "wandering star." Being born here on earth means being "star-born" and at times being star-crossed as we wander in search of connections that are our mythical inheritance as well as our inborn destiny. *Destiny* is another star word, as is *disaster*, which means to follow the wrong star and lose one's cosmological connection to the grand scheme and overall arrangement of the universe. For something deep inside each soul is threaded to the stars and tied to the cosmos in ways that are both subtle and enduring.

The human soul is mythical and cosmological by nature; thus we are unable to stop trying to imagine the entire world, top to bottom—how everything began, how it might end, and what role we might play in the unfolding of it all. Cosmology involves all the images and ideas that people have found throughout time to describe the origins and workings of the universe. Taking the human part in the drama of existence involves trying to hold a vision of the whole universe while being but a small part of the great drama. On one level we are smaller than small, each just a tiny speck in the vast universe depicted by the modern science of cosmology. Yet, on another level, as dreamers and natural storytellers imbued with a speck of the divine and tied to the stars, we are somehow equal to the whole thing.

Cosmology is storytelling on a grand and grandiose scale, a major mythologizing that attempts to make sense of the enormity of the universe and the mystery of being born within it. The instinct for cosmology inspires the study of big ideas, universal theories, and grand patterns, the entire universe seen as a whole with each thing having its place in the overall design. Traditional myths and primordial philosophies naturally place humans in the middle of the cosmic order; for a universal intuition imagines humanity as a necessary link in the subtle body and essential chain of being. Humans are the only cosmologists, and cosmological stories are a necessity for humanity.

Cosmos means "order," from the old Greek word *kosmein*, which gives us "cosmic" as well as "cosmopolitan." The outline of ancient cities often followed a cosmological design that replicated patterns seen in the night skies. Thus, being at the midpoint of the city could also mean being symbolically at the center of the universe. The issue was not simply an astronomical mistake or failure of vision that placed the earth at the center of the universe; it was more the primordial sense that for earthlings, the earth is the center from which we must view the universe. Dwelling at the center of the cultural arrangement meant being more aware of the order in the universe and thus being more *cosmopolitan*. Although such a centralizing imagination could be taken literally, the intended point was best found in a felt sense of being connected to the living core of existence.

Without a working cosmology life can lose its sense of purpose, leaving the inevitable struggles of existence to seem random, pointless, and meaningless. Without a felt sense of cosmic order, people begin to feel accidental, lost in space, abandoned "in the middle of nowhere." The sense of cosmological dislocation can make the world can seem darkly chaotic. Of course, *chaos* comes from another old Greek word meaning "chasm" or "gaping void." Chaos is the polar opposite of cosmic order and implicit design; it is the eternal darkness and endless night that is the backdrop and default state of all creation.

Chaos is the abysmal abyss, the original rend in the world, the void in the midst of creation, the black hole into which things can fall and disappear. The order of the cosmos arose from chaos, the eternal darkness, which also threatens to swallow it all again. At the human level, chaos involves all that appears confusing, disorderly, and confounding about life. Chaos is the emptiness that can suddenly be felt in the pit of one's stomach and the bottomless pit that appears in nightmares. Chaos connotes collapse, disorder, and disorientation—things slipping through our fingers and life falling apart at the seams. The chasm of chaos exists within each person as the unconscious realm that follows consciousness all around. Chaos is the presence of absence as well as the absence of presence; it is the lack of any meaning, the nullity and creeping nihilism that can be found at the edge of all that seems certain, solid, and established in this world.

The shape and motion of this world swings back and forth between cosmos and chaos, between order and the lack of it, in a continuous, subtle exchange, constantly pulsing under the skin of existence. Cosmos and chaos are the two huge and paradoxical energies that continually make, unmake, and remake the world around us. Like night and day, there cannot be one without the other, for they are the all or nothing of this world, the grand Yea and the great Nay that resound throughout creation, expressing all that can and cannot exist. The world is made and remade again and again from the dance of cosmos and chaos.

In the dark times that follow the rise of the Enlightenment and the reign of reason and positivistic science, there seems to be more chaos in the world and less cosmic order to be felt or found. Some historical eras rise on the filling tides of cosmos as the breath of inspiration launches wondrous forms over the face of the earth. Temples and cathedrals arise and rival the presence of mountains; sculptured deities are chiseled into rock walls; complete musical scores appear in the dreams of people as primordial ideas and images find conscious expression and take grand forms. At other times, chaos pulls at the threads of creation and tips the scales out of balance as everything slips towards dissolution and disarray. Empires fall into dust and desolation; whole libraries become lost in the whirling sands; languages slip unspoken from lips; and the breath of great ideas withdraws from the minds of humankind.

You can feel the nearby presence of chaos when it seems that people could destroy the entire planet with the push of a button, as if a nihilistic aspect of mankind secretly aligns with the abyss, becoming intrigued with the gaping maw at the edge of the known world. The current era— in which it seems that the final end could come from a natural disaster, a clash of overly armed societies or a showdown between extremist religious groups— can be seen as a dark turn in the unending story of the cosmos, when chaos unravels the fabric of culture and loosens the web of nature. Modern cultures use science to consider cosmological questions, and it seems no accident that contemporary theorists wind up with the "uncertainty principle" and "chaos theory" while staring into the dark mysteries of "black holes."

Human societies, large or small, ancient or modern, must fashion cosmological stories that consider the endless dance between chaos and cosmos. Whether the grand narrations are called scientific theories or religious revelations, founding myths or tribal tales, they are all stories trying to make sense of the numinous world we find ourselves within. Native American tribes tell an old tale about what happens when times become uncertain, when the threads of existence loosen and everything seems to be unraveling again. It's a story from the time when people learned directly from the natural world, when the earth was speaking and folks knew better how to listen to the surprising speech of nature. In those early times, people lived closer to the land and respected the cycles and ways of nature; more importantly, they considered the earth itself to be a living story, a veritable storehouse of knowledge as well as an abundant natural resource.

Weaving the World

The old people of the tribes would tell of a special cave where knowledge of the wonders and workings of the world could be found. Even now, some of the native people say that the cave of knowledge exists and might be discovered again. They say it is tucked away in the side of a mountain. "Not too far to go," they say, yet no one seems to find it anymore. Despite all the highways and byways, all the thoroughfares and back roads that crosscut the face of the earth, despite all the maps that detail and try to define each area, no one seems to find that old cave. That's too bad, they say, because inside the cave can be found genuine knowledge about how to act when the dark times come around again and the balance of the world tips away from order and slips towards chaos.

Inside the cave, there lives an old woman who remains unaffected by the rush of time and the confusion and strife of daily life. She attends to other things; she has a longer sense of time and a deep capacity for vision. She spends most of her time weaving in the cave where light and shadows play. She wants to fashion the most beautiful garment in the whole world. She has been at this weaving project for a long time and has reached the point of making a fringe for the edge of her exquisitely designed cloak. She wants that fringe to be special; wants it to be meaningful as well as elegant, so she weaves it with porcupine quills. She likes the idea of using something that could poke you as an element of beauty; she likes turning things around and seeing life from odd angles. In order to use the porcupine quills, she must flatten each one with her teeth. After years of biting hard on the quills, her teeth have become worn down to nubs that barely rise above her gums. Still, the old woman keeps biting down and she keeps weaving on.

The only time she interrupts her weaving work is when she goes to stir the soup that simmers in a great cauldron at the back of the cave. The old cauldron hangs over a fire that began a long time ago. The old woman cannot recall anything older than that fire; it just might be the oldest thing there is in this world. Occasionally, she does recall that she must stir the soup that simmers over those flames. For that simmering stew contains all the seeds and roots that become the grains and plants and herbs that sprout up all over the surface of the earth. If the old woman fails to stir the ancient stew once in a while, the fire will scorch the ingredients and there is no telling what troubles might result from that.

So the old woman divides her efforts between weaving the exquisite cloak and stirring the elemental soup. In a sense, she is responsible for weaving things together as well as for stirring everything up. She senses when the time has come to let the weaving go and stir things up again. Then, she leaves the weaving on the floor of the cave and turns to the task of stirring the soup. Because she is old and tired from her labors and because of the relentless passage of time, she moves slowly and it takes a while for her to amble over to the cauldron.

As the old woman shuffles across the floor and makes her way to the back of the ancient cave, a black dog watches her every move. The dog was there all along. Seemingly asleep, it awakens as soon as the old weaver turns her attention from one task to the other. As she begins stirring the soup in order to sustain the seeds, the black dog moves to where the weaving lies on the floor of the cave. The dog picks up a loose thread with its teeth and begins pulling on it. As the black dog pulls on the loose thread, the beautiful garment begins to unravel. Since each thread has been woven to another, pulling upon one begins to undo them all. As the great stew is being stirred up, the elegant garment comes apart and becomes a chaotic mess on the floor.

When the old woman returns to take up her handiwork again, she finds nothing but chaos where there had been a garment of great elegance and beauty. The cloak she has woven with such care has been pulled apart, the fringe all undone; the effort of creation has been turned to naught. The old woman sits and looks silently upon the remnants of her once-beautiful design. She ignores the presence of the black dog as she stares intently at the tangle of undone threads and distorted patterns.

After a while, she bends down, picks up a loose thread, and begins to weave the whole thing again. As she pulls thread after thread from the chaotic mess, she begins again to imagine the most beautiful garment in the whole world. As she weaves, new visions and elegant designs appear before her and her old hands begin to knowingly give them vibrant shape. Soon she has forgotten the cloak she was weaving before as she concentrates on capturing the new design and weaving it into the most beautiful garment ever seen in the world.

Black Dog Times

Upon hearing the tale, most people feel great sympathy for the old woman who labors so long and hard only to wind up having everything reduced to chaos. What a shame that she cannot finish her work; how unfair and punishing this world can be. Most people feel that if the black dog would just stop causing trouble and undoing everything, the old woman could complete her weaving. Then this world would be a proper place; things would be in order and the old woman could finally rest. Then it would be "her time," and she could stop her labors and enjoy the fruits of her work.

Of course, the old people of the tribe tended to see the story differently. They took solace in the strange tale of the cave where things unravel; they saw wisdom in the way the old woman faces the mess and deals with disaster. This is the story they recalled whenever times turned hard, when the world seemed to become a darker place and everyone became disoriented. This is the tale they told to remind themselves and instruct others how to deal with chaos, when the ends of creation seem to fray and unravel.

The old people call the persistent weaver the Old Woman of the World herself, the original weaver handling the threads of existence. They identified the ancient stew of seeds and roots as the living soup of creation that needs to be stirred up again and again or else it stagnates and spoils or overheats and boils over. They pointed out that trouble and turmoil are part of the way that this world changes, the exact process through which life alters itself and thereby renews. They considered how Nature is always cooking something up and continually shape-shifting, both devolving and evolving at the same time. They tried to remind everyone that nature means change, that change is the essence of life, and that in this old world, whatever fails to change will soon dissipate or die.

Since the old people have an instinctive grasp of symbolism, they followed the metaphorical levels of the tale and knew that the cave where the great cloak unravels and becomes woven again is the world itself, the wondrous earth with its bold creations and shining garments that slip over the naked presence of life in its many forms. The old people said that the fire in the cave reflects the necessary yet unseen fire that ever burns at the center of this green-garmented earth. They recognized the cauldron as the alchemical vessel of creation with its stew of living seeds, its troubles boiling and bubbling away, and its ancient, sacred fire hidden at the very core.

The old people had known trouble, and they saw the problems and uncertainties of this world from a different angle. Being older, they had lived through tragedies and survived many disasters. They related to the struggles of the old woman, especially how she must face the mess that remains after all her best efforts have been thoroughly undone. They saw how quickly things can unravel, how life can be wasted, and how blood can be foolishly spilled on the earth.

They liked that a little story could be used to consider such big things; they liked how it brings out many issues using only a few narrative threads. They liked the economy of that, and the way it could save time and get right to the core of the issue. They remind us that the nature of this world requires that the beauty of life be lost, that it be rediscovered only to be lost again. They said that each generation must discover the eternal patterns and that the designs of life must be recast over and over again. They knew that completion signifies death and that life keeps falling apart only to begin again from the remnants of the past and the loose threads of the present. They made the point that, should the old woman ever complete the design, the whole world would come to an end.

"Be thankful for the trouble you find in this world," the old people would say. "Be thankful for the black dog that occasionally unravels the whole thing." For the black dog acts out the role of chaos, which eventually undoes and dismantles everything made manifest in this world. They knew that the dog is black in order to remind people that this world must be repeatedly rewoven from darkness as well as light, that those are the enduring threads of existence that were separated at the beginning of creation and that must be handled again each time re-creation is required.

The old knowers knew that the black dog, so dedicated to undoing things, belongs to the Old Woman of the World just as much as the elegant garment she has woven with beauty and care. Having survived and reflected upon the trouble of their own lives, they learned to see life with a "darkened eye." They knew that prolonged innocence creates a huge shadow and that the desire for perfection causes untold damage. They were not so foolish as to think that the world could just be positive or only made of light. Yet they were not so cynical as to deny the ongoing wonder of creation. When the dark times come and the end seems near again, a darker knowledge of the world is needed if creative ways of reweaving the threads of existence are to be found again.

The old people knew that the "black dog times" come around as the world goes through its endless cycling and re-cycling. They knew that the return of the dark times means that the living people have to find a new vision for life or else become undone when the threads of nature loosen and the designs of culture start to collapse. In the midst of trouble, they would try to emulate the old woman who is also the world itself. They would try to tolerate the mess and find genuine visions of new designs and ways of being that appeared at the edges of life and on the fringe of being.

Hearing this old story, some people ask: "Is the cave real or something made up?" The old people might answer: "Yes." For everything real in this world is also made up; everything is made from "whole cloth," and all of it has been hanging by a thread all along. Those arguments about creation versus evolution miss the point; creation is ongoing, not something that simply happened in the past, and evolution happens alongside devolution as the whole world is beginning and ending all the time. Those who insist on having it one way or the other are setting the stage for a visit from the black dog that keeps bringing a little chaos into our best-laid plans, especially those of us who insist on seeing it all one way.

The mess of life is all around us and everyone contributes something to it. Forget about good intentions; the junkyard dog of chaos faithfully follows order wherever it goes, and it visits everyone. People may pretend they don't own a black dog, yet inside their lives, things repeatedly become torn and frayed. The black dog appears in the inner limp we cannot fully disguise, the loss that remains with us, the tragedy that won't release us, and the shadow that shades all knowing. Everyone has an inner shadow and the black dog knows how to undo things whenever we become pretentious or think that we are in charge of our world.

The black dog demonstrates how all notions of reality and all claims about the facts of life can one day become bare threads that unravel right before our eyes. It may be good enough to stick to the facts when things are running smoothly, but in the black dog times it becomes necessary to see past the obvious, it becomes important to glimpse behind the scenes where the issues of life get stirred up and where destruction and creation are forever changing places. After all, a hurricane can toss buildings and flatten whole towns; a sandstorm can obliterate an entire landscape; someone decides to start a war and life begins fighting with death and everything begins falling apart. The world as we know it ends all the time. The whole thing is ever on the point of re-creation, always on the edge of unraveling and slipping back into chaos. This is the world we all live in.

To be alive at this time means to be caught in the troubling mess and mass disillusionment found between the unraveling of the world as we know it and the as yet unseen revelation of new designs for life on earth. It means to be feeling what the old weaver feels when she finds her beautiful creation reduced to chaos and confusion. It means to feel the great uncertainty of the timeless moment between one world and the next. For the moment between loss and renewal, betwixt collapse and re-creation, is a span of indeterminate duration. To be alive at this time means to be caught on the threshold and trapped in the liminal space where one thing turns into another in a rhythm not of our choosing. At the cosmic level, it is but a moment among many moments of ruin and regeneration; for us, it can be a lifetime of uncertainty and radical change.

Things can seem desperate, despairing, and doomed if we look at all the losses and seemingly pointless tragedies; great institutions have become hollow and the teeth of chaos pull at the patterns of social order. In the great drama of betwixt and between, we can feel tossed back and forth as the middle ground of creation churns and often turns upside down. To be alive at this time means to be caught in a great unraveling that strands us near all the loose threads of creation; but it also means to be close to the revelation of the new design and the next paradigm. The old knowers say that the cave of knowledge can be found in the depths of the human soul, that each soul is threaded with inner qualities intended to be woven into the world and added to the garment of creation. They say that the creative energies of each soul become more important when the dark times come round again. In facing up to the enormous problems of the world and accepting the troubles that knock on our doors, we can better learn what hidden resources, deep resolves, and surprising designs we have hidden within us.

The old story depicts this process of acceptance as a matter of shifting from one task to another, yet a cosmic turn is also implied. In the cave of knowledge, we can peek in on the "routines of eternity" and see the three-step dance of the manifest world. In the existential cave where knowledge can be found, there are three essential motions that make up the cosmic rhythm of life. Creation and destruction appear as opposing and necessary poles of existence. Between them is the middle ground of sustaining life. We may experience them sequentially, but when they are perceived in their mythic proportions and their mystical reach, all three are manifested in the world at once. "Create, maintain, destroy," goes the song of life; it takes three to do the tango of existence. Nature and culture both dance to these steps and share in these eternal motions. Life is a constant re-creation at the edges of conflict and loss, and it all happens within the great mystery of continuance.

A Tale of Two Worlds

The modern world has entered a crossroads that many cultures have entered before: an era comes to its end, the basic energies of life are more intensified and polarized, and we are more exposed to extremes. The endless reports of conflict and disaster, of terror and torture cannot be easily contained by the individual psyche. In the face of chaos and radical change, there is a danger of being driven to one extreme or another. Some react by becoming cynical and being both hard-headed and hard-hearted. Cynicism grows during the black dog times as some try to protect themselves against feelings of loss and despair by tearing things down. As it happens, *cynic* is a dog word, from the Greek, *kyne* meaning "dog-like." Cynics are faultfinders who specialize in pointing out the flaws and failures of others while distancing themselves from their own dreams and hidden hopes. Eventually, a cynic winds up gnawing on the same bones of contention over and over; they rant and chew things over even after there is no marrow left. Cynics need to expand their sense of the world and rediscover the wonder and mystery that underlies everything, even themselves.

At the opposite end of the spectrum, there are those who are overly hopeful even when tragedies occur and loss demands a deeper response. *Naïveté* means "simple or artless," not simply innocent, but also artlessly foolish. Some who remain naïve will put all their faith in god; others place all their hopes in technology or science. Either way, there is an insistence on "positivity," an avoidance of supposedly negative feelings, and a lack of the gravitas natural to the human soul and to life on earth. Some insist that "every cloud has a silver lining," even when some clouds are lined with acid rain and there are nuclear clouds that could blow all the linings, all the possibilities, to kingdom come. Naïve people want simple answers when things become complex; they want the bright side of life to be the only face of existence. They forget that the paths of wisdom begin in darkness, that being lost is necessary in order to be found and to find one's true self. They forget that becoming enlightened requires entering the darkness repeatedly, not simply imagining figures of light.

At the end of an era, as the archetype of apocalypse pulls everyone to opposing extremes, there tends to be two major and contrasting stories that shape how most people view the world. Both narratives have value and each has pitfalls that can cause a person to see only one side of the dance of life. One saga involves the epic tale of progress; in it the human species climbs from a primitive state of blind instinct and ignorance to an enlightened condition of advanced civilization. When combined with notions of evolution in the natural world, this "myth of progress" develops into a firm belief in the steady triumph of humanity and the continual rise of consciousness. In this narrative, there tend to be no limits to growth along the upward and onward path to human freedom and eventual fulfillment of life on earth.

In many ways, this is a Western story that draws upon positivistic science and the rule of reason, but that also has threads connecting it to mythical tales of the Hero's Journey. The myth of progress places individual heroism and personal accomplishments as a natural parallel to an underlying process of worldwide evolution. Both tracks seem to aim at a higher order of life, an elevated state that is somehow "natural" at the same time that it is extraordinary. The myth of progress and the theory of evolution seem to fit seamlessly together, and many modern people simply believe that this story conveys the facts of the matter and presents the only way to view the course of life in this world.

When combined with religious notions of a providential god who rewards hard work and good behavior, the myth of progress can function as a "secular religion." Deeply ingrained beliefs about the never-ending arc of progress can lead to the conviction that human invention and "technological advances" will manage to save the day. Redemption takes the form of medicines that can cure all ills, genetic manipulations that can produce miracle seeds, and biological alterations that can prolong human life indefinitely. Heroic efforts, entrepreneurial innovation, and determined futurism all find a home inside the overarching themes of continuing progress and conscious evolution towards a new paradigm and a fully realized world.

The sense of predictive progress that attaches to theories of evolution derives from notions of inevitable growth made popular in Victorian times. *Evolution* means "to unfold, to unroll," especially the "unrolling of a book." The modern connotation of evolution comes from Charles Darwin's book, *On the Origins of the Species*. Ironically, like *apocalypse*, which only appears in the opening line of the Book of Revelations, the current sense of *evolution* comes from a single use of the word in the closing paragraph of Darwin's revelatory book. Darwin himself preferred the word *descent*, which seems to roll downwards through time in contrast to the notion of upward progress that soon became attached to the theory of evolution.

Of course, no single story can ever suffice to tell the tale of life on earth where diversity is the mantra of nature and there are many levels and layers to the orders of existence. Naturally, there is another widespread and deeply held narrative that depicts the world as a place of continual loss and steady decline. The "myth of decline" follows an opposite plotline in which life begins in an ideal paradise only to fall into descending periods of darkness and increasing disorder. Under this narrative, all that people can look forward to is a collapse of the current civilization along with its ruling ideas. The course of life involves a loss of order and civility as the energy of the world wears down and the lights of creation go dim. This descending or regressive arc presents a more tragic view of the world and a darker prediction for the future of humanity. Regardless of heroic efforts or spiritual exertions, the world is imagined to be declining steadily, its glory days far in the past and increasing periods of loss looming in the future.

Tales of decline that begin with an ideal world or Golden Age were common to many tribal groups and ancient cultures. Such sagas formed the foundational texts for Greek and Norse myths as well as the mythic cycles found throughout the Middle East and the Far East. Bible stories of the Garden of Eden arise from similar roots; the sense of a paradise lost leaves humanity stranded in an unredeemed realm, longing for a return to a sacred past. Something in the human soul has always dreamed of a lost paradise that existed before a fall into the trials and tribulations that come to dominate human existence. The notion of decline from an ideal era also appears as a common metaphor when people refer to the Golden Age of art, architecture, science, or fiction. Paradise turns out to be a paradoxical place that some people see in the future, but others lament as part of the past.

The age-old narrative of a fall from grace has archetypal roots that can also be seen in nature through the cycling of the seasons. Creation begins with the brightness and promise of springtime only to eventually decline and go barren as the light withdraws from the world and leaves everyone and everything in the deepened shades and cold declensions of winter. The myth of worldly decline can seem old-fashioned, darkly pessimistic, and deeply discouraging when compared to the tales of upward evolution and unending progress. Yet this world is essentially a place of mystery and what looks darkest at the beginning can have bright threads hidden within. Conversely, things that seem most positive can be found to have a dark shadow that eventually comes to the light of day and obscures what seemed so bright to begin with.

Paradox Amongst the Paradigms

Older, more traditional views and many Eastern philosophies harbor heavy doses of pessimism as well as tendencies to value the past over the future. Eastern practices tend to downplay the role of the heroic individual in favor of the group mind while offsetting any enthusiasm for progress with notions of great cycles of existence. Eastern views seem to circle around an unfathomable center that makes progress seem superficial; it even suggests an existential emptiness behind all pursuits. What some champion as progress, others consider indulgence in materialism and superficial technology that only happens at the end of a cycle, when the spiritual breath of creation withdraws from the world.

The Western worldview insists on the necessity of progress; it champions the sense of evolution aimed at steady improvements on a wide scale of existence. Thus, the West appears to be essentially positive about life and seriously optimistic about progress and the promise of a brighter future. Yet the modern sense of "enlightened destiny," with its will to dominate nature, can accelerate crises that affect the whole planet and plague the realms of ecology as well as economics, not to mention the cultural anxiety and spiritual disorientation that characterize mass cultures. The Western world, so emboldened by Enlightenment ideas and positivistic science also involves a deep shadow of entrenched religious beliefs that deny the existence of evolution and predict cataclysmic events and imminent worldwide destruction. The futuristic and often optimistic Western notions of the world seem to carry a persistent shadow of wild apocalyptic fantasies, and at times delusional beliefs, in a fallen world on the verge of self-generated disaster. Science also feels the pull towards notions of collapse and dissolution, not just in theories of entropy, but also in concerns over the destruction of the earth from a deadly asteroid or atmospheric disaster.

Modern people can, on one hand, tout the miracles of progress—which promise to redeem everyone from dangers and darkness—while, on the other hand, slip into darker thoughts and cynical feelings that arise with each new ecological disaster or mindless act of terrorism. Inside the notions of progress and the motions of evolution, there can be visions of cataclysm and a haunting of worldwide catastrophes. The promise of futurism carries with it a deep shadow of despair and a reactive pool of nihilism that can rise to the surface whenever tragedy appears.

Meanwhile, the seemingly pessimistic worldview of the East tends to include an unending cycling and recycling of existence that does not champion progress, but rather predicts renewal after each period of decline. In the West, where history tends to dominate mystery, there looms in the background the possibility of everything ending in a fury of global warming or else in a cloud of nuclear explosions. On the other hand, in the East, where many believe we have been in the "dark times" for all of what we call history, mystery tends to penetrate each little thing and the eternal can break into time at any moment and relieve the burden of existence. In the East, where the emptiness of life and the hopelessness of progress can be axiomatic, the epoch of darkness, trouble, and turmoil eventually leads to the dawning of a new era in which everything begins again.

These two contrasting narratives are like a mythical version of the opposite kinds of people who tend to see the glass of water either as half full or as half empty. Progress or regression, endless improvement or steady decline: the condition of the world is in the eye of the beholder. It might seem a matter of choice whether a person decides to be optimistic or pessimistic about life. Yet in mythic terms, such a simple choice is not inclusive of the weirdness or the wonder of the living, breathing planet we live on. Is there progress of some kind? Or is the whole thing going to hell in a hand basket? The cosmological answer is yes; both are "true stories" in some sense, and both reveal something about life on earth.

In cosmological terms, each narrative depicts something essential about life and each is necessary in its own way. Not only that, but both are happening at the same time. The opposing views are crosscurrents in the waters of existence and, like cosmos and chaos, both exist and manifest at the same time. Both views are archetypal, based in ancient images that rise from the primordial depths of the psyche, each view a natural inheritance of the body of myth and the range of human imagination. At this time, when the archetype of apocalypsis rises closer to the surface, the contrasting stories of progress and decline can be seen and felt more often and more fully. The effect of both narratives can be found wherever people consider the contemporary crises of the world that include environmental dangers, the confusing results of globalization, the increasing paralysis of politics, and the rise of fundamentalism and extremism of all kinds.

Welcome to the Chaosmos

To be alive at this time means to be in the in-between place where the tension of the opposites becomes more palpable and must be suffered more consciously if a redeeming third way is to be found. Rather than developing rationales for either view, the important point is that, like cosmos and chaos, both are archetypal forms and each plays a part in the drama of the world. The difficulty is to see both simultaneously, to hold the tension of the opposing paradigms long enough to see it all another way. The trick is to be like the old woman in the cave of knowledge who lives with the paradox, stirring the stew of existence while sustaining the seeds of change. To lose the sense of paradox means to miss the point and fail to see what all the chaos might be hinting at.

Apocalypse often appears along with images of paradise; they are the bookends of the cosmological, mythological story that inspires all religious literature. They are twin images, paired paradoxes, secretly connected like alpha and omega, like end and beginning, like chaos and cosmos. Chaos appears when the end is near, but it also appears at the very beginning before creation starts to unfold, right before paradise and the implicate order of the universe become revealed. Chaos is a paradoxical condition that includes both the emptying of familiar forms and the beginnings of renewal from the reservoir of cosmic life. Chaos is both the primal emptiness as well as the source of everything that comes into existence.

In creation myths, chaos represents the original condition, the *prima materia* from which all matter and everything that comes to matter first arise. Chaos includes the "empty fullness" of the void and is also found in the "full emptiness" at the center of all that comes into existence. Chaos can appear as a harbinger of the end, but also as a sign of renewal, as both beginnings and endings share in the great uncertainty and creative insecurity of chaos. In the end, cosmos depends on chaos; everything does—even us.

This earth is the time-bound middle ground where history suffers the endless exchange of chaos and cosmos. The cosmic middle used to be called the mesocosm, from the old Greek root *meso*, meaning "middle," as in Mesolithic, and Mesozoic. The mesocosm is the middle earth where the cosmic order and abysmal disorder frequently meet and often collide. It is the world as we know it, the ground on which we walk with the gravities that keep us grounded, the tragedies that overwhelm us, as well as the lifelong dreams and artful practices that help to sustain us. When it seems that the whole world might unravel or self-destruct it is the mesocosm that rattles and shifts as it is drawn into a cosmic turn that can seem like the end of everything, with human beings lost and stumbling in the middle of the mess.

The dance of cosmos and chaos follows its own courses while we, caught in the grip of extremes, can feel thrown back and forth on the ground of existence. For humans are cosmologically implicated, stuck in the thick of it, right in the messy middle where both cosmos and chaos, progress and decline, can be felt and must be lived. Humans inhabit the middle ground of the chain of being, set between the animals and the angels, children of the sodden earth, yet pulled by unseen spirit-threads that tie us to eternal things. Darkness and light, chaos and cosmos, lost and found: this is the world we live in. The question becomes not whether or not the world will end—for it won't—but rather what to do in the "extreme times" when it seems that it might.

The disasters that plague the modern world are real, yet they may eventually lead to a turnaround, a reversal of fortune that renews and redeems life's vitality and persistence. So, welcome to the great turning that turns everything around—the great churning that turns everything upside down so that the end becomes the beginning, and the last things last long enough for the whole thing to start over again. Welcome to the "endarkenment" that follows the Enlightenment, to the great downturn and the big upheaval, the dark ages and the black dog times. Welcome to the remains of the day and the remainders of modernity, to the turning of the cosmos and the learning of the chaos. Welcome to the "chaosmos," to the chaos and the cosmos clashing, to order and disorder dancing, as it was in the beginning and is again in the end, the world always ending and without end amen.

The Nick of Time

As things unravel in the middle and the end seems near, the two places to turn for solace and direction are deep within and out at the edge, where the imagination of the cosmos continues as a grand, never-ending story. Whatever may happen on earth, the moon continues with its hide-and-seek ways. The Milky Way whirls through the dark reaches of cosmic night. While eruptions in nature and disruptions of culture produce nightmarish scenarios and apocalyptic visions, something deep in the soul of humanity also responds to the roaring of the world. The discovery of new ways to proceed may result from the willingness to engage our greatest fears about life on earth. Great crises and impossible demands often provoke hidden resources and reveal hints of the hidden wholeness and unity of life. The threat of collapse and utter loss can provoke a deeper sense of wholeness, where nothing but total involvement and whole-heartedness will work.

Unfortunately, the modern world has fallen heavily under the spell of time being nothing but a process of loss, each passing moment falling away and further emptying the hourglass of the world and diminishing the presence of life in the process. Common time is mundane and routine; it is linear and lineal, a continuous sequence that seems also to be irreversible. Ever since people came to think and believe primarily in literal, historical terms, the sense of the sacred and eternal realm has been dislocated and removed from its hidden nest inside each moment. Common time has become rigid and *profane*, meaning that it is "outside the temple" and therefore unholy and separated from the touch of the sacred.

Whether we believe in the arc of progress or the myth of decline, we live in a period when common time is separated from timelessness, when eternity has been removed to a future place that can only be found at the end of all time. In a sense, a part of time was lost or stolen as its eternal rhythm became separated from its historical beat. The modern world is under the spell of linear time and increasingly out of touch with timeless things and therefore in fear of time running out altogether. The time that people cannot find these days is the timeless moment and eternal connection through which time itself renews.

Seeing mythically, there is always a crisis of imagination as each moment can be the critical instant in which we awaken and change the direction of life. That is a frequent message in fairy tales, where the clocks are always about to strike midnight and everything is about to either turn to stone or else be redeemed. Just before the fateful hour strikes, the hero or heroine suddenly awakens, having received an inspiration that saves the day. It all happens in the last moment and "just in the nick of time." For eternity hides near the ends of time, only appearing in revelations of the last possible minute, after all hope seems lost and time has run out on all common expectations.

The nick of time was once a notch on a stick used to measure the passing of time before a moment became but a minute and time was captured in clocks and watches. Each nick cut in the stick could also be seen as a crack in the procession of time. The nick in the stick could break open time's mortal march, allowing the redeeming energy of eternity to pour into the world through the crack in time. Time, so often considered to be exact and precisely limiting, could crack open and reveal both the past living on in the present and the threads of the future being made. The open moments when time cracks and we feel the touch of eternity allow timelessness to flow back into the world. In place of the march of decline and beyond any sense of simple progress or evolution unrolling, a mythic regeneration occurs, a re-actualization of potentials as common time, with its forms and formulations, becomes emptied out and renewed.

A Little Redemption

Myths and stories from many traditions present "little redemptions" in which the time-bound earthly realm becomes the place where transcendent energies break through and life can be ransomed and redeemed a little at a time, not in the distant future, but in the here and now. Like so many other things at this time, the word *redemption* needs to be redeemed from the monolithic sense of an afterlife reward only possible to attain after time on earth has come to an end. In folk and fairy tales "little redemptions" occur all the time in the form of spells being broken and people awakening and returning from places of isolation and exile. Redemption from a spell means a return to a sense of natural wholeness and proper orientation to the shape and meaning of one's life. Moments of wholeness in the living human soul reunite time with eternity and redeem the world a little at a time.

Redemption means "to ransom, to buy back," and we are here to help buy back the world as a place woven of wonder and mystery—where dissolution and renewal happen all the time and at the same time; where eternity hides in the cracks of time passing and the return of cosmic order always happens at the edge of the abyss, on the brink of disaster where life and beauty and meaning are snatched from the teeth of chaos; where even a little redemption helps realign the soul of the individual with the unseen soul of the world and helps to buy everyone a little more time. For redemption happens all the time in little ways—in moments that become momentous, in the little bit of time it takes for a person to awaken to the timeless knowledge of the soul.

Strange as it may seem, individual human consciousness forms the makeweight in the scales of time and eternity; living out the hidden meanings within life helps to balance the weight of the world—each living being wrapped around an invisible, eternal thread and each life-thread a meaningful story trying to break out of the wall of time and assist creation. Ultimately, the soul is the seat of imagination, the place of our ancient heritage of archetypal forms and ancestral resources. Imagination is our essential organ of being and we are constantly reimagining the world, constantly participating in its creation, collapse, and renewal. While time seems about to run out, timeless things are near at hand and ready to redeem the world, moment by moment. Behind all the roaring and confusion of this world, the otherworld of imagination and the living spirit of the eternal wait to be found again. The pressure on humanity may come down to imagining the world in ways that hold the ends and beginnings together.

We redeem ourselves and help redeem the world a little through a conscious and continuous effort to find and live the inner dream and seeded story of our lives. In the end, humans don't have to save the whole world as much as become more able to imagine the wholeness of life and the renewal of the cosmos. Despite all its massive problems and dire dilemmas, the world trembles on the edge of "once upon a time," the place where imagination breaks the spell of time and frees us from the traps of literalism so that the past can be reclaimed to the present and the future can be returned to its potential. For it is not simply a better future that we need, but also a more meaningful connection to the past and the lasting things that help the world to be in balance. When the times become dark, it is important to have a narrative feel for what is old and wise and waiting to be found again. This old world does not end because it touches eternity and finds ways to start all over again. And we, who are a microcosmic version of the cosmic presence, are the often unwitting agents of the little redemptions that ransom the world from the edge of chaos.

CHAPTER 4

STOPPING IN TIME

To see the world in a grain of sand, and to see heaven in a wild flower,
hold infinity in the palm of your hands, and eternity in an hour.
William Blake

An old idea suggests that the world inside us is greater than the world we see around us, that each person is a cosmos with all the stars hidden inside. The individual soul can be seen and held as a microcosm, a little world and realm unto itself. If penetrated deeply enough, it might turn inside out and become the living thread to the soul of the world. Amidst the current speed of life and rush towards the future, the presence and value of the individual soul is easily lost. The soul's natural horizon is the cosmos yet the modern world tends to become smaller and more horizontal as it loses the vertical dimension and the grounding depths that the soul brings to life.

In losing the soulful ways of connection, we risk losing what relates us to great nature on one hand and the eternal realm and touch of the divine on the other. Soul is the secret glue of the world and the connecting agent of existence. Soul is found where life deepens us, where meaning calls to us, where trouble deters us, wherever and however we slow down in the midst of the rushing and racing at the surface level of life. Amidst the modern fascination with newness and things that move faster and faster, there is something older and wiser trying to catch up with us. Only if we can manage to stop in time and "slow downwards" can the old soul within us catch up and help find a way through the growing darkness.

There is an old story of a young spiritual seeker who set out in the world determined to find a sacred way of life that could lead to inner meaning and spiritual fulfillment. It was a noble quest, one that can awaken at any time in life as each life longs for a true awakening. After a period of searching and encountering some of the sorrows and troubles of the world, the young seeker felt more exiled than when he first began his search for meaning. It was as if he had to lose parts of himself along the way and become truly lost before finding his true sense of self.

Eventually, he found himself in the vicinity of an old temple and managed to be accepted amongst the others there who also sought more than the common world could offer. He began to study the ways of that place, which included the practice of deep meditation. Having searched far and wide and wandered throughout the world, he now had to sit still in order to learn how to search deep within. Soon enough he learned to turn inwards and was meditating day and night. He gave himself to the work and barely stopped his inner practice long enough to eat or sleep. As time went on, he grew quite thin and often seemed on the verge of complete exhaustion.

One day he was granted an audience with the old teacher who had long been the master of that temple. After observing the avid student and inquiring about his interests and aims, the old teacher advised him to slow down, to rest more often, and to learn to take better care of himself. Of course, the young seeker ignored the advice; he even intensified his practice and doubled his efforts. When next they met, the teacher asked: "Why are you rushing so much? What is the great hurry?" The devotee answered quickly: "I am after enlightenment and spiritual fulfillment and there is no time to waste."

The teacher considered that idea for a while and then responded, "How do you know that what you seek is running somewhere before you, so that you must spend all your energy rushing after it? What if what you most need is actually behind you, trying to catch up to you? What if the knowledge and wisdom you seek is waiting for you to descend to it? What if all your haste and feverish determination turn out to be your own habitual pattern of running away from what has been trying to catch up to you all along?"

Looking inside for knowledge and grounding is an old idea that by now can seem counterintuitive and contrary to contemporary attitudes about life. Yet what we often need most, whether we are on a spiritual quest or simply trying to make our way in the world, is the soul connection that allows us to deepen and grow inwardly, to "slow downwards" enough to find who we already are at our core. Our outer life often needs to turn upside down in order to stop us in our tracks before we are ready to learn that the soul has its own sense and rhythm, its inborn style and natural way of being in this world. Having an awakened inner life means learning where we are already threaded to the world and discovering how we might be most useful to it.

"Slow" and "down" are modes of the soul; they are connective modes, ways of keeping connected to oneself and to one's environment. "Slowing downwards" refers to more than simply moving slowly, it means growing down towards the roots of one's being. Instead of outward growth and upward climb, life at times must turn inward and downward in order to grow in other ways. There is a shift to the vertical down that re-turns us to root memories, root metaphors, and timeless things that shape our lives from within. Slowing downwards creates opportunities to dwell more deeply in one's life, for the home we are looking for in this world is within us all along. The lost home that we are seeking is ourselves; it is the story we carry within our soul.

Ultimately, we turn things around by turning within and turning to the things worth risking the rest of our lives for. This is the greater risk of life; not simply surviving, but learning to grow the inner life that harbors our deepest sense of self and soul. When the outer world rattles and slips into chaos, the inner world can help us become more rooted and centered and be more able to help sustain life. The point of slowing downwards is stopping in time to catch one's own rhythm in order to change life from within. Only by stopping time can we find that which is timeless and enduring and able to help us renew our lives and, in time, help the world turn around as well. Whether the issue is a problem in one's own life or the course of life itself, in order to stop things in time, to make meaningful changes, we must stop time itself.

The ancient Greeks had two words for time and two ways of paying attention to the time each soul had on earth. *Chronos* was the term for linear, lineal time that always marches on. This is the time that flies like an arrow and waits for no one. Chronos was the name of the ancient god who came to be known as Old Father Time. He first appeared as the serpentine form wrapped around the cosmic egg, holding it closed before it cracked and creation began. Chronos gives us our chronological sense of time and all the calendars, schedules, and practical ways of keeping and counting time. This measurable, quantitative allotment of the moment-to-moment world was once seen as the sands of time falling through the narrow neck of an hourglass. In more modern imagery, we can hear the steady ticking of the clock or watch the silent rolling of digital numbers that toll the passing of each second in an increasing accuracy of the loss of time.

The other kind of time was related to Kairos, the youngest son of Zeus, most often depicted as a youthful, fleet-footed "daimon" or spirit. Poised on the toes of his feet, he carried a set of scales balanced on a razor edge, as if to suggest that the openings found in time could be fleeting and razor thin. Kairos was the opportune moment, the crack in time's relentless march. Hesitate just a bit and the moment of opportunity might be gone forever, for he who hesitates when Kairos is near, is lost. On the other hand, respond to the little crack or nick in time and become suddenly open to new possibilities through which everything might change, including the direction of time.

Kairos is the old Greek term for a moment of "great time," the unpredictable instant in which opportunity knocks and the doors of time can swing wide open and reveal all that exists on the other side of the daily rounds of life. Kairos is the other side of time, the hidden well of timelessness that exists alongside each moment in common time. Kairos is time outside time; we can feel it in those moments when we slip free from the reins of time and become truly inspired, when we fall in love, or wake up to our calling in life. In the "kairos moment," every situation becomes full of meaning and of infinite worth, for the moment has become momentous and we become capable of eternity. Those who learn the true value of time use it to prepare for the arrival of eternity.

The Awakened Moment

The kairos moment involves qualitative time, a shift in the very nature and duration of time as the moment becomes an indeterminate period and uncountable interval outside of the spell and trap of common time. Our entire lives can pass before us in the blink of an eye, opened wide by the cracking of time. A kairos moment is "syn-chronos time," thus it is ancient and immediate at the same time; it is a moment of synchronicity in which all parts of time become available at once. In the moment of synchronicity, we become prophetic and see in all directions at once. For prophecy means more than simply glimpsing a part of the future. The genuine prophet sees into the past and brings ancient knowledge back to the present as well as looking forward in time.

The open moment in time becomes the river in which time flows both ways and the present is immersed in timelessness. In such moments, we are called to awaken further; not simply to hear the alarm of time passing and leaving us behind, but more to find the depth and meaning of the present. Kairos is "awakened time," the moment trying to awaken us, the moments in which we awaken to a greater sense of the world and our place in it. Both the East and the West at one time paid close attention to the ways in which time could stop and be reversed so that life could be renewed; the Sanskrit word for such an awakened moment is *ksana*.

Ksana means "a unique instant," literally "the time it takes to cut a thread," or the little time it takes to pick up a loose thread and begin to weave the web of life again. It used to be said that such an instance includes nine hundred circles of life that touch upon all the underlying patterns that sustain this old world. Ksana refers to the opportune time that can appear at any time. It involves a paradoxical escape from time by entering the given moment more fully. In so doing, we slip through the crack in time and step upon a threshold that connects us to the eternal realm on the other side of time. This threshold moment puts us in a "liminal state" of betwixt and between that is neither here nor there and thus can lead to anywhere.

The most animated, surprising, and soulful places are those spaces found betwixt and between one thing and another—between sleeping and waking, between culture and nature, where the inner and outer and the above and below entwine. The world may be made of days and nights, but it changes from one to the other through the liminal moments and gloaming times of dawn and sunset. The soul understands the nature of bridges and shores, doorways and crossroads that gather the contradictions and oppositions that exist between one thing and another in this world. In such places and times, the laws of nature do not hold as the light of day dims to reveal a dusky realm that is neither night nor day, neither one thing nor another.

These liminal places and spaces exist at the extremes of time and in the margins of life. We may become disoriented in finding ourselves on the threshold between one thing and another, yet that is also the place where the divine that is hidden in us can be felt and become better known. The human soul is a betwixt and between thing that ties us to the time-bound world on one side and weaves us to eternity on the other. Each moment in time is pregnant with eternity waiting to be released and to release us from the strictures of time's relentless march. We are pulled into broken moments and exaggerated conditions that compel us to awaken to a greater imagination of the world and of our place within it. In the places of betwixt and between, life becomes more animated as both great nature and our own inner nature intensify before us and become revealed.

In contrast to the common sense of "reality" and the measurable world of facts and figures, the most Real moments in life are Timeless and Mythic and open to the Sacred. We live in extraordinary times and extraordinary moments are more real than common reality because "the Real" breaks through linear time and a common moment can become a momentous occasion. The problem with the "real world" is that it is not real enough to give people a genuine sense of meaning and purpose in life. That which is most real is also timeless, whether it be beautiful or terrible to behold; something happens that opens us to a world that has more presence and we become more present to ourselves. In the great loosening that happens when time turns over, there is also a thinning of the veil between the common world and the otherworld. On the threshold between one era and the next, things become more liminal as they become less certain; the normal rules of life are suspended and the trajectory of one's life can be altered. The most real moments in life alter us and change us forever. Such occasions have a timeless quality and a mythic sense that continues to live inside us. No matter how many years might pass we "remember it as if it was yesterday."

The most memorable times in our lives are those occasions when time seems to stop altogether and we enter another time and space. In that moment, we become an outsider; we live on the margins, in an indeterminate state that can involve both disillusionment and disorientation. Yet we also become more able to see; in a kairos moment, whatever we perceive becomes revelatory, even prophetic, as each nuance reveals hidden aspects of the world otherwise unseen. In such moments, the plotline of the soul can clarify and become more visible as we are propelled further into the life-story we came to live when we first came to life.

In fully entering the moment, we can live more fully; such an intensification of being can change not just the quality of time, but the arc and direction of one's life. Such moments of awakening become "lived time," time fully lived into, leading to a life fully lived out. We live for such moments, live most truly in such moments, and secretly long for such openings in time, all the time. The open moments of awakening break apart any over identification with the "things of this world" and remove us from the traps of history and the spell of linear time. In that time that is no time at all, the soul grows and unfolds the story trying to live into the world through us. In stopping time we see the way our soul would have us see; we find the genuine vision of our lives. In learning to truly see we become both younger and older, both more visionary and wiser at the same time. When we are running out of time the point is not to be running faster to make up for lost time, but to stop in time to let the unseen and the timeless qualities of life catch up to us.

The Original Mind

Regardless of the narrowing of imagination and loss of the immediate sense of spirit that characterize modern life, we still have an old knowing mind within us. Not the "old brain" that contemporary science studies but the ancient mind, untouched by the passage of time—the intuitive and instinctive mind that knows both basic survival and greater awareness. It is the deep mind, with its narrative intelligence and mother wit, the creative force sewn inside each person born that makes life and beauty and love possible. It is the old story-mind that knows how things can turn around in the last minute and how the last can become first in the back and forth between time and eternity.

There comes a time when the most important thing in life is for us to allow something older and wiser to catch up to us, as if the only way forward involves a step back—away from the competing disasters of the world and into the dusky realms of imagination, where things take new shape before entering the barrenness and glare of the daily world. Those living at a particular time are never simply the denizens of history or the pawns of time, they are also the only possible recipients of the messages of eternity trying to slip into the world and sustain the discourse of the eternal drama of life, death, and rebirth. Before a meaningful future can be found, something ancient and enduring about the world must be rediscovered. The balance of the future depends upon the presence of ancient things. By turning within and growing down, we find the original mind and old soul within us. In the depths of our lives we are each already an old soul capable of living meaningfully and, at times, able to lend a hand to creation.

Whatever survives the ravages of time and the threats of extinction involves the old mind within and the ancient inheritance of humankind. The old and original mind has a primordial sense of survival that permeates all of history without believing in any of it. The old mind is the poetic core that is naturally abundant with ideas and images, that which remains eternally threaded to the animistic, altruistic, ever-abundant source of life. Each person feels weary of life and more tired of the world when distant from the vital wellspring and fecund mud of the old mind within us. It is the original mind that returns things to their origins and keeps finding original ways to survive the disasters of life and learn anew. Any originality we might manifest arises from the roots of this original self and old soul that was seeded within us to begin with.

Under the rule of reason and the trap of history, the old mind seems illogical and irrational; yet it is our first way of being in the world and the original way of knowing anything about the world. This original mind is logical in its own way; it is mythological, psychological, and cosmological. The old mind within us is tied to the mythical, mystical thread upon which everything hangs in the end. In the eternal Lascaux of the old mind, life slows down and ancient ways of imagining the world can suddenly appear, the way a torch can reveal potent images on an ancient cave wall.

The old mind carries messages between the brain and the heart, allowing thought and feeling to meet. It is the ancient lord and inner sage hidden in the deeper self, trying to awaken and release the inner dream of one's life. *Mind* comes from old roots meaning "loving memory;" it is related to the Sanskrit root *munih*, which also gives us sage and seer, and the Greek *mantis*, which indicates "one who divines." The unfettered mind is naturally in touch with ancient memories and deep roots of imagination that touch the divine in us and in the world around us. The old mind can divine things that are necessary for the world to survive and for nature to revive.

With the old mind we perceive the world around us in ways that are pre-systematic thus more immediate and revealing. Being both ancient and immediate at the same time, the old mind is the "inner indigenous self" that instinctively connects us to the elemental forces of the earth and to the organic energies of our bodies. It is what connects each person to the dream of life as well as the pulse of nature. The old philosophers knew it when they carved "Know thyself" at the entrance of caves and places of oracle. The point of all oracles and most attempts to divine the secrets of life is to come to a deeper knowledge of one's true self, and that self is already an old and knowing soul. The deeper, instinctive, and intuitive self is wise about who we already are at the core of our lives and knowing about the purpose and aim of our soul.

Secretly, we each seek the greater personality seeded within us, the true self that is naturally gifted and uniquely formed. This primary self becomes accessible through passionate adventures in life and through deep thought and self-reflection that allow the speech of destiny to rise and murmur from the blood and bone, oracle-like and original within us. Thinking in this manner is also imagining; in the end we become what we can truly imagine ourselves to be. This requires a second courage, for true reflection and active thought are usually more difficult to face up to than the first courage needed for stepping into life.

Through the old mind we participate in the life of the soul; we become an "old soul" capable of knowing again the old ideas and images that keep this old world going. We become original, living closer to the origins of life, to the inner movements of creation, and to the dance of spirit with the soul of the world. This way of knowing requires the old way of thinking—thinking in blood and bone, an embodied thinking that stirs both the mind and heart. Thought becomes a combination of body, emotion, and mind—not simply brain and nerves, but the nerve to think in the blood and feel in the mind. There is a mind behind the brain, one that carries messages between brain and heart and allows thought and feeling to meet. It is the mind within the brain, the heart within the heart. It speaks of the poetic unity and secret history hidden in man. It whispers the mythical presence that was there at our beginnings and that keeps us threaded to the beginning of the world.

A separation from this primordial sense of being—a loss of meaningful connection and intuitive relation to the old mind and ancient soul within us—is the basic split in human life from which all conflicts arise and within which all anguish develops. *Primordial* refers to the prime sources of life energy and deep imagination that do not simply disappear, wear out over time, or run out of energy. Primordial indicates the underlying, pre-systematic way we were intended to feel, think, and be in this world. When in touch with the old mind within us, we become creative, original, and able to contribute to life. To be *original* means to be connected to the origins, to tap the potentials of the beginning and the ever-inventive, renewing capacity of the old soul and old mind within us.

The old mind offers us second chances no matter how long we have avoided our calling in life or been lost on the roads of despair. To any who would listen, it says: "You can't help but be who you are... and where." From that small notion of awareness and implicit motion of forgiveness, the old mind offers a thousand ways to step further into life and begin the whole thing again. When in touch with the old mind, we become indigenous to the world and dwell in the wonder of discovery. The original mind is the "inner indigenous" part of us that can feel at home anywhere and be ready to go on a great adventure at any moment. When in touch with it, we think as our ancestors did; we find new versions of old stories, become prototypical and unique instead of typical or normal.

Paradoxically, the "young at heart" part of each person is also part of the old mind. The eternal inner youth that carries the dream of one's life and knows how to connect it to the dream of the world is part of the old soul within us. Together they make up the inner imagination needed to survive the dark times. Thus, in the synchronicity of the soul, two things are trying to catch up to us at the same time: the ancient knowing inner sage as well as the ever-young, dream-making eternal youth of the soul. For the old mind is also the "beginner's mind" that is ever ready to begin again and learn new ways of being present and picking up a thread of meaning, beauty, or imagination that can help the reweaving of this troubled world.

The Cave of Knowledge

When the black dog stirs and the dark times come round again, the old mind tries to catch up to us in order to reconnect us to threads of imagination woven into us from before birth. For the cave of knowledge resides in the human soul, where the threads of the eternal can twine with the moments of time. The wise old woman sits in the eternal moment with the mess of chaos on one hand and the next design of life on the other. She represents the old mind and the inner mind that is abundantly veined with the gold of imagination. Her cave is the liminal space that is nowhere and everywhere at the same time; it is nowhere to be found and it exists wherever and whenever we allow the old dreaming mind and ever-imagining soul to awaken within us.

The old weaving woman is a primordial figure found in the realm of myth and in the deep imagination of the human soul. She is part of the old mind, a symbolic presence that connects great nature with the inner nature of humanity. She is an archetypal presentation of the living Soul of the World as well as a part of the human inheritance that resides in the cave of the mind and in the crevices of the heart, where the designs of life wait to be discovered and rediscovered again. She has many names including Mother Earth, Old Mother Nature, and Gaia; but she is also called Mnemosyne, Mother of Memory, and Mistress of the Muses, for she cares for the roots of culture as well as the seeds of nature.

She is old like the world and wise in the deep, feminine ways of weaving unlike things together and she is deeply resilient when things fall apart. She has human form, but she is timeless and able to transcend human limitations. She has seen it all before, yet she can feel it all anew. She knows that the hound of chaos will undo all life's beautiful designs whenever things get too close to perfection or when the greed and violence, the hypocrisy and the deceit, become too great. She has observed where good intentions pave the road to hell and how the righteous usually fail to do the right thing when it counts the most. She has witnessed the unjust wars and the rigged elections and watched the grand schemes, intended to save everyone, collapse into foolishness and mean-spirited plots.

She knows that chaos shadows all the manifestations of creation; she is not surprised when the black dog pulls again at the threads of existence. She has been there all along, behind the scenes, spinning, weaving, and recycling the threads of existence whenever things become threadbare. She is an essential part of the oldness that sustains this mysterious world, for what we call "the world" was old to begin with. The word *world* has *old* in it, and oldness has been a part of the world all along; something ancient and enduring was rooted in the world from the very beginning. The original word was *werold* with the root *wer*, meaning "woman or man," and the root *old*, meaning "aged" or "worn out." But *old* can also mean "ancient, primeval, and experienced;" as a verb it suggests "to grow, to nourish, to bring up." To be properly old is to be truly ancient and long-standing, to be close to the origins of life and near the mysterious place where things keep ending and beginning again and again.

On one level the world evolved as it grew up and it continues to evolve in both predictable and mysterious ways. On another level it was fully there, fully manifest, ripened and bearing fruit, from the very beginning. Call it paradise, call it a paradox; the world was old and ripe to begin with. It evolves and dissolves at the same time; it renews as it ends; it is old with origins and new with virginal inspirations at the same time. This old world presents itself paradoxically, and the paradise that we lost and endlessly seek is near us all along, for it exists within us while we search for it all around us. For something ancient and original dwells in the human soul as well.

Oldness is essential to the presence of the world and anything new in it rests upon the oldness of it. Anything truly original must touch the origins of life in order to surface in the world. New ideas arise from old radical roots hidden in the ancient ground of being. Knowingly or not, new inventions and innovations touch and tap into original archetypal patterns and ancient powers of imagination before ever appearing in the realm of time. Thus, scientific revelations often come in dreams or in visionary states that draw upon unseen, unconscious, and primordial sources of both thought and imagination. Of necessity, the "new paradigm" arises from the old archetypes as the world renews itself from original things and from the endless imagination that is the natural inheritance of the human soul.

Necessity

The old woman is the ancient and original recycler; she understands all the cycles of existence and knows when the time has come to recycle it all again. She knows the dance of life, the place of death, and the three-step waltz of creation, maintenance, and destruction. The ancient Greeks called her Ananke, or Necessity. As primordial goddess, she was present at the breaking open of the cosmic egg when it came time for the world to be born into the gap between eternity and time. She was the primordial personification of destiny, of inevitability, and fate, and all the gods had to bow to her out of necessity. She represents a universal principle and natural order that the other gods could not alter.

She spins the wheel of life, weaves the intricate web of the world, and at times allows the whole thing to fall apart; for in this world, creation and destruction are both parts of Necessity. She understands the importance of the unraveling as well as the necessity of the reweaving. "All of this has happened before, but you have to become old enough to know that," says the old woman as she looks upon the chaotic mess that was once the vibrant and elegant garment of the living world. Of necessity, the world becomes messy and confusing, and life can be full of anguish and loss; it can be by turns deeply tragic and wildly comic, and it is all necessary.

The old woman represents the enormity and the specificity of this old world. She is Old Mother Nature attending to the great cycles of existence, and she is also the source of the instinct that nourishes and nurtures each individual life. She is the mother of necessity at the beginning of time, but she is also the ancient weaver who winds each soul into the web of existence. She is depicted with a spindle in her hand as she continually weaves together the threads of fate and destiny, giving each soul its necessary limitations as well as its thread of destiny to transcend them.

When all seems lost and about to slip into the abyss of chaos, she is ready to start the whole thing over again. All she needs is some loose threads to begin with. From old remnants and odd remainders of all that went before, she can shape new designs for life to inhabit. Naturally, the most elegant and enduring designs will combine ancient forms with new shapes. Recycling is a component of the complex of apocalypsis; near the end "what goes around, comes around," and it does so more quickly. While the literal practice of recycling becomes essential for reducing the burdens of the earth, the symbolic sense of recycling involves a review of the stories we tell ourselves about the world and our place in it.

The exact medicine for the dissociation that has become so characteristic of the modern mind lies in finding again the ancient continuity of human thought and the underlying unity of life. Facing the end of an era with psychological awareness may be the way to wake up to the time we live in and find the inspirations needed to help turn things around. Times of apocalyptic intensity involve a mythic recapitulation, a reconsideration of what is most important, a re-visioning of what is most valuable and worth saving as things turn upside down before everything turns around again. Like the old woman in the cave of knowledge, we must accept the black dog times, yet not succumb to cynicism or despair about the world. We must find ways to imagine and assist new designs and nascent forms yet not ignore how suffering and loss plague most people in the world, or how denial delays the work of assisting nature to heal.

When things unravel before our very eyes, when the whole world seems to have lost its bearings, it is the ancient imagination of creation that seeks to be found again. It is not simply that the garments of culture have worn thin, exposing everyone to the raw greed of materialists and the fanaticism of fundamentalists; it is not simply that something completely new must be invented, rather it is that something ancient and enduring must be touched for things to be made anew and fashioned again. It is the ancient way of this world to make itself anew from the enduring threads that have been woven and rewoven many times before. DNA suggests the same thing, as does the renewal of entire forests from fallen trunks, branches, and tendrils that once danced in the wind and waved at time.

There is a level of existence where objectivity can be studied, where gravity rules the day and everything has its limits. There is a level of reality where people are necessarily responsible for the viability of life and the ecological well-being of natural environments. And there is another world: the world behind the world that transcends common limits, that extends beyond the rules of gravity and outside the clutches of time. It is this timeless and eternal realm that originally produced the time-bound world and that secretly sustains it as well. What we call the world is a living, breathing, ongoing experiment in which everything is recycled but nothing is ever repeated exactly. The world is a unique, ever-changing place of ongoing creation that renews itself by touching eternity and redeeming reality in both small and profound ways.

Seen mythically and psychologically, this old world is a wise old woman or sage old man; it knows how to return to the origins of life and nourish its own roots when things become torn down or worn out. The idea of renewal being an original element of the world is an important notion to have when everything begins to spin and speed up and all the world seems about to fall apart. If we have been born to a dark time it becomes all the more important for us to awaken to the threads of meaning and imagination woven into our individual souls. We are not just the passive witnesses of the world around us but also the recyclers of the threads of existence and the agents of renewal for our time on earth.

Through living fully we realize and transform the earth's silent potential. We become part of the ongoing creation of the world, for creativity is at the heart and soul of each of us. In imagining and creating, we make more life and add to the enduring presence of the world. In the darkest times something woven within us tries to become known and be expressed, a new articulation of beauty that allows us to discover the beauty hidden in ourselves. Amidst the rapid changes and reckless speed of life at the end of the era, something ancient and knowing keeps trying to reach us. In order to find the wisdom of the earth and feel the touch of the eternal, we have to stop in time and stop time's relentless march. When there seems to be no time left at all, the old ideas and ancient ways that help the world survive are close at hand and waiting to be touched by us and become known again.

CHAPTER 5

THE SECOND ADVENTURE OF LIFE

If a person wishes to be sure of the road they tread upon, they must close their eyes and walk in the dark.

St. John of the Cross

Each soul that arrives in this world carries a hidden spark that burns with varying levels of intensity throughout life. The spark of life is the inner nature of the person seen in its fiery form. This spark of the soul generates both bodily heat and inner intensities. It burns with the heat of libido or vital life energy that makes us warm-blooded as well as prone to heated passions. The more aware we become of the specific nature of the spark within us, the more it becomes an inner light able to lead us in the direction our souls are aimed at. For the soul's inner spark is also the seed of destiny that can illuminate a way through life even when the darkness around us grows deep.

Everyone has an inner spark and speck of star, though it is more visible in some than in others. When it does shine forth, it reveals something different in each person; the spark of life is the uniqueness in each soul. The inner spark would light the way of greater destiny in each life, yet it must find its fuel in the here and now of daily existence. It must shape the inner flame from the raw material of experience, from the challenges of the outer world and the burning questions and deep reflections found within. Thus, two of the greatest errors in life are running from the effects of the past and shrinking from the potentials of the future. Making either mistake takes us partly out of the present; it removes the specific matters intended to ignite the spark and cause it to flare, flame, and blaze within us.

We suffer the tensions from the effects of the past and face the uncertainties of the future in order to widen and deepen our sense of self and learn the way our souls would have us live. Those who try to run from the past often run right into it, while those who try to avoid facing that which is new or strange fail to learn what life has in store for them. Either way, we become trapped in too narrow a sense of self and can become increasingly estranged from the inner spark of awareness that alone can light the way we were intended to go. For there is no outer map that can outline the true adventure of the individual self or mark the surprising trail of darkness and light that the soul would have us walk.

Because each soul carries the spark of uniqueness, each life becomes a distinct experiment that can never be repeated exactly. We enter life aimed in a certain way, and we must find that way in our own way. Therein lies both the beauty of each life as well as the problem that results when one does not have a general map that can lead to the destination of the soul. The soul prefers detours that include the deeper, darker places where hidden gold can be found. Whoever shrinks from life will see only darkness and fear. They will be overwhelmed when opportune moments occur and will miss the synchronicities that make sense of the past and open the paths before them.

There is an old story about Mullah Nasrudin that illustrates the point. The old holy man appears at times to be wise and at other times to be quite foolish. It is never clear which side of him will respond when life takes an unexpected turn. In that sense he seems to represent each of us when we are faced with loss or opportunity or the need to change and see life anew.

On one occasion, Nasrudin arrived home quite late after being at the tavern. A neighbor found him squatting on the ground under a street lamp, evidently looking for something.

"What's the matter Mullah?" asked the concerned friend.

"I have lost the only key to my house," replied Mullah.

"Let me help you," said the kindly neighbor, who proceeded to get down on his knees and search for the key as well.

After some time searching the neighbor straightened up and asked:

"Are you sure you dropped your key here?"

"Oh, I didn't drop it here," replied Mullah.

"Where did you drop it then?!?" asked the bewildered neighbor.

"Over there," said the Mullah as he pointed near his house which was enshrouded in darkness.

"Why are you looking for it here!!??" exclaimed the now exasperated friend.

"Because this is where the light is," replied the Mullah.

The Key is in the Dark

Nasrudin is a holy man and supposed to be wise, yet he has all the weaknesses, fears, and failings of a common person. He represents the part of each of us that knows that something is missing and can be found nearby. He wants to search for the key that can unlock the mystery of life, but he also wishes to avoid the darker places and the deeper issues. Nasrudin as the holy fool illustrates the persistent human tendency to go where the light is and avoid the troubling places of darkness. Of course, the key we are really searching for can only be found by entering where the world looks darkest to us. That is the way of this world, which is divided into opposing things like darkness and light, day and night, order and chaos.

Everyone has access to a key that can open the door to a meaningful life; that is the basic setup on earth and a good reason not to give up on people. The psychic fact of the inner key is also a reason not to despair in times of loss. Each life is aimed at something worthwhile, and there are keys nearby and subtle filaments of the soul waiting to be found and followed. The problem is not that people are empty, hopeless, or intrinsically bad; the problem is that each must enter their own darkness in order to locate the key that opens the paths of meaning and genuine purpose. Not only is there no general map for the necessary journey of life, but the key needed to unlock the mystery of the self tends to be hidden exactly where we prefer not to look.

Parts of us prefer dwelling with manufactured light and are quite willing to stay within its predictable circle of limited radiance rather than enter the dark to learn the nature of the spark hidden within. Like old Nasrudin, most prefer looking for the keys to understanding in obvious places, like under the light, where the answers to the essential questions simply cannot be found. If the missing keys to a greater life were somewhere in the light, everyone would already have found them; fewer people would be lost in confusion, stuck in violence or apathy, or dwelling in places of denial.

Even when people reach the point of having to acknowledge that something essential has been lost, most prefer looking where the light shines. This is especially true now, in the afterglow of the Enlightenment, when the lights stay on twenty-four hours a day as if even facing the darkness might lead to overwhelming despair. In addition to the usual fear of facing the deeper issues of life, there is now a greater disorientation to life; mass culture makes it more difficult for individuals to trust that there can be a genuine orientation set within them. It is one thing to be anxious when facing a particular challenge, but quite another when general anxiety levels increase the collective sense of being helpless and out of control.

The extraordinary stress that develops amidst the flood of changes and hollowing of institutions that characterize the current world condition leaves everyone more disoriented and exposed to collective trauma. It is not simply that there are massive problems, but also that they come from all directions and leave no time to digest the results or to fully consider the effects on the future. The storms of change create an accumulation of shock that gathers into clouds of anxiety and fear. The speed of change and the experience of sudden losses and radical reversals are part and parcel of the end of an era and the intensification of the archetypal presence of apocalypse. A wide range of phobias, wild visions, and extreme fantasies can manifest as the catastrophic sense of collapse takes on greater immediacy.

Periods of radical change either develop maturity in people or else cause them to regress. One either becomes deeper and wiser about the nature of this ever-changing world or else becomes more rigid and fearful in the face of overwhelming change. As things cycle faster and faster and one major crisis quickly replaces another, the more restrictive attitudes of an individual or a group can become increasingly resistant to change. Inside a person, the archetype of apocalypse can manifest as a profound increase of anxiety; the ego fears it will be completely overwhelmed or simply obliterated by the nature of repeated shocks and unexpected changes. The areas in which each person or group are most literal or feel most constricted will be the places where they feel most threatened by the sense of loosening and the patterns of exposure and disclosure that accompany the rise of the archetype.

The more distant we are from the unique spark of life in our soul, the more devastating and isolating the growing darkness and uncertainty in the world will seem to be. The more stubborn or narrow, the more rationalistic or compulsive the ego attitudes are, the more catastrophic events will seem to be. The more limited and restrictive we feel, the more negative and nihilistic things will appear to us. The more narrow and fixated we are inside, the more it seems that the whole world outside us will end. However, all these changes might simply be aimed at trying to put an end to our willful confusions, rigid ideas, and fixated attitudes.

Amidst the rapidity of change and massive disorientation, one of the few ways to find sense and meaning is to find the inner order, the shape and style of one's own being. Even in times of chaos the soul instinctively seeks to awaken and grow the original design that it carried to life. When truly oriented from within, our choices become more meaningful, even if they are limited by outer circumstances. If we remain in touch with the inner spark and light of the soul, our experiences can become revelatory and our responses more spontaneous and life enhancing. Otherwise, we become more reactionary; both more impulsive and more compulsive. Either way, we find ourselves increasingly traumatized.

As in the story of the missing key, there is darkness and there is light in this world, but there is also a light found in the darkness. Those who try to avoid facing darkness miss the guidance of the inner light and become more subject to the collective anxiety. Those who avoid chaos at any cost wind up more subject to it. The light found inside the dark is a description of the human soul which tries to shine from within a person, especially in the darkest hours of life. In the dark times, the eye begins to see in other ways; we must be willing to bend low, enter the shadows, and learn to see with a darkened eye if we are to recover the key that unlocks the mystery of the deeper self and soul—a key that strangely belongs to us yet keeps getting lost.

When trouble can no longer be avoided, the issue becomes the willingness to enter the darkness. At certain times in the course of life, we must wander amongst the paradoxes and feel our way along by an inner Braille and a willingness to stumble and fall into the truth of things. The lost home and true dwelling we seek to find is in ourselves, and when we feel that something is missing, it is likely to be found there. We are hunting the deeper sense and greater being of the self within us that has the energy we lack and the ideas and imagination we most need. The divine spark within us waits to be found and be fueled with the matters of the world, and it knows what in this world matters most to each of us.

The Soul's Great Adventure

No matter the conditions around us, there are two great adventures that the soul would have us undertake. Our life-project involves both making a way in the outer world and awakening to the way of being already planted within us as a divine spark-seed. The first adventure of life begins with the first breath we take; it concerns the course of human development that leads to "growing up" and eventually entering the world on our own two feet and establishing ourselves in the marketplace of life. The first arc of adventure requires that we produce something, achieve in some way, and "make something of ourselves." While following this initial arc we make a life, find a livelihood, and adopt a lifestyle.

On the first adventure we take up the common challenges of life and often do so while following paths that others choose for us. We follow an education track or a career course that "runs in the family" or seems most likely to lead to security or worldly success. Whether we succeed or fail, we become socialized in certain ways that inevitably lead away from the inner design and true aim of our intended personality. For what allows us to adapt to the culture around us most often leads to an over-adaptation in regard to our deeper sense of how to dwell in this world.

The first adventure of life is necessary for us as well as for the culture around us. Yet the deep psyche has a better design than the ego's plan, the family's requirements, or the culture's map. Whereas the first adventure may involve the pursuit of happiness and the recognition that comes from outer accomplishments, the second adventure of life involves the fulfillment of the inner longings and hidden destiny of the soul.

The second adventure aims at a path that leads beyond the concerns of the daily world, yet it is of great importance for the continuance of that world. It involves stepping off the common pathways and going off the map that others have given us. It involves finding a way that takes us further into life rather than simply adapting to available lifestyles. We are here to decipher and live up to what life asks of us, not what others might ask us to live up to for them. This idea does not arise from simple rebellion or egocentricity, rather it is the essence of spiritual growth. We all have something to give to the world from our essential nature, and when the world around us becomes dark and increasingly uncertain, it becomes more essential for us to live the adventure of the soul.

The second arc of life involves taking up the inner-directed path and following the thread of destiny that truly orients us to life and to our genuine destination. This more radical path leads to a spiritual journey, not because it is religious in nature, but because it serves the uniqueness in one's soul, the "spirit that is already there." The first adventure tends to involve gathering information about the world and common knowledge of how to survive in it. The second adventure involves a kind of "gnosis," a deeper knowledge of life that becomes available once we awaken to the nature of the inner spark and the greater calling set within the soul. It involves finding and learning to give one's god-given talents, skills, and gifts in ways that make life in general more meaningful and genuine human community more possible. The second adventure leads to the pursuit of wisdom, the kind of transcendent knowledge that enlivens individual life, nourishes genuine community, and helps re-create culture.

Outer success, common expectations, and evident achievements usually reign over the course of the first arc of life, but the second arc is a deeper venture that values things differently. Our worst failures in the course of life's first adventure can become the fecund soil from which the second adventure grows. Places of struggle, loss, and suffering can be revalued as the inner arc of awakening revisits core life experiences to reclaim meaning, even from seemingly wasted aspects of life. The key to understanding our true nature often resides where we have fallen the hardest yet somehow have survived. The often avoided places of loss and collapse, of abandonment and rejection, are where the inner light of soul waits to be found. The soul values depth and the darker knowledge of understanding that often grows more from failure than from success. In the dark times it becomes important to value the darker knowledge found in trials and tribulations that reveal the spark burning and glowing within us all along.

Another tale told of old Nasrudin involves the time when he lost a gold ring. Being poor most of his life, the old fellow had few valuable possessions. One day his cherished ring slipped from his fingers and fell through a crack in the boards of his old hut. Of course, he took the whole house apart looking for the lost gold and made quite a display of his anguish. Inevitably, someone asked where exactly the object of concern had been dropped. Nasrudin had to admit that the gold ring fell through the crack into the darkness below his dwelling place. He knew the gold was down there, but feared what else he might find if he dared to descend into the darkness. Once again, the old Mullah stands for the part of us that is wise enough to know where the gold can be found, but foolish enough to pretend that it might just pop up in a less-troubling place.

The golden ring represents a wholeness and unity waiting to be found in just those places where we feel the deepest sense of loss. The gifts that make the second adventure of life possible tend to reside right next to the wounds that we receive in trying to grow up and make our life unique and meaningful. Growing down the soul and nourishing the spark within us means facing up to failures and old fears; it means admitting to deep longings that show what we value the most yet often fear to pursue. In this life everyone is wounded, and those who claim not to be are usually the most wounded of all. The second adventure of our life requires that we recognize our deepest longings and find some healing for our essential wounds.

This second arc of living is the primary adventure our souls would have us undertake. It requires a second level of courage that allows us to enter dark places in order to recover a deeper sense of self and greater sense of soul. This soulful journey intends to serve something beyond simple self-interest as it involves a calling that asks each of us to contribute something essential to life. At critical junctures and in times of trouble, we are repeatedly called to choose; either we accept the life that has been given to us or we undertake the greater adventure of the soul.

In the dark times we encounter the crossroads of life more often as the common paths of daily life become less stable, more subject to sudden alterations, and more impeded by obstacles. The necessity of change produces a greater frequency of kairos moments that offer both challenges and opportunities. Each crossroad brings us back to the choice between life's two adventures. At such times the key will more likely be found where things seem most dark before us. Each initiatory passage requires that we step into the unknown and become lost again before finding ourselves at a deeper level. The second adventure requires that we risk all that we have in order to learn the destination our life is aimed at. If we fear letting go of who we think we have become, if we hesitate too long before stepping further along the road our soul would have us travel, we miss our star and the spark of life can grow dim within us.

Filaments of Eternity

We may be limited by aspects of our body and bound for death every day that we are alive, but we are also fashioned with the filaments of eternity. Each soul is woven onto the loom of life and held together by a "warp thread" that makes it unique and purposeful, even if a bit strange and weird. The mythic thread connects us to the world behind this world and nourishes the soul throughout its life with dreams and intimations of spirit, inklings of originality, and insistent desires for change. Too often it remains the least-known aspect of our lives. When we hold to the inner pattern and innate rhythms, all the moments of our lives make sense; without those guides, all can seem accidental and pointless.

Amidst the increasing uncertainties of the world, many try to reduce life to simple survival and blind belief; yet others awaken to a second adventure of life, a path of genuine purpose and lived imagination. The second adventure seeks one's true life purpose, but also reveals one's best way of contributing to the life of others and to the ongoing creation of the world. For each person desires to be part of something "larger than life," each expects to be above the ordinary because each secretly knows that the gift of life is in each extraordinary case. Whether through a grass roots project, a spiritual awakening, a creative endeavor, or a great love affair, we seek to transcend the horizontal world of simple reality and blind normality. In these critical and extraordinary times the soul expects to find moments of transcendence along a true path of discovery and revelation. In the end all paths lead to the door of death; the trick in this life is to learn who and what we are at our core before we find ourselves standing at that dark door. The point of all the trouble that can be found in life is to locate the key to understanding the life we have been given before it is taken from us.

Upavita, Initiation of the Soul

The second adventure leads to discovering inclinations that have been below the surface of our lives all along. It is the road of emotional and spiritual growth rather than worldly fulfillment; it is the inward arc through which we turn fully to the inner dream that the soul has harbored all along. The second adventure would rediscover and renew the dream that made each person come to life to begin with. It arises from the inner myth and passionate story set within each soul, the dream that tries to awaken throughout the course of one's life. It involves one's true calling and intended work in this world that is sustained by dreams as much as it is by sweat and tears. The inner dream first appears during youthful adventures and moments of seeking meaning and purpose, but it tries to reappear at each turning point in life. The inner dream is the subtle thread that ties each soul to the web of life in specific ways and in a unique arrangement.

In ancient India there was a rite of passage that involved removing young people from the daily course and common demands of life and placing them in a temple or holy place. In ancient times, learning was considered a sacred task most often associated with sanctuaries and holy places found in nature. In the sacred precincts the young souls would attend to spiritual longings and learn practices that could open up the inner life and reveal one's true nature. For a time, the young people would look within and learn something of their intended personality and the shape of the second adventure trying to unfold from within them. For the point of genuine learning is not the simple task of following a religious map or simply learning what others have done, but also awakening to the specific spark of intelligence and wisdom trying to grow from within.

Eventually, the young seekers would return to the common world and take up the issues and concerns as well as the responsibilities that characterize the first adventure of life. They would immerse in the back and forth of the daily realm and establish themselves in one way or another. Meanwhile, they would have gained an inner sense of who they might be in their essence and what greater order of life they might one day come to serve. The idea was that after making a way in the world and fulfilling the duties common to family and community, they might turn again and return to the deeper path and greater service indicated by their inner nature. In order to ensure that the young seekers would not forget the nature and inclination of their inner life, they would be given a sacred cord to wear. A red thread would be tied across their body as a reminder to them and to those who cared for them that they had a deeper calling and greater way to be in this world where it is always easy to lose one's way.

The Sanskrit term for the thread that ties a person to the inner life of spirit and soul is *upavita*. The ceremonies for investing the young seekers with the vital thread of life varied widely, and over time the practice became mostly associated with the higher castes and upper classes. However, the origins were more basic and essential; the red thread served as a visible reminder of the unseen world and of the inner thread that connects each soul to the life of spirit and to the living soul of the world. The upavita was imagined as the red thread of passion that runs within the blood of everything that breathes; it could also be envisioned as the green thread of existence dancing through the endless windings of the vegetal realm. Either way it was the vine of eternity that secretly united the living tendrils and the embodied souls to the web of life as well as the unseen world behind this world. For the slim thread showed that each soul was claimed by something beyond the demands and responsibilities of the daily world.

When worn by initiates, it represented the hidden eternity within each life and the capacity of each person to awaken to how and where they were threaded to the chain of being. The simple red thread indicated that each life was sacred and that becoming conscious and fully human meant taking on meaningful and sacred tasks at some point in life. The initiatory thread would be draped so that it fell over the heart and marked the young ones as seekers on the deeper paths that can open the mysteries of that exact heart. The thread of initiation would be placed by those who had found a genuine sense of direction in their own lives, the older ones helping to tie the young seekers to the living threads of imagination and genuine practices of conscious human culture.

When the dark times come round again, old ideas like the upavita and the chain of being become more important. When the world becomes darker the inner light of the soul becomes more important; when even nature seems about to unravel the inner pattern, the thread of meaning can be the only way to feel woven into life and bound for some valuable purpose that can assist the world in distress. When the world becomes dark with endings it becomes time to turn to the inner thread that first brought each soul to this life. Although it cannot be found by common observers, as long as we hold the inner thread of being we cannot be completely lost in this world.

Taking up the second adventure can mean that we get a second chance at the same life. Like the thread of upavita, we are called back to pick up the essential life-thread that first surfaced somewhere in youth. We might have to search around in the depths within us to find the thread of the dream that brought us to life; yet even if it has been ignored for a long time, it remains tied to us in some way. Like the ring that fell between the cracks, the original dream and potential unity of our life waits to be found again. From inside life comes a "second calling" that keeps calling us back to the imagination and dreams first experienced in youth. The point of such a calling is not a literal return to youthful ways, but a re-calling that touches again the dream of life and sense of purpose first found in youthful adventures.

What we really seek is the greater personality seeded within. In many traditions this great self within us was imagined to be in the heart, where the dream of one's life and symbolic core also resides. Thus, the instinct to tie the upavita over the heart. When we take up the second adventure, we become more wholehearted and can more readily find a path with heart and soul. Following a path with heart also means opening the vital arteries of libido and releasing the vial energies of life. The second adventure involves an increase of love as well as an intensification of spiritual awareness. For the heart is the seat of love as well as the dwelling of spiritual knowledge.

Each seeker of truth and beauty must hunt the place where conscious energy is trapped. The energy needed to change one's life can be trapped in "wrong-headed" ideas about the aim and direction of one's life, and it can be blocked by a lack of instinctive connection to the wisdom of the body. The second adventure involves all the ways that the soul can grow, for it is the soul that keeps spirit and body together. Growth of the soul intensifies one's natural spirit for life while also deepening the vitality that sustains the organs of life. In following the inner gradient of the soul, we descend further into the life of the body even as we become more threaded to the life of spirit. In learning the true nature of our inner nature, we become more able to contribute something unique and meaningful to the world. For it is not something abstract or general that can answer all the burning questions and solve the increasing dilemmas of the world around us.

The Old Man Reflects

There is an old tale about an old man who sat in a tea shop looking back over the trail of his life. Around him sat younger friends who listened as he considered the way his life had gone. "When I was young my spirit was on fire. I wanted to awaken everyone to the vision I had of the world. I prayed fervently to god to give me the strength to change this world where suffering, injustice, and greed too often rule. Years later, I awakened to the evidence that my life was half over. The truth was that I had not managed to change anyone and the world seemed to be in worse shape than ever before.

So I prayed to god to give me the strength to change those who were close around me and suffered in particular ways that I could plainly see. Sadly I learned that people must truly desire to change in meaningful ways before they find healing and the purpose of their own lives. Having now become old enough to be considered an elder, my prayers have become quite simple and more direct. When I pray, I say: God, give me the strength to change myself and find the way I am intended to live during this lifetime."

No solitary idea, no matter how great, no single notion nor shared belief can shift the weight of the world towards a meaningful future, but the accumulated vitality of many lives lived more fully might become a meaningful counterweight in the balance between time and eternity. Strange as it may seem, individual consciousness forms the counterweight, and living out the hidden meanings within life helps to balance the weight of the world—each living being wrapped around an invisible, eternal thread, each a story breaking out of the wall of time to become a genuine story that adds to the ongoing story of creation.

In following the threads of the soul, we find the spark intended to grow within our lives and learn to follow the thread woven within us to begin with. Some innately know how to preserve the forests and rivers and subtle ecologies that sustain the pulse of the earth; others are just as naturally threaded to the fabric of culture intended to preserve and nourish human life. Some have a natural way of reassuring children, while others know enough about death to be able to offer hospice to those at the opposite end of life. Some who have struggled just to survive or find a way to enter society know the true meaning of refuge and how to help those who are literally homeless as well as those who have a home but are lost just the same.

The second adventure of life intends to lead us to the exact places where our innate spirit and genius best fit into the struggle and dance of life, the exact places where we can become an agent of healing and change in this world. In the end the only true satisfaction comes from knowing that we have lived out the dream of life that was seeded and sewn within in us to begin with.

The Only Design We Must Learn

The Old Woman of the World was also known as the triple goddess of Fate who spins, weaves, and fixes the threads by which each person becomes set into the extravagant tapestry of the world. In addition to her cosmic weaving responsibilities and pot-stirring tasks, the old woman takes an interest in each soul that enters the nets of earthly existence. As mistress of fate, she sets within each soul a core pattern and inner image that gives essential shape to that life. The inner pattern contains a plotline intended to unfold as the essential living story of that soul. To each soul born she also gives a "twist of fate" that makes its story specific, unique, and unrepeatable.

This inner, coded pattern is the key to understanding the purpose and destiny of the individual soul. While we are near that inborn thread of meaning and understanding our lives make sense and even our mistakes can be meaningful. If we neglect to awaken or fail to learn how to trust the pattern set within us, we will fail to find the places where our life energy can be most rewarding to us and most helpful to others. For that which the soul came to life to give is of necessity valuable to others and to the meaning of the world around us. Lacking a connection to the pattern trying to unfold from within causes many people to follow maps made by others and lives not of their own making. When they come to the end of the road it will be revealed that they have followed the wrong path; that they have failed to find their inner gifts and have wasted the most valuable aspects of themselves.

Each of our lives is wrapped around a soul that is threaded through with a mystery trying to unfold and become known to us. Some old stories describe how the thread of our lives leads us back to the place where the old woman first gave us our inner design and wove us into the world of time and space. They say that the old woman who was present at the very beginning also waits at the end of the great adventure of life. She sits at the entrance of a cave—a threshold between this realm of night and day and the otherworld that is forever behind this world. The unique adventure having come to its conclusion, the soul returns to the cave of knowledge. The lifelong journey having come to its inevitable end, the wanderer feels an old longing to join the community of souls on the other side.

Of course, modern people argue over the issue of an afterlife that continues on the other side of this world so often seen to be limited to things that are measurable and can be proven by facts. Modern thought often begins with the facts of birth and ends with the death of the body, even though the exact moment of death, like the first moment of life, still proves to be an elusive mystery. Death may be the most predictable thing in this earthly world, yet modern cultures tend to avoid real knowledge of such an important subject. In favoring "objective thought" over imagination and the deeper knowledge of the old mind, the modern mind falters at both ends of life, not intuiting the intricacies of birth and not sensing that life continues after death has claimed the body.

The modern world tends to be historical in its thinking rather than psychological or philosophical. Philosophy begins with the knowledge of death. This was also the idea held by the old mind, the one that prevailed when philosophy was closer to its original sense of pre-systematic thinking and "felt thought." Philosophy begins with considerations of death not because it is morbid or fearful, but because knowing something about darkness and loss, about impermanence and death, can lead a person to a greater appreciation of the gift of life. Philosophy means "love of knowledge or wisdom." A genuine philosopher loves knowledge and meaning, but is also wise enough to become a lover of life before the gift of life is taken away.

Each person is supposed to become a philosopher insofar as they seek knowledge of who they are at their core and learn to decipher the meaning woven into their own soul. For the soul knows from the beginning what it loves, and what the soul loves is often the cure for what most ails a person. The old philosophies say that those who learn what their souls truly love in life can meet death with less fear and no anger. Those who manage to live life fully have usually faced death in more ways than one. Having died in little ways along the way, they value the gift and the meaning of the life that they have been given. Strange to say, but a conscious way of approaching death is one proof of a life fully lived.

Death may be the darkest door, but it is not simply the end as many would have it, for the soul is not simply of this world. The body is formed of earth and must eventually return to it—dust to dust, mud to mud, clay to clay. The soul, made of more subtle threads, slips past the gates of mortality, destined for a postmortem appointment on the other side of life. After shedding the sheath of the body, the soul continues on and crosses to the other realm. Once on the other side, the tale of one's life continues as the recently departed soul finds itself on a path that approaches the cave—both a womb and a tomb. At the threshold of the cave of knowledge, the Old Woman of the World awaits the arrival of the newly deceased.

The Final Test

The Old Woman of the World recognizes one of the children of fate coming along. She perceives the pattern that was woven into that soul at the very beginning, when the cave was the womb of life and the pathway led into the embodied world of incarnation. Being the old mother of fate, she played her part when the weaving, setting, and aiming of that life began. Now she wonders what that soul did with the fine thread of imagination and destiny that it carried knowingly or unknowingly all through its days and nights on earth. Did the wanderer awaken to the story trying to unfold from within? How did he or she handle the twist of fate that led it to the fateful occasions of trouble and darkness in which the inner light of the soul must be found?

What remains after the bodily remains have been placed in the earth is the shape of the life lived and the outline of what was truly learned. Now that death has cut the body thread and brought a conclusion to life's fervent fever, it is time to review how that story went, how much of the inner tale became known and lived out consciously. So the old woman traces the design originally set within that soul in the dust at the entrance to the cave. However, she reproduces only half of the soul's original design, for the life actually lived is intended to become the conscious representation of the other half.

At the time of death, the wealth and riches of this world, the power and fame accumulated here, do not count; all we have left to offer is the life we lived while we had the gift of life. Death turns out to be the great equalizer; finally no one has any advantage over others, except the original advantage of being a unique soul on the road of life and death. There is no school for becoming oneself; one can only allow the inner life to express itself and live its way into the world. All along the way each person is pulled by hidden threads and subjected to twists of fate that secretly wind close to the core of inner meanings. Although this cannot be proven in an overt way, these inner tendencies and patterns are the true subject of life's frequent tests, and they are the core issue once life is over.

The inner pattern of the soul was there all along; the answer to life's puzzling test was woven within. The answer—so often sought in the external world—existed in outline form in the depths of the soul. It was woven into the inner fabric of life from the very beginning. Now, upon death, the time has come for laying out the genuine facts of life, the consideration of what happened between the intended self and the outer world. Was the dream imbedded in the soul actually brought to life? Was the inner purpose discovered? Was the genius expressed? Did the individual handle the elements of fate and find the threads of destiny? And how did the loving go? For each attempt at loving helps to reveal a part of the design that is hidden in the heart, that which also whispers in the blood and sings quietly in the soul.

It may seem surprising that love is part of the final review, but the life project cannot proceed without it, and each soul's way of loving has virtues that make more sense when seen from the other side of life. In following the spark of life, we find the genuine paths with heart and learn what we naturally love in this world. Loving frees the soul and makes a person bigger and, in the long run, wiser as well. In the end it turns out that there were no small lives, only people too hung up with the worries of the little self or too afraid of outer authorities to follow the thread of existence all the way. At this point it has become too late for excuses or justifications. It doesn't matter what others did or should have done; we have to face the music we have made with the talents and instruments we were given.

At the end of life the question is not whether people obeyed certain rules or avoided certain vices. After death the question becomes whether or not they found the threads of their inner life often enough to learn the destiny that brought them to life to begin with. In this primordial meeting between life and death the inner threads of the soul become revealed and the old woman waits to see what the wanderer learned of the intended personality and the destiny that was carried into the common world. This is the final test that so many have worried over and it turns out that the answer was within us all along; the only preparation for the final test being the life already lived. If the soul can match the design laid out by the old woman with etchings shaped from the life they lived on earth, then it qualifies to pass into the cave of knowing and on to the trail of the ancestors. If not, the old people say that it returns to the common world again attached to aspects of the original design that went unlived.

This is just a little story about what happens after death; nothing in it can be proven one way or another. It does however show how stories can build bridges between the worlds and that, even at the very end, the story of life goes on. It also reminds us that each life has its inborn purpose and its natural way of being woven into the world. When the end has come, either a person can say: I lived the life I was given, gave the gifts that were mine to give, and followed where the thread of soul led me; or else: I failed to awaken to the spark of life that was originally given to me and followed instead a map made by others.

In the soul adventure, we become fully alive from within, more gifted in serving our community, more capable of living with dignity and, when the time comes, more able to die with grace. We become more like ourselves, more of who we are supposed to be in this world before it becomes time to leave it. Even if we are born to a dark time, surrounded by strife and riddled with loss and conflict, we have been given the unique gift of life. The second adventure involves the divine spark hidden in each soul and the dark times require that the inner light of soul be found again. Perhaps there is no greater time to awaken to the adventure the soul would have us live and become agents of the divine in this world.

What survives the adventures and tragedies, the challenges and demands of life, is the old soul in each of us that would have us take up the second adventure of life and become fully threaded to the ongoing creation of this world before the time comes for us to leave it. Although it grows from inward reflection and deeper self-awareness, the second adventure of our lives affects both the course of nature and the direction of culture.

II

Wisdom of the Earth

CHAPTER 6

THE GIFT OF LIFE

Gratitude is the parent of all virtues.
Cicero

In the strange way that life can reverse itself over time, myth has come to mean something false or illusionary. Meanwhile history, which is always being rewritten and proven to be wrong, has come to be considered the true story. Myths are timeless tales that remain separate from *historia*, which changes based upon who is telling the tale. Myths narrate the sacred dramas that take place before time begins, in the beginning that is also present throughout time. They are intended to reveal the sacred and essential stories that are not altered by the passing of time. Myths are neither history nor something of the past. They keep the present open to the possibilities of another world nearby, a transcendent realm of archetypal forms—paradigms for all human actions and sacred realities that underlie the common world.

The history of the past as well as news of the current day concerns the *exoteric* or external elements of the world of facts and figures. Under the rule of literalism the outer aspects of the world can seem to be the only meaningful elements of life. The *esoteric* or inner levels that shape the outer world and define the individual life can be underestimated and even dismissed when viewed from the limited perspective of the march of history. Myths are not intended to simply commemorate or attempt to explain things that happened at the origins of time, but to evoke the presence of original things at *this* time. Mythic tales are vehicles of imagination that can reconnect the passing moment with the eternal ground from which all of time arises.

Living myths are always nearby waiting to be rediscovered. They are able to reveal truths that shed light upon the past as well as illuminate the present moment in time. Myths are intended to break the spell of time and release us from the immediate pressures and limitations of daily life. The great narratives of the eternal dramas of life are intended to dispel the blindness created by the rapid passing of things at the surface of the world. Myth speaks to the esoteric parts within us that are also the extraordinary things about us. The archetypal dramas that constitute mythic narrations are living vehicles of creation intended to reconnect us to that which is most noble and imaginative within our souls. Hearing or reading a mythic story awakens the myth already living inside each of us. As the story enters us, we enter the timeless territory of myth. Being in such a mythic condition allows us to reconnect to the core imagination at the center of our soul. We become mythic again, a knowing participant in our own story and a seeker of the greater knowledge found near the source of all stories, at the ever-present origins of life.

The modern world requires that most things be sacrificed in service of linear time; yet in order to touch timeless things and become renewed, *time* is exactly what must be sacrificed. Only when time becomes broken can the "once upon a time" realm of renewable potentials appear again. Then, creation becomes not a thing of the past, not even a sacred history of religion, but something capable of erupting into each passing moment. Thus, creation stories used to be told at critical junctures—the beginning of a new year, or when things seemed dark and troubling—in order to bring things back to the place of origins, renewing potentials and inspiring creativity.

There are endless stories of how the world began, though no story of creation can tell the whole story. The world is too mysterious and wondrous to be captured in a single tale. At the same time, each genuine story has a wholeness to it, as everything it needs can be found within its shape of beginning, middle, and end. Thus, entering the territory of a myth can give a person a sense of wholeness. The creative aspect of our soul would have us touch the esoteric ground where creation remains ongoing and life renews itself from within. Creation wishes to continue, yet can only work through the souls of those who are alive at a given time.

When viewed from the outside, myths can seem patently false; of course the same can be said of love. Only those who surrender to something beyond themselves know what love means, how it heals and reveals and how it teaches a person to grow. Learning what myths have to offer also requires some surrender and, like love, a little sacrifice of the common ways of viewing life. Myths and stories are evocative of the deep passions, great emotions, and spiritual aspirations natural to all peoples. Myths involve the holy longings of the human soul as well as the eternal fountain of emotions that fuel those longings. They live through the lives of people whether they know it or not. Myths involve the underlying stories of life and the secret histories of the soul.

Myth includes all the invisible aspects of life—the missing parts and the hidden themes, the epic qualities and emotional tenors, and all the mute and musical tones that shape the inward ground of being. Stories offer mythic contexts, psychic subtexts, and subtle backgrounds for viewing and interpreting the world around us and the inevitable dramas and tragedies that befall us. Myth is both a remembering and a making anew, as the narrative roads bring the primordial imagination into the present in ways that make wonder, beauty, and spontaneous intelligence available at once.

Myth opens immediate feelings for the great wonders of spirit as well as for the intricate territories of the soul. Mythic imagination can awaken the soul and fill it with energies and images. A myth can bring us to the heart of our subjectivity, to the imaginative core that is the dream of our life and the language of our soul. When the key images and core ideas that reside in myths are allowed to speak for themselves they shed light on both the conditions of the world and the plight of living souls. Simply listening to a myth can release a person from profane conditions and historical situations.

Mayan Creation

The ancient Mayan people have become known as master calendar makers and precise keepers of time, yet they were also great singers and poets who studied myths and preserved stories. The Mayan creation story, known as the *Popul Vuh* or Council Book, offers an unusual way of viewing the role of humanity in the great drama of the world. It also offers glimpses of how such things as literalism and technology might have entered this world. More importantly it depicts a vision of how the great imagination at the root of creation keeps getting lost, yet can always be found again.

The Mayans, like most ancient peoples, considered creation to be an ongoing project. Their intricate and accurate calendars might come to an end, but time would begin by touching the origins again. They imagined the initial act of creation to be an original sound that reverberates throughout everything that exists in the world, unlike the notion that holds that "in the beginning was the word." Whereas the *word* may be considered something that can be written down and be determined to have a fixed meaning, the sound of creation becomes an eternal resonance that continues to ripple and flow through all of existence, from the music of the spheres to the song in the human soul.

There are other versions of sonic creation stories that depict divine figures instigating the onset of creation by singing or humming—even by snoring while dreaming up the world. And indeed, everything in this world carries a particular vibration and pitch. Modern scientists have begun recording the sounds of planets and the surprising humming that comes from black holes in space that permit no visibility and emit no light yet seem to exude music. Modern studies also show that hearing is the last sense to go just before the moment of death. The world begins in sound and a sound may be the last thing we experience before leaving it. It is not that myth tries to explain the world, rather the world proves the intuitive grasp of myths.

In the ancient Mayan tale the world was conceived as a sound and a song from which everything that exists began to take on contours and find shape. From that original song of making, the earth came to be, as did the creatures that continue to murmur and sigh and sing as the sound of creation continues to vibrate and hum. The Mayans imagined that the original eloquence of creation secretly speaks its many-tongued, living language through all that endures in the world to this day.

They said that the original articulation of life was hidden behind the darkness of appearances that was there at the very beginning when the sky was not yet open and the face of the earth had not yet appeared. At that time, there was only the heavenly world above and its soft reflection upon the dark sea that lay below it. The world was a hidden unity waiting to be fully expressed and enunciated with the breath of life. The murmur of the first intonation—the sound that would change everything by bringing that which was hidden into expression—had not yet occurred. It was before time and tide began, when nothing stirred, for everything was waiting, still held back behind a veil of silence.

It was then that the original thinkers joined their breath, thoughts, and words and composed the first expression of existence that flowed into shapes and forms that continue to be seen in the manifest world. Those first thinkers and original dreamers had names like Heart of Heaven, Heart of Sky, Heart of Earth, Hurricane, and Sudden Thunderbolt. Some say that there was only one being breathing life and sound into the world, others say that the creator spoke with many voices at one time. One or many: take your choice. Even now the world can be seen as a hidden unity, as a single divine principle, or else as a diverse expression of many living voices.

Just as people who try to create things today tend to worry, the original thinkers thought deeply and worried over creation. From their own unknown depths they conceived the quiet growth and stability of mountains, the endless generation of trees and forests, the rushing of rivers and reflection of lakes, and the fervent pulsing of animals. Their inner thoughts and effective imaginations gave shape, style, and resonance to the gift of life as it reverberated in many forms when "being" was just beginning and everything was possible to "be."

Once everything had been given a shape and become set in the world, the pulse of life continued in constant changes that rippled throughout the garment of nature, humming in the flowing of rivers and lapping in the back and forth of tides. The song of creation and the productions of time were underway and the gods of creation felt satisfied with the beauty and elegance of all that they saw before them. However, there seemed to be one thing wanting in this world, the sense of one thing being missing was there right at the beginning and the gods could sense it, even if they had not yet found and sounded out the name of it.

The Missing Ingredients

Something was missing in the great garden of life and that caused Heart of Heaven to ponder and worry and consider that absence. Eventually, Heart of Heaven declared that although the animals were able to express many sounds, they were unable to pronounce something that the creators now desired to hear. Even the elegant songs of the birds could not express a certain knowledge that was needed to complete the song of creation. After being at the work and play of creation for a while, Heart of Heaven experienced a clear desire for the beauty and wonder of life to become consciously known and fully recognized by the creatures of creation. It also seemed that some kind of gratitude for the gift of life was needed in order for the eloquence of existence to be fully expressed.

With the idea of more knowing and expressive creatures in mind, Heart of Heaven shaped some beings from the mud and clay of the earth. These "mud beings" were interesting to look at; they had unique shapes and soft contours that seemed to highlight the sonorous waves of created life. However, it was the softness of those first people that turned out to be a great problem when the rains fell from the sky. The compromised integrity of those mud beings could not withstand the rain, any contact with water made them soften and soon enough they would melt right back into the earth from which they had come.

Heart of Heaven allowed the rain to melt them down and soon began fashioning some new beings from sticks of wood and hollow reeds. The new creatures were an improvement; they were able to walk about and pick things up. In some ways they reflected the ongoing energy of creation as they began making things themselves. They spent their time shaping and fashioning things, even developing a kind of primitive technology. These "wood people" were superior to the mud beings. They did not melt when it rained; they stood up for themselves and added something to the ongoing rhythm of creation.

However, it turned out that the wood people also had something wrong with them. Their hearts were closed and their minds could be as narrow and restrictive as reeds. The wood people turned out to be hardheaded and obstinate and it became clear that they could not manage to be open to the world around them or to the other creatures in it. In their narrowness and stiffness they were like "doll people." Yes, they could make things, but they did not remember their own maker and they could not provide the expression of gratitude and appreciation for life that had been the inspiration for their own creation.

Even the animals sensed that something was wrong with the wood people and eventually they rebelled against them and their hard-edged, narrow-minded technologies. It was as if everything in creation began to speak out against them; the animals and the trees and even their own utensils eventually turned upon them. Soon, Heart of Heaven caused a thick rain of black water to fall and, in the flood that followed, the wood people were scattered and destroyed. Some say that a few survivors of those creatures made from wood became the monkeys that continue to live in this world.

Meanwhile, Heart of Heaven was not finished; for the third time he set about shaping creatures that might become conscious of the gift of life and be able to express gratitude for it. Even at the beginning, it seems that some things had to be attempted three times before the hidden could become visible. This time Heart of Heaven decided to fashion some new creatures by using maize, or corn, as the basic material. Having mixed some maize with water, he shaped it into dough and breathed some life into it. In that way, the "corn people" were born and they began to inhabit the earth.

From the beginning, the people made of maize were different. The primary distinction was their ability to see clearly, for they had a great capacity for vision. The corn people were the first creatures to look past their immediate condition and see something beyond their initial hungers and basic needs. They had enough insight to recognize the gift of life and be conscious witnesses to the wonder and beauty of creation. They not only survived when the storms of life came, they found ways to be grateful amidst the floods of change that often alter the course of life. It was those corn people who became the ancestors of all the human beings and all the cultures that later resonated the eloquence of creation.

Because the corn people were able to feel gratitude in their hearts, they approached the world and their fellow creatures with respect. They survived and thrived on earth because of their conscious awareness of the gift of life and the necessity of change. They found artful ways to express their appreciation for life and they contributed to the ongoing creation of the world. Heart of Heaven felt greatly pleased with this turn of events as it became clear that the missing piece of creation had finally been added. All seemed good with the world, until another problem developed. One problem after another seems to be the way of this world. Some even believe that it is the problems in this world that keep creation going along, just like the sense of something missing that inspired the conception of humans.

It turned out that the power of vision and knowledge that had been implanted in the original ancestors involved a capacity to see into the very heart of existence. The corn people could see far beyond the circumstances in which they dwelt and they could look inside themselves and find a deep knowledge that dwelt within them. They were farsighted and able at times to see into the future, and they had the kind of second sight that revealed things hidden under the skin of the present moment. They had dreams that revealed things directly to them and they had inherent imagination and deep thoughts like those that occurred to the ones who created the earth. Not only could they recognize the creators, but they could see in ways that were similar to the vision of the early deities.

An Instrument for Seeing

The capacity for great vision, genuine knowledge, and inspired imagination formed the core powers and creative abilities of the first ancestors of humanity. However, it was the presence of those powers that became the source of some discomfort amongst the gods of creation. Heart of Heaven might have been pleased with the inner qualities of the corn people, but the other deities feared that the new creatures would become the equals of the gods. That troubling possibility caused the early deities to ask Heart of Heaven to reduce the vision of the new kind of people. They asked that the corn people have more short-term vision and less ability to see with the eye of imagination that allowed the original creators to shape the forms of life from the reverberations of existence.

Heart of Heaven found himself caught in a tension between the gods of creation and the creatures that had been created. Ever since then, people can become caught in the tense vibrations experienced between things that are divine and things that are limited and earthbound. In the end, Heart of Heaven knew that he had to agree to reduce the vision of the ancestors, but he also knew that the only satisfactory outcome of the tension of opposing forces was something truly creative. Heart of Heaven bowed to the concerns and demands of the other gods and agreed to reduce the visionary capacities of the corn people.

After having experienced knowledge and vision like the gods of creation, the corn people would begin to look at the world with short-term vision and limited imagination. The adjustment that limited the vision of the original humans satisfied the concerns of the gods of creation, but there was one more thing. Heart of Heaven added one stipulation to the agreement that reduced the power of the first genuine people. Humans would have their vision diminished, but they would have access to the core of imagination that continued to generate life and reverberate through this world. Humans would have a deep capacity for knowledge and an ability to see what was behind the skin of the evident world. They would have a "seeing instrument" that would allow them to see again in the way that the gods see. The seeing instrument was a kind of living book of stories, an array of essential tales that could be recalled and used to approach again the original energies of life and ongoing resonance of creation.

Humans would tend to be short-sighted and self-interested and they would also have a tendency to fashion utensils that caused trouble at all levels of existence. But they could also access the origins of life—where the thoughts of creation continue to be thought, where the eloquence of existence continues to resonate and resound, where the pulse of life continues to conceive and express the wonder of creation. Because of that original stipulation, each person that enters this world continues to carry an innate capacity to imagine and see beyond the immediate needs and past the limits of self-involvement. As direct descendants of the corn people, humans remain capable of foresight, insight, and second-sight.

However, this capacity for great vision and imagination tends to awaken only after other approaches have failed. Often it takes three or even more tries before that which is hidden from human sight and veiled from human thought can become revealed. Not only that, but people must open their hearts as well as their minds and return to the great stories again in order to see the world in its divine proportions and as being capable of renewal. Like the vestigial tail that reminds people that they are connected to animals at one end, the capacity for great imagination connects people to the gods at the other extreme of embodiment. When living people can hold those extremes together they become the friends of creation, the companions of the animals and all of nature. They also become the living organs of consciousness, the only creatures able to feel and give a full expression of gratitude for the gift of life.

Regressive Tendencies

The beginning sets the pattern for all that follows. For better or worse, humans sometimes see as the gods see, for what was originally given cannot simply be taken away. What happened then continues to happen now; that is a core conception of myth. Myths are instructive and revelatory because people continue to act out the original drama whether they know it or not. When the dark rain comes and times are hard, humanity seems to regress and walk backwards through the phases of creation. Some simply melt when life demands change, while others resist all change and cling to narrow ideas and rigid systems of belief. The threat of change makes them more hardheaded and more hard-hearted or else blindly dedicated to simple technologies that endanger and offend other creatures.

In the great recycling of time, the old story comes around again as the blindness of human invention causes great troubles for the creatures of the world and for the rhythms of all of nature. Under the guise of progress or claims of necessity, clever utensils and "technological advancements" are raised up as if they were miracles made by the gods of creation. The notion that technology alone might save the world misses the point that shortsighted inventions and technological solutions often isolate us from nature while making life more mechanical and less soulful. Unless the capacity for technical invention can be placed in service of the long vision and the ongoing story of creation, then the inclination will continue to turn the natural world against us.

We keep forgetting that we are the conscious witnesses of creation and the living vehicles of gratitude for the gift of life. We lose the animal connections as well as the felt sense of being part of the living world and the ongoing reverberations of creation. We become overly soft with fears and anxieties or else so self-involved and hard of heart that we offend the animals, damage the earth, and even threaten to explode nuclear weapons that can tear apart the underlying resonance of the created world.

When times become troubled and the hard rain falls people tend to regress, reverting to old behaviors rather than seeing more deeply into current issues. Some wither in the winds of change; they become softheaded about ideas and halfhearted about engaging life's problems. They are too easily dismayed and cannot seem to stand for something meaningful. They think that someone should be outraged enough to do something, just not them. They mostly wish to be left alone to simply exist and not have to respond to all that troubles the world around them.

Faced with great challenges they become overly adaptive and thus too easily manipulated by outside forces. They become putty in the hands of those who promise quick solutions and painless transitions. As the signs of trouble intensify they are ready to melt into the background and become part of the crowd, neither responsible for anything nor fully responsive to life. Of course, we each have some of this softness within us; how else can we identify it so readily? If it were just others that acted in such undeveloped ways, soft-headedness and empty heartedness would not be nearly so troubling and disheartening.

While some melt in the face of difficulty, others go to the opposite extreme and become rigid in their attitudes and fundamentalists in their beliefs. They would rather hold tight to some dogma or abstract principle or system of belief rather than learn to flow with the changes, bend with the wind, and learn where creation might be taking us. Like the doll people, they lack insight into their own behaviors and fail to develop open minds or have genuine feelings when trouble threatens everyone. They prefer to attack what they don't understand and try to master fear with tools of dominance or even terror.

Unable to see the way nature constantly shifts, changes, and recycles, they cling to a single, reed-like vision of the world and wind up at odds with the rest of creation. Blinded by the obvious they fail to see that another vision of the world has already begun. Convinced that the end is near they either dedicate themselves to short-term gains or else look for an exit that promises a return to the paradise of the beginning. Blinded in one eye they fail to read the small print that says "what you find here, you will also find there."

The ways in which we as people present a strange mixture of godlike vision and mud like limitations—how we can be capable of penetrating insights as well as mindless urges for destruction—is an old story told many times. Instead of seeking greater insights and trying to imagine paths of healing and renovation, a part of each of us can become heartless and closed-minded when we feel threatened by challenges or radical change, for instance those of us who are in denial of things like climate change or in favor of weapons of mass destruction, and the threat of nuclear warfare. There are even those who justify the slaughter of innocents through various forms of terrorism. A part of humanity continues to invent faulty technologies and indulge in hard-headed, hard-hearted patterns that threaten the very elements of creation.

By virtue of the original dispensation of creation, each person enters the world with at least a speck of "god-sight." Of course, each will also have a tendency to regress into muddy confusion and each will have specific ways of being blind to the world and their place within it. Like the original creators, humans experiment with the essential elements of this world and make puzzling mistakes as well as fashion dazzling inventions. Just as it was for the original creators, seemingly important ideas can turn to mud in our hands. Each person inherits a connection to the creative energies that make life a gift like no other, yet most fail to live creatively. Each has an inborn capacity for surpassing vision, yet it is often the case that most cannot see the forest for the trees.

The Original Mistake

Humans are made from the mud of the earth and the infinite heart of heaven. Creation repeats itself as people struggle mightily to become genuine individuals, learn to open their minds, and follow the way of their own heart. No matter what precautions might be taken, mistakes will be made and will have to be corrected. After all, artists often destroy what they make with their own hands before finding the proper shape and meaning of their work. Meanwhile, great encouragement can be found in the notion that the gods of creation made mistakes at the beginning. There is hope in the idea that people could awaken from the wooden-headed conditions that generate harsh technologies, threaten the animals, and offend the deities. There is always a possibility that, after recognizing how hardheaded and hard-hearted culture has become, people might find renewed insights into the heart of the earth and the meaning of the gift of life and cease to offend the rest of creation.

Some religions and religious thinkers have trouble with the notion that the creator of the universe made mistakes and had to learn the ropes of creating. Mythic sense includes the notion that everything has to start somewhere and each thing that exists has to be present in some form at the beginning. The idea that mistakes were made during creation gives us an explanation for all the errors that continue to be made. The idea of an original mistake offers an alternative to the more punishing idea of an "original sin." If the problems of the world stem from original mistakes, then all of our mistaken ideas and mindless pursuits become more understandable and in the end more forgivable.

The ancient Mayan tale of the gift of life gives us the gift of forgiveness when it lays responsibility for mistakes at the feet and hands of those divine figures who first handled the elements of life. Instead of an original word that must be understood a certain way or else great punishments will be handed down, there is a capacity to start over again and keep trying until appropriate forms are found and heaven and earth can be creatively connected. Accepting that even big errors were part of the world from the beginning allows creation to continue despite all the common mistakes and false steps and; regardless of the damning errors, the ongoing tragedies and the persistent fallibilities.

Paradise Revisited

Revisit the famous story of the Garden of Eden with the notion that mistakes must occur when things are just beginning. This paradise story, with its interpretation of original sin, continues to be the background tale for much of the world at a time when the earthly realm seems threatened in many ways and big mistakes have already been made. Just as in the Mayan story, a point is reached when the beauty of the earth had been established but something more was required. As was also the case in the Mayan tale, knowledge and god-like vision were at the core of the trouble that developed at the inception of human beings.

In the case of the Garden of Eden, the cause of all the trouble and the responsibility for mistakes seems to fall heavily upon the first human ancestors. Eve and Adam seemed to make the first big mistake that thereafter became the most common human mistake. They desired to know; especially to know what god knew. That desire separates humans from all other creatures. Whether it turns out to be right or wrong in the end, the desire to truly know was there at the very beginning and it troubles humanity and disturbs the stability of creation even now.

In the Mayan myth, the human interest in transcendent knowledge begins with the gods' own desire to have conscious, knowing creatures that can witness creation and be grateful for it. In the bible tale the origin of the desire for knowledge seems less clear. It seems that the longing for deep knowledge might never have awakened had not the serpent induced the first humans to take the fateful bites of the forbidden fruit. In one tale, knowledge is first given and then withheld; in the other, knowledge is first forbidden and then taken anyway. In the Garden of Eden knowledge turns out to be a sin as well as a gift that makes humans more conscious of both good and evil. Similarly, in the Mayan tale knowledge is both a gift from the gods and an offense to them. The kind of knowledge that sees into the heart of creation is a problem for the divine as well as for the human inheritors of this garden of a world. Knowledge can be seen as a troublesome gift— the forbidden fruit of creation. To this day, if you want people to desire something strongly, just call it forbidden fruit. In mythic terms the original situation was not simply back at the beginning, it also reverberates and resonates in the present moment.

Something deeply rooted in the human soul desires to know the divine and see the eternal. Forbidding any taste of the original fruit of the tree of knowledge turns out to be the most certain way to initiate the harvesting of it. Becoming intrigued with something that is forbidden is axiomatic in human psychology; it is part of the setup and was built into people from the start. God must have known that at the beginning. Either god made a mistake that required severe correction or else the divine used human psychology to provoke and initiate a desire for knowledge that was there to begin with.

It is one thing to fashion an abundance of earthly creatures—to shape a natural world that reverberates with life and beauty—but it is quite another to forge beings capable of awakening to the knowledge that exists at the center of creation. This attempt upset the original garden and it continues to trouble the world to this day. In order to share the knowledge of creation and the beauty of existence, the creators' had to take a risk. In order that creatures might awaken to genuine gratitude, the creators' made new beings wander close to divine vision. Unless such risks are taken there can be no conscious witnesses to creation and no real gratitude for the gift of life.

One way or the other, making big mistakes was part of the original job of making the world; if the gods didn't do it, then the first people would have. It might be useful to consider that Eve and Adam made a necessary mistake. They triggered the search for knowledge and that turns out to be the only way to learn genuine gratitude for the gift of life. Humans have an inborn desire to see into the workings of the world, to know and see as the gods do. How else could they become conscious witnesses to creation and be able to express gratitude for life?

The gods may resent the searching vision of humankind, yet creation seems to require such visionaries. Call it a sin, call it an unavoidable mistake; either way humans are implicated in the problems of creation and in the solutions that keep the song of creation going along. No matter which story sets the scene, humans are central to the ongoing drama of creation and the reverberations of the original song of life. The stories of creation indicate elements of life on earth that inhabit the present and continue to call our attention to the issues of awakening more fully and developing conscious ways of handling the gift of life.

Friends of Creation

Some modern people caught up in random notions of the accidental universe consider humans to be an afterthought of creation and a questionable idea altogether. Because we make such grand and tragic mistakes, they imagine that the world might be better off if the most troubling species of all failed to remain in the world. In a way they continue the kind of questioning and fears found in creation tales. The trouble first found back at the beginning continues to reverberate in the current time. Yet, as the stories indicate, what was given cannot be taken away. Humans are a great risk taken by the forces of creation in the interest of conscious awareness and genuine vision on earth. In order to make beings that could understand the value of life, the gods had to generate them from the very heart of creation and then run the risk that they would trouble the world with their visionary powers, forceful attitudes, and even delusional states.

We as humans may have come last on the scene, but inevitably we wind up in the center of the beauty and the trouble of creation ongoing. We see in ways that can either help sustain life or else damage existence. We are creatures who long for knowledge, yet we forget the stories of creation and lose the basic instruments for truly seeing, readily becoming inflated and thinking that we are the gods and can lord it over the earth. When chaos ripples again and the underlying issues of creation rise closer to the surface, humans tend to repeat the original patterns that include serious mistakes as well as the possibility of penetrating visions. The eloquence of the beginning resides in the human soul, but only awakens in critical times and in creative moments when deeper knowledge and greater visions become essential again.

In a strange way, humans are the friends as well as the enemies of creation and, at some level, also the envy of the gods. Remember old Prometheus? He stole the fire of the gods and gave it to humans. Prometheus means "farsighted, able to see ahead." Whether it is the fruit of knowledge or the fire of heaven, the inner star-spark or the gift of divine sight, most old stories depict the human ancestors as burning with longings and burdened with visions. Humans enter the song of creation both gifted and wounded, both inspired and mistaken—the paradoxical inheritors of paradise found and of paradise lost. Call them the corn people or the first couple, the First People or the Ancients Ones; they have many names and many stories are needed to keep the possibility of awakening to genuine knowledge present.

The Heart of the Matter

It seems to be no accident that an early version of humanity was simply too hard-hearted or that the deity that shaped the core human organ was called Heart of Heaven. The human heart is often the organ at issue in the dilemmas of life, just as it was a question at the very beginning. Having a genuine vision for one's life requires an open heart as well as an open mind. Some might argue that the heart and the eye are completely separate organs that shouldn't be confused. One receives impressions of light and movement; the other, deeply encased in the body, is there to pump blood.

Yet, there are organs within organs. The mind can operate anywhere in the body and a blind person can often see many things clearly.

There is a heart within the heart that holds a deeper capacity for vision. There is an eye in the heart that sees beauty and envisions things that cannot be proven by logic or be simply explained or easily understood. The eye within has its own sense of purpose and direction, just as the heart has its own thoughts that began long before the mud body formed and all the kicking and crying started. The heart is a subtle organ that mythically remains connected to the Heart of Heaven as well as to the Heart of the Earth. The eye of the heart is shaped for seeing the mysteries of life and love and for sighting new ways for making both.

The heart has foresight as well as hindsight. It has insight and remains subject to visions right up to the end. The heart is a measureless territory trying to open to greater and greater awareness. The heart's eye was open before birth; it saw otherworldly things and seeks to perceive them again. The pain of birth closed that visionary eye of imagination, yet it expects to open again in the course of life. The heart is first of all a metaphorical organ; *metaphor* means to "carry beyond" and the heart's eye would cause us to see beyond all that is obvious in the world and be carried beyond all that divides and fragments the world.

When we see with the eye of the heart, we see what we love in the world and find the beauty within us as well. In the fullness of that knowledge we become grateful for the gift of life, even if only for a moment. In the moment of gratefulness we become whole again; we fulfill the desire of the divine that we might consciously witness the beauty of creation and express gratitude for the gift of life. In such moments we are both ancient and immediate—we are fully human. Being ungrateful means taking life for granted and remaining ignorant of the knowledge hidden in the heart. Until we know the fullness of that knowledge and the enduring visions that can come from it, we are always in danger of being too soft and undeveloped, or else too hard and unapproachable.

The eye of the heart is made to see beyond, to glimpse the whole cosmos and perceive its own paradoxical place in that great arrangement. Trying to see that way again requires that the heart crack wider open, which can bring back all the painful separations of life including the original pain of separation from the divine. Many try to avoid that heartbreaking pain; but it used to be better known that the only heart worth having is a broken heart. Only then can others find a way in, only then do people develop insight into their own wound and its healing.

The human heart is a great inner territory that participates in creation and makes mistakes, yet can learn to forgive itself and forgive others as well. If the heart fails to open to its own vision and learn the meaning already hidden within, it can harden and become a weapon that battles with all of creation. Many things serve to close and harden the heart. Extremes of poverty can dry the heart and turn it bitter. Too much rejection can cause it to reject its own inner vision. Violation of the subtle tissues of the heart can turn it away from love and towards violence, and too much sorrow makes a stone of the heart.

When the space between common reality and the greater vision of the human heart becomes too great, people no longer perceive the inner resonance and continuing eloquence of life or the subtle presence of the unseen energy of creation in this earthly world. There follows a loss of genuine imagination followed by a willful blindness that causes people to become both hardheaded and hard-hearted. Soon people are suffering from such a narrowness of vision that they only see what might be useful in the moment. Once again people begin having ideas that alienate them from the rest of creation and inventing utensils, gadgets, and technologies that cause the rest of creation to turn against them.

Restoring the World

In many myths the first genuine people were also the last experiment of creation. Seen in this way, humans are the culmination of the creative effort as well as the vehicles of creation ongoing. Humans are the last born and therefore the youngest children of the earth. Continuing the paradox, humans are endowed with the imagination and vision that served to create the world, but generally suffer reduced vision and blindness until the inner vision is awakened. Although heartfelt vision and genuine imagination are always what is most needed, they are also the aspects of the human soul that are most easily forgotten and most readily dismissed.

Something original that is ancient and eternally young at the same time tries to see into the world through our eyes. When we see with that god-given vision we become able to join the ongoing eloquence of creation again. This mythic sense of hidden vision and imagination appears in many fairy stories and folk tales in which the youngest sister or brother seems most out of touch with the concerns of everyday life and least able to be helpful in the conventional world. The youngest just doesn't measure up to the expectations of others. They are too caught up in dreams or too weird in their ways. They seem aimed some other way and they don't fit the common molds. Yet when it all seems about to end and end badly, the visionary capacities and surprising resources of the youngest souls become necessary for the survival of everyone else.

When everything seems most threatened and all the usual methods and practical attitudes lead to increasing disaster and dead ends, when many people melt into the masses or else harden their attitudes and narrow their minds, the youngest sister and brother hidden in the heart try to awaken. It is the eternal youth within the heart that remains connected to both the heart of heaven and the heart of earth. If we allow that visionary heart within the heart to awaken, we can find the courage of beginnings as well as the wisdom of survival. For what survives the dark rains and storms of change is not the softness of conventional thinking or the hardness of self-involvement. What survives the storms of life and allows us to envision a future are the imagination and original inspirations that are set within the soul from before we were shaped and given life.

We cannot rescind this ancient and immediate heritage of imagination, for it is buried in the bones and laced into the body, cell by cell. We are imaginative beings doused with eternity before our eyes, ever opened upon this earth. From the beginning we see more than we can express and our last words fail to conclude the stories that live through us. We are lived through by energies, ideas, and emotions that flow from the unseen world behind this world. We are overloaded by our own dreams, saddled with unusual fates, and driven by unseen destinies. Were it not for the gravity of this earth that rests in our bones and vital organs, we would take flight. Were it not for the tangled relationships of past, present, and future, we would escape every atmosphere and become the Unseen.

Despite the collapse of the immediacy of mystery into the confines of history, this down-to-earth world is also a mythic place, an ongoing production fashioned and staged by eternity. Despite the pressing problems and mounting concerns, the issue is not so much saving the planet as saving humanity from itself again. When times become dark and difficult the issue for those on earth comes down to living authentically, to authenticating the purpose and meaning already present in each soul. The eloquence of creation and meaningful imagination continues to resonate and reverberate through the world and waits to be found where it has always resided in the heart within the heart, in the living stories that reconnect the mind and the heart as well as each heart to both heaven and earth.

In mythic terms the issue is not simply the end of the planet, but the danger of a further loss of the earth as a magical, mythical, imaginal realm. The issue is the growing poverty of imagination, the wound of separation from the subtle levels of life, the loss of tender connections to unseen things and the felt sense for the presence of beauty. The loss of the soul connection leaves humans in the lurch, falling out into a sullen void that avoids both the healing touch of genuine culture and the enlivening spirit of the natural world.

Myth makes sense by holding things in the rhythm of beginning, middle, and end and placing each person in the patterns and plots of the eternal drama. Mythic sense reveals the themes that secretly run all the way through life, the hidden threads that can draw disparate pieces together and shape them into a coherent, renewable story. Myth invites us and involves us in the necessary project of finding enough imagination and vision to keep restoring and "re-storying" the world. Whenever the end seems near it is important to have a mythic sense, a story-mind, an awareness of imaginal things; not a fantasy to escape with, but a sense of living imagination that can connect us to the hidden unity and ongoing eloquence of creation.

CHAPTER 7

OPEN SECRETS

We are more closely connected to the invisible than to the visible.
Novalis

Whereas the grand myths and epic sagas of civilization tend towards dramatic conclusions and apocalyptic endings, more humble folk myths and folktales tend to escape the grand finales in order to live another day. Survival is a keynote of folktales and a habit of the common folk; it is also a core practice of nature itself. The folk of folklore tend to have little myths of how the world survives rather than grand dramas of how it all comes to an end. Folktales and folk myths carry elements of earthly wisdom. They offer artful ways of understanding times of radical change and offer hints of how to survive the inevitable periods of collapse that come along with the elevated moments of great civilizations and high culture.

Alongside the parade of major civilizations and the processions of the great religions, the tracks of the common folk can be found, a bit in the shadows and certainly closer to the dust of the road. They carry the folklore and local tales more closely connected to the land and to the knowledge of specific places. Attending more to earthly lore than codified law, they draw upon traditional wisdom and the old roots of earth knowledge. When the great civilizations lose their civility and collapse upon the historical heap, the folk continue along intuitively, instinctively making do with remnants, loose ends, and leftovers that remain when everything else falls apart. When the end seems near it might be wiser to turn to the lore of survival and the humble but enduring tapestries of stories that cannot quite end.

High cultures tend to lose touch with root stories and the core metaphors of primordial imagination. Meanwhile, village tales and folk myths linger on the edges of civilization like intelligent animals waiting to be recalled, or like seed memories tucked away until a time of need arrives. They wait for the trouble to get deep and for people to wonder whether it has ever happened before. Like the animals, the folk of folktales represent the long-term memory and primal imagination of humanity. Though often simple and rough in appearance, folk and fairy tales carry basic and essential knowledge of the world and how to survive in it. The folk of folktales are the original survivalists and they survive by remembering the age-old pattern of life, death, and renewal that ultimately sustains both great nature and human culture. They try to remind us that all this has happened before and that people have faced the End many times and lived to tell the tale.

In folktales it is not uncommon for animals and humans to communicate, as if to suggest that the wisdom lacking in culture might be waiting to be found in the realms of nature. The animals and the "little folk," the wise old women and sage old men found in stories, carry threads of knowing that constitute the wisdom of the earth. Remaining close to nature, they defy logic and tend to champion magic. Like dreams and poetry, they are part of the "there-not-there" quality of this world. They are an aspect of culture, yet not too cultivated. They are connected to nature and have a strong sense of place, yet they deal with shape-shifting and radical transformations.

Folktales are a part of the open secrets of life, part of an earthly wisdom that avoids the dizzying heights of culture by keeping close to the ground of being. They inhabit an intermediate realm between mystical ideas and common sense. They shelter an uncommon sensibility that involves both a sense of survival and an awareness of the little redemptions that keep things going along even when everything seems about to collapse altogether.

Unlike religious narratives or scientific theories, folk myths do not require that we believe in them at all. They are more like companions that desire that we simply keep in touch and occasionally listen carefully to what they have to say. Although they are frequently drafted into parables of morality and religious books, no one can truly own them. They are easily handled, readily translated, and suffer misuse rather casually. No matter, they survive and recall to us what is so often forgotten in the centers of the great cultures and overlooked in the long-shadowed halls of academia.

Folk myths form a "loose literature" that inhabits the soul of the world and that survives the ravaging of the temples of knowledge by unbelievers and believers alike. Being neither great literature nor divine word, they persist like those mysterious paintings hidden deep in the caves of old Mother Earth. When the ideas and beliefs of a given time wear thin and fail to carry the collective imagination of people, the old stories can continue to encourage, inspire, and instruct those willing to listen. Their wisdom is only available to those foolish enough to wander off the beaten paths and step beyond the maps that try to contain the constantly changing face of the earth.

Although often indigenous to a particular area to begin with, the mythic motifs of folktales can suddenly appear anywhere in the world. The essential characters of folk myths are both indigenous and indigent; they wander from place to place, yet remain connected to invisible roots that tie them to the living soul of the world. Flood stories, for instance, have been found all over the earth, even in landlocked places, as if to say that it is not only the literal seas that are being addressed, but the psychic waters of the unconscious that can flood forth and overwhelm an individual or a culture at any time. In the time of apocalypsis, the earth becomes flooded with changes and the soul of humanity is challenged to rise to the occasion and change with the times.

A Folk Tale Condition

These days we are in a folktale condition again as we face seemingly impossible challenges and overwhelming tasks. Like characters in an old story, we cannot escape the trouble that we find ourselves in. The only way out is to go through it and the only way to go through it is to find some wisdom right here on earth, the kind of wisdom offered by the enduring characters found in the timeless territories of folk myths. Remember old Noah who had to hold onto a dream and foolishly fashion a ship for a flood that had not yet appeared? He was a mythical character in folk traditions long before he was drafted to play a role in religious stories. He set sail many times before winding up in the biblical seas. The idea of important undertakings beginning with a dream, the need to accept that great changes are underway, the importance of relating to animals that often anticipate changes on earth, and the whole notion of surviving what seems to be the end are features of folk myths also found throughout the world.

The name *Noah* is very old and carries meanings of "rest" as well as "sea." Noah is an old name for the survivor in the human soul who rests in the waters of the unconscious until the floods of change threaten to wash over everything. Noah is the native survivor in the human soul who keeps close to animals and who relates to the elements of nature even when the earth rattles. Old Noah is part of the inner nature of human nature, part of the original nature and enduring capacity of the human soul. Rather than being an historical figure or a religious model, old Noah represents an inner resource of humanity. He is an indelible, unsinkable inhabitant of the human story and part of the imaginative inheritance of every living person.

Noah is the ancient mariner of the human soul, ever willing to set sail on the swollen seas of change, ready to follow a dream at the behest of the divine. He stands for the timeless dreamer in the human soul who knows what to do when the winds of change gather and the sense of dissolution begins to spread. When people start to talk again about the collapse of culture, the loss of the world or the end of time, the old dreamer stirs again inside the human psyche. Noah is only one of many names for the ancestral faculty for invention and the internal instinct for survival that continue to inhabit the old soul hidden within humanity.

There were others who dreamed big dreams and set sail amidst the seas of change. Some say that Utnapishtim was the first Noah, a primal predecessor who faced an earlier flood. At that time, the earth was troubled by overpopulation as well as a shocking increase of ignorance. There were growing numbers of people who increasingly failed to recognize the presence of the divine in the world around them. Short-term thinking began to dominate all the important areas of life and threatened to overrule the greater imagination that is also native to the human soul. People took nature for granted; they exploited the earth and gave no consideration to future generations or to the need for culture to seek balance with nature. Amidst a decrease of gratitude, a coarsening of culture, and widespread greed and cynicism, things were steadily going from bad to worse.

At that time, Enlil was considered the supreme deity and leader of the gods. Enlil had been formed from a union of the sky and the earth. Because of that pedigree, the chief deity had both a capacity to be distant and an inclination to get personally involved in what transpired on earth. As in so many old tales the divine figure came to earth and wandered amidst the creatures of creation. After a particularly disturbing visit to mankind, the god of heaven and earth reached the conclusion that a time of sweeping change was necessary. The title *Enlil* means "lord wind" and, true to his nature, the god decided to clean things up and wash everything pure again by sending great winds and torrential storms that would thoroughly flood the earth with water.

Amongst the people of that time, *Utnapishtim* was an exception to the rule. Somehow he retained a sense of wonder about the gift of life and had a genuine awe for the elements of nature. Despite the increasing blindness of most people, Utnapishtim could sense and see the presence of the divine in the things of the world. He felt at home in nature, was mostly at peace with himself and, needless to say, was also a great dreamer. People have always dreamed, often having little dreams that simply recast the events of the previous day in a different light. At other times big dreams arrive, the kind that revise people's understanding of the world and can define their role in it. Utnapishtim began to be visited by big dreams and he was wise enough to pay attention to them.

One night he dreamed of a wild wind followed by a great deluge that flooded over the entire face of the earth. Since the dream included the image of a sturdy ship that weathered the storm, he lost no time in beginning to build such a vessel. He gathered some friends to help and together they managed to fashion a large ship. Soon after, they boarded it along with their families and other friends. They also gathered "the seed of all living creatures," including the wild animals as well as the domesticated ones.

It was not long before strong winds began to blow and heavy rains began to fall. For six wild days the storm raged in every direction and the seas began to rise all around them. Soon the waters covered the entire earth except for the very top of a sacred mountain that remained above the flooding tide. As the fury of the deluge intensified and the earth grew darker and darker, even the gods became frightened. As hordes of people and herds of animals drowned day after day, the massive loss of life caused even the gods to weep amongst themselves.

People have trouble imagining that the gods can weep, yet depictions of weeping gods are found in many old stories. Weeping had to begin somewhere and most things began with the gods. In ancient Egypt, Isis was revered as the goddess of fertility and patron of all living beings. The great Nile River was said to flood from tears that she shed over the loss of Osiris, who was the "lord of love" as well as ruler of the cycles of nature. Isis was beloved by all the people but especially revered by the poor and oppressed, who felt most battered by the storms of life. They felt that in the midst of an unfeeling world the goddess felt mercy for them and wept at the pain that people had to bear. In the midst of trouble, in times of injustice, and when radical change is on the wind, it is encouraging to imagine that the divine can be merciful.

As the great winds blew across the earth and the waters continued to flood the gods wept at the plight of humankind. Eventually, the torrential storm carried the ship—laden with dreams, people, and animals—right to the high peak that alone stood above the dark and turbulent waters. Utnapishtim means "he who found life" and it was he who had to find a way to bring life back to the earth when the seas finally settled and the flood began to subside. He decided to release a dove to see if it would find some dry land, but the dove soon returned to the ship having found nowhere else to settle. After a time he sent a sparrow out, but it too flew wearily back. Finally, Utnapishtim released a black-feathered raven. When it did not return he knew that the waters had receded enough for the people and the animals to emerge from the vessel and find a place to rest on earth again.

Holy Waters

Many creation myths begin with an endless expanse of dark water and flood stories depict the idea that everything must return to a fluid state before the next phase of life can take form. Tales of the great flood are a form of re-creation myths, which show the process of upheaval and dissolution that eventually leads to a new start for humanity. In mythic terms, the time comes when the world cannot simply be repaired, but must be renewed. Change comes like a flood and a storm that wipe everything clear so that things must begin again. As it was in the beginning, the earth must separate from the waters and people must start shaping the ways of culture again.

One does not have to believe in a particular version of the flood story. Rather, the point of myths of loss and renewal is to awaken the dreamer in the soul and remind people that the divine has an interest in human survival as well as a need to transform things when the time comes. Whether it is an individual life that needs to change or an entire culture that has become stuck, a genuine solution is often preceded by a period of dissolution. Often things must dissolve back to the primal seas before taking on a new form on earth.

Flood stories are connected to old practices of cleansing and purification, where intentional immersion in water served to cleanse the troubled heart as well as to remove disturbances from the mind. Those who believe in being born again from the waters of baptism are repeating a primordial idea and ancient practice. However, before it became a ceremony that happens only once in a lifetime, baptism was a ritual that could be repeated whenever a person or a group became stuck in life. It could be brought to bear whenever people became overly conflicted or deeply confused. Thus, a person would undergo baptism at critical junctures in life and be reborn again and again. The idea of a radical cleansing and renewal was both a personal and a collective experience of the possibilities of renewal of life on earth.

The basic elements of nature offer core symbols for understanding the true nature of this world. The earth is more than two-thirds water as is the human body. Water has always been a sacred element, as the number of holy wells and sacred rivers throughout the world attest. Water has always been sacred to humanity and reflective of the presence of the soul. Water is the element of flow and reconciliation; yet its power to unify often comes after things have been torn asunder.

Instinctively, people have immersed themselves in water as a way of reconciling their spirit with the circumstances of their lives. And people have frequently intuited that sometimes it is too late to repair things and a new way of life must be found. Immersion in the sacred waters represents a return to the original acts of creation; the initiate disappears into the primal sea and emerges like a newborn, cleansed of the troubles of time and ready to start life over again.

In the midst of all the flooding waters of dissolution and change, there stood an ancient mountaintop. Mountains are the opposite of all that water stands for. Water runs deep and flows downwards like the soul, but a mountain rises upwards like the spirit trying to touch heaven. Water is the essence of alteration as it literally changes from one form to another, appearing sometimes as ice or mist or rain. Alternately, mountains stand for that which remains unchanging amidst all the changing elements of the world. A mountain offers the oldest image of an earthly temple, the natural template, and a primordial symbol from which cathedrals, mosques, and synagogues all take their shape. There may be floods that change the face of the earth and cause most people to relocate, yet something must remain unchanged. Even when the world floods with turmoil and change, there is a holy place from which the earth can gather itself again.

Being on top of a mountain has always meant being closer to the heavenly realms where the deities dwell. Temples replicate the shape of mountains imitating that uplifting form where the divine presence may be more readily felt. In many old stories a single tree, representing the Tree of Life, stands atop the highest peak. It shapes the template for all the steeples and minarets that can be seen rising above the domes of cathedrals and temples and points above the turmoil and troubles of the earth. At the center of all the storms of life there is the mountain-temple that holds up the Tree of Life that must remain above the floods of change and from which nature and culture can begin to branch out again and again.

The old flood story is trying to remind us that when everything has become dark and threatening, and when even the earth itself seems about to be overwhelmed, the temple at the center withstands the storms. When things become dark and treacherous on earth and it seems that everything might be destroyed, it is time to find the center again. For at the center, life can renew itself and new solutions can be found amidst the great dissolution that turns everything upside down. In mythic terms, the center and the beginning are the same place; if we find the center we are also near the origins of life.

The story of Utnapishtim and the great flood ends with the old dreamer having reached the symbolic center of the earth. After disembarking from the ark, Utnapishtim made a sacrifice to all the gods for allowing the people and the animals to be saved from extinction. In making prayers of gratitude, he included all the gods that were known and any that might be unknown, for that was the oldest-known way of praying. In the intensity of all the turmoil and in the midst of all the changes, the old dreamer intuited that if things were to start over again everything known and unknown had to be included. Having made appropriate prayers, Utnapishtim and the company of survivors began to populate the earth again. The story tells that the old dreamer and his wife received the gift of immortality and were given a place to dwell in peace at the "ends of the earth."

The Dream of Life

When the seas of change and times of loss sweep over the world again, the inner dream of life must be awakened. Like Noah and Utnapishtim, each soul begins the great journey of life with a dream. Each soul sails forth from the Unseen on a dream that carries it across the threshold between the worlds at the moment when the waters break and the onset of the labors of life begin. The inner dream is the vessel for each uniquely formed life. When we lose touch with the inner dream, we can become lost in life or simply float from one place to another. Our dreams come from the center and would have us return there again. Often enough, people must begin a foolish project like Utnapishtim or old Noah in order to find the center again and reconnect to the imaginal roots that brought them to life to begin with.

When the storms of life rage all around us, the floods of change threaten to drown us, and even the gods begin to weep, the only safe haven may be the dream that brought us each to life to begin with. When the usual solutions fail to keep things afloat and the mainstream becomes flooded with anomalies, it becomes more important to follow a dream than to seek safety in some isolated corner of the earth. It becomes wiser to reconnect to the intuitive and instinctive realm, the way animals sense a storm coming and head for higher ground. Noah is the part of each person that intuits when to depart from the mainstream and seek unfamiliar tributaries of knowledge.

Those who believe in literal versions of what were once old mythical stories may try to prove when the world actually began; they may try to calculate the exact time of the flood and go looking for historical evidence of Noah's ark. In their literalism they miss the whole message of surviving the flood by following a dream or a whisper from the divine. In searching only in the measurable world, they miss the point of "it came in a dream," or "god whispered in his ear." In taking the old texts as literal reports, they miss the subtleties that place humans and animals "in the same boat." In fixating on the surface of this world, they miss the inner conversation that can lead to finding little redemptions in the here and now.

Each person comes to this world with a meaningful dream that first formed in the otherworld, and it is that inner dream of life that is intended to become the vessel that allows us to align ourselves and navigate the rough waters. As the floods of uncertainty rise in the world again, it helps to remember old Noah, Utnapishtim, and all the old dreamers and survivors that are the true ancestors of humanity. Even in the midst of destruction and radical change, they maintained the secret bond with nature and the ancient relationship with the animals. They held the earth to be a temple and found baptism in the floods of change. In the end each person must learn the language through which the unseen world speaks to them or else miss their star and become lost in the storms of the world and the flood of life.

Manu and the Little Fish

In ancient Hindu myths, Manu was the first human. His name suggests "man," not simply as first male ancestor as much as the first example of "mankind." *Manu* also has roots that mean "to think," so Manu was the first human ancestor as well as the original thinker. As human prototype, Manu presents an archetypal pattern in which choices made by the individual human soul lead to grand projects that affect other people as well as other species. The story begins near the beginning of time with Manu having something on his mind. The old tale does not tell us what the nature of his problem was at that time, yet it is the nature of people to have problems that burden the mind and weigh heavy on the heart.

With a thought weighing on him, Manu set off to walk along the shore where the solid earth was washed by the endless waves of the sea. To this day, people feel more free and open when walking the shores of oceans and lakes, or even sitting by streams. Thoughts flow more easily in the proximity of waters that also flow. The subtle edge that forms where earth and water meet is a betwixt and between area that is neither one thing nor the other. In such liminal spaces things can more readily shift and take new shape and change. Instinctively, Manu bent down to touch the water and wash his hands in the old gesture of libation that can purify one's hands and heart. He also bent in natural submission to something essential and greater than himself. As he bent low to the ground and close to the water, a small fish appeared in the waves and spoke to him.

It may seem surprising now that a fish could talk to a person, but this happened long ago, close to the origins of life, when it was easier for animals and humans to communicate directly with each other. The little fish begged Manu, the first human, for protection from the larger fish in the sea that were intent on swallowing it. From the earliest times the pattern of the big fish eating the smaller ones has prevailed in this world—big fish eats little, large devours small, in the teeming seas of life where one thing feeds upon another. The old pattern continues and can be found throughout nature, and it exists in every culture on earth as well.

Manu listened as the fish explained that if he offered help on this occasion it would return the favor when it was mankind's time to be faced with death and disaster. As the first human, Manu had a decision to make. He already had something on his mind and here was another creature asking for help. Things could go many ways: he could claim that he was too busy to help; he could argue that he was already preoccupied; he could simply ignore the plea for help. Something in the first ancestor responded to the plea and Manu bent down again; no reason is given, and perhaps none is needed. He collected the little fish in his hands and carried it home. It was a small thing to do, a simple gesture of sympathy; yet there was something significant in the connection between the two species and the way they carried on together.

Upon reaching his dwelling place Manu placed the fish in a jar and began to care for it. A little nourishment and some attention caused the fish to grow rapidly and it soon outgrew its little jar. Manu placed the fish in a well, but it again outgrew the container in no time. He dropped the fish into a pond and it rapidly became a big fish in a little pond. Next he placed the fish in a lake, only to have it continue to grow and become too big for those waters as well. Manu had to carry the fish from one place to another in search of bigger and bigger reservoirs for the ever-expanding being. Manu thought about the surprising developments and noticed that even when it grew to a huge size, it remained pleasant to hold and relatively easy to carry. Despite its evident growth in size, the fish was not significantly more troublesome for him to bear.

Finally, the fish was so great in size that Manu realized that it could only be held in the arms of the wide ocean. So our ancestor carried the little fish, now grown huge, all the way back to the shore of the great sea. Arriving there, he gave it back to the waters from which it had first appeared. As soon as it was released, the fish spoke to the man again. It revealed to Manu that a great storm and deluge was coming. It told him that everything solid would soon disappear in a wide flood that would change everything and would purify all of existence. Then the fish advised Manu to prepare for the gathering storm by building a vessel that could ride on the wild seas and carry him to safety amidst the flooding tide.

Manu did not argue with the fish or question the validity of the message. He remembered that when the fish was small and feeling threatened itself, it told him it would one day repay his kindness. So Manu took the advice of the fish and began building a large ship. He invited family and friends, gathered animals, collected the seeds of the earth, and waited to see what might develop. Just as had been predicted, the flood-times came and the winds blew and the waters began to roil and rise. In the midst of the raging winds and the broiling sea, the fish appeared again. This time it told Manu to tie the ship to the great horn on top of its head. Once that was done, the huge fish began to pull the ship across the raging seas until it reached a mountain peak that remained dry above the flooding waters.

Before departing, the fish revealed itself to be Vishnu, the original creator who breathed life into the dream of existence while floating on the original expanse of the endless ocean of time. The little fish who had asked for refuge from the troubled seas of life had been none other than the deity who had first dreamed up this world, where solid land and swollen seas must meet. In helping the fish survive the troubled waters where big devours little, the first human had not only lent a hand to another species, but had also assisted the god of creation. Having served life in a seemingly small way, the original human received a great reprieve when the hard times and the great dissolution came around.

After the flood waters receded and the surface of the earth became visible and inhabitable again, Manu practiced all that he learned from the deity. For before departing, Vishnu had revealed to our ancestor certain practices for keeping close to the breath of creation. Through those arts and practices, Manu learned that the creation of the world was an ongoing process and that he could participate in it. Just as he had lent a hand to the little fish that felt threatened by bigger forces, Manu could lend his hand to assist the ongoing creation of the world. Our ancestor also learned that although big can devour small, a little help offered at the right time and in the right way can have a huge effect and even change the typical patterns that govern this world.

Like old Manu, humanity continues to stroll through the middle of existence, sometimes listening to the subtle voice that indicates how and where to be helpful and creative, at other times mindlessly devouring the resources of the earth and risking being devoured in turn. Life on earth ever hangs in the balance and it turns out that humanity plays a crucial part in the drama. This fact was settled a long time ago, back when things were just beginning and critical choices had to be made. Of course, the beginning keeps trying to begin again, especially when it seems that the end of everything is near at hand.

What was true at the beginning is also true now: either people learn to lend a hand to creation or else they tend to unconsciously swim in the realm of the fishes. It is an important thing to know about, especially when the floods of change come and everything familiar seems about to be washed away. At certain times, in the great back and forth of the tides of creation and destruction, nature needs a little helping hand and culture needs to return to practices that assist the song of creation to continue. For human beings are intended to be the friends of this world and often are the counterweights in the scales between time and eternity, between needless destruction and ongoing creation.

The Realm of the Fishes

The little fish that calls to the first human is caught in one of the great dramas of this world that unfolds in all the oceans and seas, in what the ancients called the "realm of the fishes." Day after day, night after night, year after year, the living oceans teem with great operas of devouring. Big fish feed on smaller species in numbers that cannot be counted as life endlessly devours life, as life grows from death in the great, blind back and forth from which even we emerged. The realm of the fishes has existed from the very beginning and remains a necessary part of the continuing dynamic between creation and destruction that characterizes and sustains life on earth.

What happens in the drama of nature is often replicated in realms of culture, where every pond has its big fish and the small fry continually become fodder for the big shots. In the first level of life, where people practice "survival of the fittest" and believe that personal needs must dominate all concerns, the big fish make all the rules. Those who hold power often hold everyone else at bay and usually indulge in their own appetites. Call it the world of "dog eat dog," call it hard reality; all too often in this world "might makes right" and the powers that be tend to claim whatever they desire. In nature the conflicts and devouring happen automatically and quite naturally; in culture it happens both unconsciously and with the conscious intention to rise above everyone else and even rival the gods.

The old story names this process of aggression and domination as a natural and necessary aspect of the world; yet it also includes a plea from nature to interrupt the common patterns. The first human is placed exactly in the middle of the tension between blind aggression and service to something beyond oneself. Humanity remains in that elemental tension between simply consuming the resources of life and becoming a friend of nature and of other species and thereby assisting the gods of creation. In the end, fact and myth approach each other and the ancient and the modern overlap. By now, the most powerful nations of the world consume the resources of the earth with reckless abandon. Huge multinational corporations act out the role of the big fish devouring everything in its path while justifying all manner of destructive behavior as being necessary to feed the bottom line.

The whole idea of a "consumer society" mimics the realm of the fishes, where consumption is blind and ongoing—night and day, day and night. Terms like "gross national product" and "free market" reflect the level where life consumes life in the endless economy of unreflected existence. Only people who are wealthy enough to play can experience life as a free market and, once becoming the big fish, they willfully adjust the rules to suit their own sense of freedom. Call it the free market, the world economy, or the reality of the marketplace; in the end it will be another version of the realm of the fishes, where big eats small and life grows from suffering and death.

In the realm of the fishes, in the seas of competition, the bottom line is death and consumption, just as it is in the oceans. Mass culture is the latest version of the realm of the fishes as the value of individual life becomes diminished amidst the flood tide of mass communications, massive advertising campaigns, as well as massive debts. The enemies of life are not simply whoever might have weapons of mass destruction; the huge problems do not end with the puzzle of radical climate change; the issues are not just the massive health crisis and the growing masses of refugees. One of the enemies of life at this time is mass culture itself. Big means better and huge is great and massive is now considered the best of all.

We live in a time of "giantism;" we swim in the waters of tyranny where abstract ideas and mass-mindedness as well as monolithic religions and corporations blinded with greed take up all the oxygen and threaten to swallow everything. Yet the ancient story of Manu and the fish depicts a second powerful force in the world. The plea of the little fish is the sound of something that is frequently overlooked but can be a source of surprising change and meaningful growth. At the edge of life, where the predictable patterns and the waves of change meet, there are devouring energies but also possibilities of surprising alliances that can alter the outcome of what otherwise appears to be blind consumption and massive waste of life.

The drama of this world has more than one level and sometimes a small change can lead to a great effect and turn things around. There are exceptional times when things run *contra naturum*, when something in nature goes against what seems most natural and predictable. Something in Manu responded to the desperate call of the little fish. He could have ignored the plea or dismissed it as irrational or impossible. After all, the endless devouring is natural. What difference can one person make in a world so large and so dedicated to basic forms of aggression and consumption? How can a single person faced with the overwhelming dramas and persistent complexities of life do anything meaningful?

It turns out that there is a powerful, underlying theme of life that goes against typical patterns, a hidden aspect that goes against the grain in the way that certain fish swim upstream no matter what. Yes, bigger devours smaller, and larger seems better to most; no one can change that. Yet at times a little change in awareness can alter the way that people exist and act in this world. Manu felt some immediate sympathy for the endangered fish.

Rather than turn away or deny what was being asked for, the first human protagonist bent down and entered the drama of life at a deeper level. And we are the living descendants of the original ancestor. When we listen to the subtle voices that can come from any part of life, it becomes possible to awaken more fully to the creative impulses that sleep within us. It turns out that being truly creative means going against the flow and against the tide no matter how stormy the seas become.

The Wild Card of Creation

The human soul is the wild card in the game of life and human imagination can act *contra naturum*, going against the blind needs and unconscious drives that dominate most of the world and the realm of the fishes. Manu represents that capacity in each person to respond to a particular call and calling in life, for something calls to the inner genius in each soul. The world may be increasingly a place of distraction and confusion, and we may suffer greater onslaughts of mass communications, massive denials, and mass delusions. Yet something elemental in life on earth and essential to its continuance still calls to us and calls us individually to awaken to a greater purpose and specific aim.

The human soul is imbued with a dream and aimed at a destination; this purpose can be ignored or be denied, but it cannot simply be revoked. There is a second adventure that is possible in each life and that is valuable by its very nature. If and when we respond to the call—that call which, of its nature, keeps calling throughout our lives—we become like Manu and can be a friend to nature as well as a progenitor of humane culture. The old story tells the tale of how we can learn to bow to something other than simple self-interest and can serve something beyond ourselves. Despite the disorientation of modern life and the increasing blindness of mass culture, humanity remains capable of bending to the earth again and learning to assist the little fish of creation to find some refuge and ways to survive the great changes already underway.

In bending down and lifting up the little fish, Manu plays the wild card of creation as he acts in cross-species sympathy with the one close to being devoured by the blind engine of life. In offering a little help he shifts the balance in a way that creates meaningful change. By responding to the unusual request of nature, he plays part in a regeneration of culture as the god of all creation also responds. This is the mystery of creation ongoing, it is the open secret of life on earth trying to get our attention and draw us into the mysteries and wonder of the world. Those who are blinded by self-importance or are trapped in the fears of danger cannot hear the subtle voices nearby or within themselves. They miss the whisper that runs every day in their mind and in the world around them.

Remember, old Manu was already troubled by something when he heard the call. In bending down and lending a hand in response to what called to him for help, his life began to grow. He moved closer to the breath of creation and to the dream of life. Helping the "other," it turns out, secretly helps oneself. The act of genuinely serving something beyond and seemingly below oneself can have a hidden benefit. A little help can be repaid tenfold. Saving that which seems helpless redeems the redeemer as well. Of course, if the help is offered in hopes of a greater return, all bets are off. Such expectations are the realm of the fishes slipping back in, as self-interest has a habit of doing. It may be part of human nature to make a deal in hopes of a good return, but it is also part of one's inner nature to sacrifice personal comfort and immediate needs in order to become involved with the greater project of creation.

In ancient India the Sanskrit name for the realm of the fishes was *artha*, meaning the ground of conflict and competition, the fields of life where people struggle to achieve something recognizable and tangible in the common world. Thus, artha includes the realms of politics and war as well as the arenas of business and sports. The energy of artha appears wherever achievement is attempted and it plays out in both competent and brutal ways. Many in the modern world seem to think that the territory of competition and achievement is the entire world. Some people spend their whole lives building greater and greater monuments to their own achievements. For them, the realm of outer accomplishment and reward, whether it is seen in the goals of fortune or of fame, constitutes the whole world. They have not heard the more subtle callings from the other areas of life, and they risk arriving at the end with nothing to show but capital that cannot be spent in the otherworld.

The drive to survive and achieve, to master life and establish oneself must be limited, or else a person becomes either a small fish endlessly struggling for survival or a big fish endlessly dominating others. Neither mode can make for a full life; each eventually leads to being a fish out of water. In ancient philosophy, there was another realm besides the realm of the fishes, an area with contrasting practices and altogether different aims. Opposite the territory of striving for achievement and social power there was the area of *dharma*, which means "service," especially service to something greater than oneself. Whereas artha tends to serve one's personal ambitions, dharma serves others and even otherness.

Dharma involves giving generously instead of taking endlessly. The old idea was that each person has a proportion of achievement to accomplish in one lifetime as well as a duty to serve something greater than pure self-interest. Thus, the wealthy have not just a duty to support the poor, but also the opportunity to balance themselves by growing in generosity and deepening through a greater understanding of life. Those fortunate enough to handle power are also called to place it in service of something genuine beyond personal prestige.

Humans carry opposing energies—not just competing instincts, but also conflicting interests. Sometimes achievement is required, sometimes selfless service must be offered. Sometimes it is best to reach high, sometimes better to bend low. Each person must live in a tension between opposing energies. No one gets it completely right; we are a mixture of good and bad, just like the world around us. When the times become dark and troubled, when the underlying archetype of apocalypse rises to the surface, it becomes important to follow the urgings of the soul. It may be *contra naturum*, but the saving grace is more likely found when we take up the inner aims of the soul and pursue the second adventure of life.

The Greater Self Within Us

When Manu bends down to lend a helping hand to the little fish a great liberation of life energy is occurring. For millennia the symbol of a fish has been used to represent the deep self that swims in the inner seas of the unconscious. The psychological idea is that there is a little-self, or ego self, that formed early in life in order to keep us from being completely overwhelmed and swallowed by the world around us. The little-self comes to think that it is the whole self, the real self, and the master of our world. Yet there is a deeper and wiser Self hidden within us that would have us live a greater life than the ego knows. There comes a time when that which helped a person adapt to life and survive the rough waters to begin with must be put aside. For that which first saved our lives and gave us a little sense of self and self-esteem, one day becomes a danger to inner growth and the life of one's soul.

Manu bent down when he was asked for help and acted from the big Self within. He found a sympathy that runs deep inside humanity, an age-old quality equal to, and at times greater than, the devouring energy of the realm of the fishes. The bigger and deeper Self within us is the little fish that can grow rapidly and it is our instinctive connection to the divine. In order to fulfill our genuine potential and innate sense of destiny, we must put aside the little self, with its deep insecurities and underlying fears, and risk swimming in greater and greater containers. The really big fish is one that had to be neglected early on that later tries to call us to the great adventure of our lives. Picking up the genuine project of the soul can seem like a little thing, yet from this project the true dream of our lives can grow. While in touch with that inner dream and great project, the need to devour others diminishes and the deeper compassion for all levels of life emerges.

Acting from the big Self, or the deep soul, makes a person original, like Manu who lived close to the origins and was able to be of assistance to the endangered species as well as become a servant to the divine. The deeper Self has a capacity to grow great and it is connected to the very source of creation. In the story of Manu, the source is depicted as Vishnu, the cosmic dreamer who dreamed up the world. Manu turns out to be a friend of a god, and god turns out to be dwelling in little things that might be overlooked or dismissed as unworthy of our full attention. When the world is faced with huge problems and mass cultures have come to dominate human society, the smaller aspects of life tend to be overlooked to our own detriment.

There is a famous story about someone who asked a holy man why it was that no one could see god anymore. The world had come upon hard times and people were afraid that there would not be enough to go around; most were simply looking out for themselves and taking whatever they could grab. Naturally, some folks wondered whether god had become tired of the world and had withdrawn from all that was offensive and troubling in human societies. The holy man did not deliberate long before answering. No one saw god anymore, he suggested, because people were unwilling to bend down low enough.

Once again, people were looking in the wrong direction; they expected help from above when the redeeming energy was inside them or inside the earth, found near those most threatened in the world. Looking down to find something holy can seem patently unorthodox and possibly blasphemous. Yet sometimes the higher elements must be sought in lowly places. By its very nature, the divine often goes against the grain. That which comes to be considered holy is often anything but orthodox to begin with. Manu, Noah, and all the old thinkers who came to be considered the founders of orthodox traditions were themselves quite unorthodox to begin with. All the great makers, founders, and pathfinders start out in contrary ways; it is this very quality that makes them unique and open to the sacred. Not only that, but the wise ones become smart enough to find the divine elements right here on earth where it most often hides in things that are commonly overlooked.

The tale of Manu and the little fish serves as a reminder of the immediate and immanent connections between the divine and the natural word. The divine, so longed for and sought after, has been hiding nearby in the realm of nature and in the inner nature of humanity, often the last places where people look for it. In order for things in this world to change, people might have to listen to little things, learn to hear again the language of nature and learn to trust the little voice that speaks from within the human soul. Noah had to follow the dream that awakened in him whether or not others understood his calling. Manu had to listen to a little creature in order to make contact with the god who was seeking him.

Flood stories do not simply point back at what might have happened before. They are intended to call us to the creative projects we came here to undertake now. These are Noahic times during which whole species disappear each day, ethnic languages go mute, forests fall unnecessarily, and people increasingly forget who they are before they die. We are forced to look at the ways in which things end and disappear. It is a time of loss, a period of destruction, an epoch rampant with refugees fleeing the floods of change. Everyone becomes a refugee when life changes so rapidly, so tragically, so inexplicably.

Yet in times of great change the dream of overarching, life-saving projects tries to get our attention again. When the end seems near old ideas return in order to be known again. Subtle voices hint at unseen designs. If we begin listening as Manu and old Noah did, we become gainfully employed and find the exact projects and practices needed to keep things afloat for a long time to come. Our job is not to comprehend or control everything, but to learn which story we are in and which of the many things calling out in the world is calling to us. Our job is to be fully alive in the life we have, to pick up the invisible thread of our own story and follow where it leads. Our job is to find the thread of our own dream and live it all the way to the end. In order to be fully alive we have to be a little foolish, a little bit listening to something divine, a little bit hanging out with the animals.

We are the descendants of old characters like Manu and Noah. We are the current inheritors of the dream of life and witnesses to the mystery of creation. The world as we know it has ended many times only to begin again. When the end seems near, seemingly small changes and little redemptions can shift the underlying patterns of both nature and culture. When the world around us seems about to collapse, the threads of renewal are nearby. When the world seems old with worry, ancient ideas are also near and trying to become known again. Despite feeling overwhelmed by the dramas and challenges of change, our hands are never far from finding again the old practices for being agents of creation. Like intelligent little fish, stories of renewal whisper that the time has come again to bend down and find the divine connection and the old ways of wisdom right here on earth.

CHAPTER 8

SWIMMING TOWARDS GOD

Renewal is inherent in dissolution
but is often preceded by disillusionment.

Something deep in the human soul awakens as things fall apart. Something in the soul knows that everything in this world can become lost. And something in the soul knows how to survive periods of devastation, disorientation and loss. Descent and falling is the way of the soul from its beginning. We each fell from the womb of life when the waters of the inner sea broke and it came time for us to breathe on our own. We continue to descend in order to become ourselves more fully, in order to find our own inner depths and be born again from within. A specific gravity brought each of us here and at times we must descend further, for our soul would have us understand who we already are at our core and in our depths.

We arrive wrapped in dreams with soft and subtle eyes of vision, used to floating on inner seas. If we do not learn to see in that way again, we can drift through the world, lacking purpose, despairing of finding meaning, or else pretending to have found our way while all the while lamenting inside our lives. Life is the journey we undertake in order to reach the center of ourselves; it is the pilgrimage we must undergo in order to learn who we already are and what we are intended to do. When the world around us seems to be falling apart and all seems headed for disaster, the journey to the center of the self becomes all the more important. For in finding what is essential and central to ourselves, we become more able to serve the dream of life ongoing.

The idea of a pilgrimage that leads to a holy place or a natural wonder has been part of human imagination from the very beginning. People long to be near a hallowed place, to be in the presence of a natural wonder, or to approach some revered person. Some dream throughout their whole lives of going to a particular place that represents the center of the world for them. Seen another way, every pilgrimage is secretly a journey to the center of oneself. When we risk seeking what we most long for, we also begin the path of self-discovery. In arriving where we long to be, we also approach our own center. The real pilgrimage involves awakening the deep self and soul set within us. Meanwhile, every journey must begin with the first step. An old story tells of an ancient sage named Markandeya who took the initial step on the first pilgrimage from which all subsequent journeys derive and proceed.

Markandeya was another one of those progenitors that were said to have appeared near the beginning when the world was just being dreamed up by the god Vishnu. At that time, Vishnu was resting on the infinite coils of a serpent that floated on the cosmic sea. The god reclined in comfort on the expansive waters while meditating and sleeping as the dream of the world took shape within the deity. Most gods have many names and one of Vishnu's titles was *Narayana*, meaning the "one who moves the waters" and in so doing moves all of life. The great serpent on which the deity rested was called *Ananta*, meaning "endless." Vishnu was dreaming up the world while sleeping upon the coils of the endless serpent resting on the limitless ocean. The three aspects of the beginning, the god, the endless serpent and the ocean of eternity are each distinct, yet they also depict an essential unity. This world, in which we must make the journey of life, continues to be a place of distinct experiences that secretly rest upon an underlying unity.

This version of the creation of the dream of this world involves the giant figure of a deity in human form, a serpent of countless coils capable of continuous change, and the formless, endless ocean of night that surrounds everything that exists. All were there at the beginning and each was an aspect of Vishnu, the one at the center who meditates on existence, moves the waters of change, and dreams the dream that becomes life on earth.

The vibrant terrains of the earth first took shape within the dreaming god and began to manifest a wondrous array and extensive display of elemental beauty. And there, in the pristine landscapes of the beginning, the first seeker and human seer could be seen as he wandered about, enacting the original pilgrimage from which all the wanderings of humanity have come.

Markandeya, the first pilgrim, was viewing the earth as it initially appeared in the cosmic dream. He beheld the pristine rivers and forests and the mountains that seemed to rise up to touch the heavens. He felt the flowing waters and the still pools that reflect the rapids of life and the places of inner stillness. Each natural setting he came upon became a revelation that caused him to bow in awe to the intricate beauty and wonder of existence. He saw each earthly habitat as part of a living network of natural shrines and wonders that naturally inclined him towards acts of devotion.

The first wanderer and seeker began to worship at each place in a generous, easy way, enacting the ideal role of the human devotee doing the essential work of exploring the world and reflecting upon the wonder of creation. The first sage instinctively felt the delight of existence and the abundance of creation; he experienced the joy of life repeatedly and felt that all was right and fine with the world. Of course, in this world things can only remain right and fine for a limited time. If everything was perfect nothing much would happen; if life is to be a pilgrimage it must involve some difficult terrain and some obstacles that produce meaningful change and greater awareness or nothing much would be learned.

Slipping Off the Path

At a certain point Markandeya somehow tripped and stumbled and began to fall. For some unexplained reason, the first little slipup happened, the first misstep on life's journey occurred, and with it the first hint of a nightmare appeared inside the dream of the world. It was the first blunder, a kind of primal pratfall, and some say that we have been falling ever since. Despite the ideal conditions and the assumption of good intentions, Markandeya stumbled and fell off the path and that may explain why so many who take up a spiritual path fall from grace even now.

To make matters worse, great Vishnu was sleeping with his mouth open; not only that, the dreaming god was snoring. Everything first happened at the beginning, even snoring had to start somewhere. Vishnu slept with his mouth open and snored away while the dream of life took shape within him. From the dreaming god there came a deep, sonorous sound that softly broke the silence of the limitless ocean of existence. Then, inadvertently, accidentally, and unexpectedly the first seeker slipped and fell and tumbled right out of the mouth of the all-containing god.

Mortally astonished and thoroughly shocked, the original saint dropped from the tongue of god and landed in the cosmic sea. After being expelled by the sleeping, snoring god there was nowhere else to fall except into the great void. Markandeya had fallen right out of the dream of life and into the emptiness that surrounds it. It was one of those things that was bound to happen at some time and ever since, people can experience a sinking feeling in the pit of the stomach whenever something starts to slip, go sideways or go seriously awry. Whether it comes from an unintended slip of the tongue or an unintentional loss of the way, each soul that enters the dream of life eventually repeats and continues that original slip and comes to know the free fall feeling that follows from it. For the human soul is intended to experience the heights of spiritual vision and the depths of emotional turmoil.

The first person to lay eyes on the wonders and beatitudes of creation was also the first to look straight into the emptiness of the void. As an image, it was the primal sea; as an idea, it was the void. In the beginning, ideas and images were entwined. As time has moved on, it has become more difficult to hold the image and the idea— the dream of life and its origin in the eternal void. At certain times, everything seems about to slip and slide so severely that the entire world might just topple into the darkness that surrounds it. It is helpful to know that things have slipped severely and fallen dramatically before.

Markandeya fell into nothing and he also fell into the wine-dark sea. He drifted blind and unknowing amidst the starless expanse of an endless night and boundless water. Feeling an existential level of abandonment and being completely disoriented in darkness, he became plagued with waves of doubt and flooded with torturous questions. He knew the world to be a harmonious and beautiful place, but where were the moon and stars that wrote stories across the sky? Where was the sun that taught each day to see anew? Where were the determined stands of mountains and the terra firma? Even the wind that had whispered of subtle movements and promised changes was absent now. Nothing moved and no sound could be heard.

Cast upon the limitless waters and alone in the unrelenting obscurity, the seer was adrift in the emptiness and awash with anxieties and a growing sense of dread. Each direction he turned to appeared empty and forbidding and Markandeya began to drown in the depths of despair. He felt overexposed in all his parts and found himself almost suffocating in a fear that seemed to chase his life down through the narrow shapes of his bones. More than anything the first seeker felt a growing sense of exile from the beauty of the world and the felt presence of the divine from which it came.

Soaking with confusion he floated along and pondered in fear. All that he had known before seemed impossible now; everything that was substantial was now but a mirage, all of it an empty illusion. Was he even alive? Had he ever been? Was this exile into oblivion all a dream? Had it been a dream before when the world had seemed so solid and clearly defined? Which was real and which the unreality: the endless void or the well-shaped world that he once wandered and worshipped within?

Before he could consider the situation further, Markandeya realized that the weight of the questions that echoed within him seemed to be pulling him down. Not knowing what else to do or where else to turn, the sinking sage began to look inside himself. Being unable to see anything beyond himself, the seer was forced to look inward and draw any sense of being from the depths within or else sink heavily into the blind sea. To his immediate relief and great surprise, he found essential images and cogent ideas within himself. He found the dream of life within himself; found a core imagination that seemed able to keep him afloat when there was nothing else to depend upon. Soon, the fallen saint found a way to slow his breathing and steady his attention while contemplating the images within his soul.

When he did return his gaze to the sea around him, Markandeya has become able to perceive a vague shape somewhere beyond wherever it was that he was. There seemed to be something submerged but partly visible in the expanse of water, as if a mountain range was vaguely breaking the dark horizon in the distance. As he gazed intently upon that distant shape, it seemed to glow from an inner radiance that softened the edges of darkness. With a growing sense of amazement and feeling an inner glimmer of promise, the solitary sage began to move towards the glowing shape in the distance.

Soon, instinctively swimming and reaching forth with all his might, the first seeker drew closer to the apparition. He became flooded with joy as his eyes began to realize that the shape he found in the void was the immense form of the sleeping, dreaming god. Feeling wildly inspired and enthused, the sage swam closer and closer to the deity. Moved by a renewed sense of awe, he opened his lips to ask aloud if it was indeed the creator. But before he could form the words and speak, a giant hand seized him up and he found himself being swallowed back into the mouth of god.

Betwixt and Between

Markandeya, wet with doubts and still dripping with some despair, found himself once again wandering a path within the surprising dream of the earth. Although back on familiar and welcome ground, the saint was a bit unsteady. He had seen the void, had tasted of it and had been immersed in it. He had seen the other side of existence and part of him felt a great distance from the beauty that was once again all around him. He had also perceived the form of god, a giant shape— manlike or womanlike, so huge it was hard to tell. He had glimpsed the divine, yet could not comprehend it. He had felt both the warm breath of the divinity and the penetrating chill of the void. He remembered both but understood neither, and felt himself internally suspended between one thing and another.

The first pilgrim had fallen into oblivion and had been saved from it; he had suffered an existential exile but also felt redeemed a little. For an uncountable period of time he had lost all orientation to life; now he felt disoriented in a new way. He found himself carrying on the questioning that had begun in the great sea of doubts. He still puzzled over which was real and which the dream. Although he could feel the path again beneath his feet, he knew he could slip at any moment and fall again from the grace of god and from the dream of the world. Now, he pondered as he prayed and made his way along the path before him more carefully. He began to notice the silence between the notes of birdsongs. At night he felt the distance between stars and at times he knew again a gnawing emptiness deep within himself. How quickly the world could disappear, how slight the veil between things could be, and how close the hand of god.

Is this world a reality or all an illusion? Can it disappear in a moment and be found again? Myths tend to answer: Yes. It is all real and all an illusion, all a dream and a nightmare, all there and not there —the breath within the breath. Then, does what happen in the world matter or not? The answer comes again: Yes. Those who think the whole world to be a simple illusion fail to realize that it is the great illusion, the living illusion that is both reality and dream, both full and empty at once. We are the living, breathing pilgrims bound to wander amidst the dream of the earth and equally bound to question the meaning and purpose of it all. It is a great mistake to take it all at face value and an error of another sort to dismiss the wonder of it all as a simple dream or an empty illusion. Any attempt to deny the human condition of being in the tension between the essential opposites in this world eventually leads to some kind of disaster.

There is a story of a man who went to a spiritual teacher in order to learn about the true nature of the world. All his life he had been a pragmatist and a realist, yet things had begun to slip away from him and life no longer seemed so exact or certain. He decided to learn what the spiritual seekers had to say about the world. He found an old teacher who quickly perceived how the new student habitually overvalued things that could be measured and often tried to reduce complicated issues to the bare facts of life. The teacher welcomed the man of facts and introduced him to basic spiritual practices. When the realist unexpectedly appeared at a session for advanced students, the teacher did not send him away. He continued his discourse on the notion that the divine presence exists in this world and can be found in all the things around us.

"Everything is god," said the teacher, "the divine can be found in all that exists, even in those things that appear to be completely opposite energies to each other. That is the unifying nature and true essence of the divine. God is everywhere even if hard for most people to see." The teacher went on to describe the world as a place of illusion, where the divine wears uncountable disguises that look to the unenlightened to be hard reality. The new pupil seemed to grasp the ideas, even altered by hearing them. "God is the sole reality," he said in response to the teacher's discourse. "The divine can be found in all forms as everything that exists is the abode of god," he repeated the ideas as he experienced a wave of expansion and delight that he had never felt before.

When the teaching session concluded, the new student of divinity walked off in a cloud of delight. Each thing he saw looked radiant and appeared to be imbued with the divine. He moved through the world more slowly than ever before and wished to bow to everything that moved before him. Caught in the new spell of wonder, he walked unwittingly straight down the middle of the road. He only realized where he was when he heard the voice of an elephant driver shouting for everyone to clear the way as he tried to control the enormous body of the animal he rode upon. The elephant was moving rapidly down the same road and silvery bells were ringing forth at each ponderous step it took. The self-exalted seeker of true knowledge could hear the ringing of the warning bells and could see the huge animal rapidly coming directly towards him.

As others moved swiftly out of the way, the former realist thought to himself, "Why should I make way for an elephant? Certainly the elephant is a manifestation of the divine, for everything is— even me. I am god. The elephant is god. Why should god be afraid of god?" Fearlessly continuing his reverie about the beauty of the world and the wonders that could be found in it, the new devotee continued undaunted down the middle of the road. Soon enough, god came to god, and in that meeting the elephant swung its trunk around the waist of the great thinker and simply tossed him out of the way. The poor fellow landed heavily on hard ground and was quite shaken. More than that however, he felt a great shock. He had been in a state of beauty and wonder in one minute and found himself crashing hard against the ground of reality in the next.

After a time he picked himself up, and still covered with the dust of the road, began to limp back to the dwelling of the old teacher. As he dragged himself along he wondered aloud how it could be that the world was but an illusion and a disguise in which the divine was hidden, yet also the ground of hard reality that can bring a person down quickly or even crush them. When he found the teacher he gave an impassioned account of his state of delight and the subsequent encounter with the elephant that brought him back down to earth. He asked aloud how this confusion of states could exist in one world.

The teacher listened serenely until the entire tale was told. Then he replied directly, "It is true that the divine is everywhere, even to be found in you. In that sense, you *are* god. So also is the elephant a representation of god. You have that equation drawn correctly. However, there is always a third thing that shifts the ground when two opposing forces meet. In this case, the third and essential thing was the elephant driver. Why did you not listen to the voice of god calling to you from the driver, who was also god telling you to clear the way and save yourself?"

The Grand Illusion

This world is both reality and illusion; it is a place of gravity and hard limitations, but also a place of revelation and transcendence. This world is the grand illusion that expresses the eternal dream of the divine manifesting in itself in all the intricacies and entanglements of time and space. We come along like unwitting pilgrims and often thinking like the new student who has been schooled on the operations of gravity and the realities of a world divided into subject and object. At one level, that perception is quite true; an encounter with an elephant and falling to the ground prove it to be so. On another level it is all a wondrous dream that keeps being lost and needs to be recovered or else we become lost in another way. Lose the dream and lose the sense of the divine nearby. Follow only dreams and encounter harsh realities or experience a fall into the void which is also part of the necessary conditions of being conscious and alive on the face of the earth.

Mankind has always been soaked with divine imagination and been wet with fears of emptiness, absence, and abandonment. The "all and nothing" of this world has always been whispering at the edges of human awareness and intriguing people to explore further and examine things in detail. Followers of the positivistic sciences went looking for the absolute cause and exact beginning of the universe. They shined sharp laser lights into the great unknown and found themselves looking at a mystery of grand proportions. Their studies indicate that the visible, provable aspects of the universe— the humans and animals, the oceans and mountains, the planets and stars, and all the spiraling galaxies— represents a mere 4 percent of what might actually exist. The rest remains a mystery that has become the new study of dark matter and dark energy. Those on the cutting edge of astrophysics now believe that the universe contains 23 percent dark matter and 73 percent of something even more mysterious and about which they have few clues for understanding. They call this unseen force which may be the predominant factor in the universe- dark energy.

Ancient seekers after knowledge and greater awareness found similar mysterious forces through more intuitive ways of observing life. The Sanskrit word for the mysterious force of life that can be matter on one hand and pure energy on the other was *maya*. In the Western world, *maya* has often been translated to mean "just an illusion," as if the whole mystery of life could be reduced and dismissed as a kind of trick from which people might simply escape or extricate themselves. Yet *maya* is itself a tricky word and concept. On one hand maya means "magic," a kind of cosmic sleight of hand that produces all the forms and illusions of the world. On the other hand it means "matter" and also "mother" and it involves all that matters to us. Maya is the magic of existence and the wonder of the material world that continually bubbles up from the void. Maya involves the great trick of existence and the grand illusion of life that produces and sustains everything that matters in this world.

The word *illusion* comes from a stem meaning "to play with" and nearby is the root *ludic*, which points to the essential spontaneity of life. As the magic of life Maya is in play everywhere, particularly in the many forms of water. Like the force of maya, the essential liquid of life can appear in many forms and readily change from one to another. Water can fall as rain that sustains everything that grows or cause things to disappear in a mist. Water can freeze and harden into solid ice then melt and rush down mountainsides cutting relentlessly through massive rocks while also polishing little stones. Water can also appear as the great and dark expanse of the unconscious that sits inside each conscious being trying to make a way though this world of hard facts and shape-shifting mysteries.

Vishnu was sometimes called Lord of Maya, but more often *Maya* referred to the mother of creation; Maya as the unfathomable, as the original substance from which all dreams as well as the thousand forms of things came to be. Thus, diving or falling into the waters of darkness also meant delving into the mysteries of Maya and swimming in the unfathomable. Maya meant the *one* ever becoming the many, as she brings forth each phenomenal realm of life and pervades it as well. As the Weaver of the World, she is the mother of enchantment ever hidden behind all the veils and illusions. As Maya-Shakti, she personifies the spontaneous energy that permeates all of tangible reality and the playful delirium of the dream of life in its multiple, manifest forms.

The great goddess of illusion was seen as the seductress of love and mistress of beauty, the source of the creative joy of life, the fount of grace, as well as the mother of the Muses. *Maya* means magic and magic means change, especially the capacity to transform and shape-shift. Modern science also seems to come upon this aspect of the grand illusion and great mystery when discovering an intimate exchange at the nuclear level, where matter can suddenly become energy and energy becomes matter again. Maya, energy, and matter are the stuff of dreams and the elements of cosmic play, and we are made of the stuff that dreams are made of.

Maya was also called the Queen of the World, and as such, she was present in every nuance of feeling as well as in each moment of conscious perception. Feelings and perceptions are the gestures that bring her present and primary ways of awakening. Maya is the unity of all opposites, the yoke inside yoga, as well as the inspiration in works of art. For art is made of combining unlike things and so is magic and life for that matter. The point of creative art and of spiritual practice is to cut through the simple illusions of life in order to find deeper ways of being and of touching the underlying unity of life.

Dark Matters and Dark Times

Maya could also appear as Kali, the Dark Lady, mistress of time, death, and the tomb. *Kali* means "black" and also "time;" especially it means the darkness that existed before light was shed upon the world. *Kali Ma* is the "dark mother" and *Kali Yuga* refers to the "dark times," when the waters of oblivion seem closer and the darkness around us seems deeper. As cutting edge scientists gaze into the expanse of creation they find the mysteries of dark matter, black holes and dark energy. Here on earth the darkness around us becomes deeper.

It is a dark time when all the questions about life and death appear on the nightly news as well as in the scientific journals. Reports of holes in the ozone layer, intended to protect us, and stories about the melting ices caps raising the levels of water over the face of the earth bring the sense of existential dread closer. As do the reckless threats from nihilistic terrorists and the growing tensions around nuclear weapons that might throw the whole dream of life into the waters of oblivion. In the dark times, the dark matters and dark energies appear closer at hand as the center can no longer hold and we can feel tossed back and forth by the extremes of life.

Not only does every issue tend to polarize into fierce oppositions, but everything must be taken to the extreme. Not only are there extreme changes in the weather, but extremists of all kinds abound and exaggerated feelings develop inside people as well. Irrational influences and undue pressures become common and people feel driven to extremities, like it or not. It becomes difficult to avoid intense feelings and edgy thoughts as inner fears compete with outer threats. The chill of the void seems ever closer and the nightmare of destruction threatens both the beauty of nature and the promise of culture. It seems as if everyone might fall out of the mouth of god and wind up in the waters of despair.

In the dark times it is easier to feel the presence of the void nearby and the dull pull of oblivion. Amidst increasing confusion and tragedy, there is an increasing dis-location of the self, even a sense of cosmic homelessness. The world can lose its sense of magic and it can become difficult to remember the deep honesty of standing before a natural wonder and instinctively bowing to the awe and beauty and mystery of life. The crack in existence becomes bigger and the darkness grows greater and we can slip more often and find ourselves falling like Markandeya. Like the first pilgrim, it is our human fate to ride on the breath of the divine, to wander in the dream of life and to fall from grace and land in the seas of oblivion. Call it losing our way, call it falling into the unconscious or simply being born during a dark time. Everyone must feel it at one time or another for it is part of the human experience that knows the presence of the divine, but also must suffer a loss of the enchantment and magical sense of this world.

The Kali Yuga was also called the Last Throw as in the last roll of the dice in the great game of life. The dark times signified the end of an era, the conclusion of a grand cycle and cosmic dream. The saving grace in the midst of the diminishing of the cosmic dream comes from the fact   that each moment near the end represents a greater proportion of time as the time of that cycle runs out. In the dark times, a small effort in the direction of creation has a greater effect than it would have at another time. When the darkness around us grows deeper, it is important to know how to swim in the rough waters of life. As was the case with Markandeya, the divine is closer than we think, especially when we allow ourselves to be near the core imagination of our own life.

Sometimes we have to willingly enter the waters of uncertainty and find the inner dream and living story that can keep us buoyant and learning to swim in the direction of the divine. At certain points in life it becomes necessary to accept the darkness and descend into the deep waters of the soul and learn what has kept us afloat all along. It is like the tale of the scholar who was traveling from one place to another carrying his load of heavy books and weighty questions. His long journey led him to the shore of a great body of water and he began to look for a ship that could safely carry him across it. After doing some research and locating a suitable vessel, the scholar wanted to know who was in charge of the crossing. Being a man of questions and answers, he wanted to know what was what in this business of sailing and crossing over.

Upon being introduced to the captain of the ship, the scholar asked if he was familiar with the ideas of philosophy, with the current issues of science, and with the precise arguments of the theologians. The man of the sea had to admit that he had not read any of these subjects in detail and that he was not schooled in the latest theories. The scholar promptly informed him that without developing such knowledge he had wasted most of his life. Be that as it may, the captain informed him that the course for the journey had been arranged and the time had come for the ship to set sail.

Not long after the vessel had reached the open seas, a storm began to blow across the surface of the water. The skies darkened all around, the winds blew wildly, and the waves surged greater and greater about the ship. When the gale did not abate but grew more treacherous moment to moment, the captain went to check on the scholar. He asked the learned man if, in the course of his studies, he had mastered the art of swimming. The man of books and big ideas explained that he had never taken the time to learn swimming or practice any other exercise. "Then all of your life has been wasted," said the captain, "for this ship is going down."

The problem with the scholar was not simply that he had an interest in ideas; the problem was that the ideas he carried could not keep him afloat in the seas of change. The issue was not that he took religious issues or scientific theories seriously, but that he believed more in the word written down than in the living practices that make change meaningful. Books are a wonderful thing, but they can be a little heavy and obtuse when immediate knowledge of the world becomes necessary in the moment. Fixed ideas and accepted beliefs may look like life rings, but in the long run it is better to learn how the soul would have us swim. The solutions to life's dilemmas most often lie in an inward experience of one's own soul, not in a doctrine or belief found outside it.

At times the world grows dark, the ship goes down or we simply slip and lose our footing in the daily world and fall out of the dream of life. Here on earth the sinking feeling is never far away and sometimes we have to abandon all designs, forsake all studies, and jump into the waters of life and swim with all our instincts and intuitions and our own intimations about life. People drown in the seas of change because they cling to abstract notions or conventional patterns that lack true buoyancy when the time for changing comes. People become numb or paralyzed with fear instead of letting go of familiar but uninspired things. A person cannot swim and hold on at the same time. A genuine awakening implies both making a greater commitment to life and letting go of those things that are not in fact life enhancing.

Swimming is a form of surrender that requires trusting the waters we find ourselves in and letting go of all prior beliefs. In the moment of jumping or falling overboard, everything seems lost and we do die in some fashion. Yet it becomes easier to swim and aim for the divine horizon once the full implications of drowning in the darkness have been accepted. Swimming, like breathing and loving, requires some surrender and a practice of letting go. As we try to swim and make our way amidst all the uncertainty, something old and resourceful in the soul can awaken in us.

Self-Revelation

In falling out of the dream of life, Markandeya had a life-changing experience. He found himself in an existential crisis, having to face the great tension between the abundant dream of life and the endless void. In order to survive, he had to find the dream of life as it was formed and set within himself by facing inner fears and layers of despair. In a metaphysical version of sink or swim, he had to learn how to let go, yet not abandon himself. The first seer and seeker had to learn the way in which he was meant to swim in the troubled waters that ultimately lead back to the beauty of life. In order to get his feet back on the ground, he had to learn to swim with the force of his own unique life dream. Learning how we are supposed to swim and reconnect to the divine energy of life becomes the issue of survival when the dark times come and everything seems headed for oblivion.

The trick in this realm of illusion and disillusionment is to learn what really carries us when the seas of life get rough— to recognize what brought us here and what has secretly carried us all along. Finding a genuine orientation to life involves the difficult journey from the outer world to the inner realm. It requires a conscious turning to the depths of being found in the individual human soul. Only by turning inward can we find the deep subjectivity of the soul and experience a true way of being present in the world.

Markandeya found inside himself the way in which he was secretly threaded to the divine. In becoming conscious of his innate connection to the dream of the world, he became able to swim in his own way and style. In moving closer to his own essence, he also began glimpsing the divine at the edge of his awareness. Then the essence in him began to move towards the divine from which it came. As the swimmer moved closer to the divine image, it moved to gather him in. There is an important lesson here; it is not necessary to make it all the way to the divine source of life, rather, the willingness to swim the dark waters and the effort made to awaken to our own inner being and life vision moves the divine closer to us. What we are seeking in the troubled waters of life is also seeking for us.

The fall into darkness places us outside creation looking in. That shift begins the process of seeing into ourselves, but also makes us more visible to the divine. Once we have fallen, our job is to learn how our soul would have us swim in the ever-changing waters of life. Swimming towards god means finding the way we are aimed in this world. We do not have to make it all the way, but must simply surrender to the way we are intended to be in this world. Something of a divine nature is trying to reclaim us even as we despair of finding it. And the dream of the world, so easily lost and forgotten, is also trying to be found again. There is no proof or scholarly certification that can be offered for this, only the evidence found inside the soul when trying to survive the waters of doubt and despair.

There is something deep within that knows the divine and longs for it and can at times recognize it in the world. The pilgrimage of life has always aimed at the center and deep self within each soul. In the midst of all the collapse and familiar things falling apart there can be more revelations of the deep self within us. When the little self becomes overwhelmed with fears and uncertainties, the greater self within us is also near. The deep self and old soul within us carries the inner dream, the god-given pattern and guiding force of our life. The self within the soul is the god connection, the indelible inner sense of how we are threaded and magnetically drawn to the divine.

Times of great change and experiences of apocalypse can be viewed as the exact conditions under which a primal eruption and genuine revelation of the deep self can occur. Instinctively, the soul knows that, when all seems lost, the "only way out" is a greater revelation of what and who we are at the core of ourselves. The trick in this life has always been a matter of discovering what is already seeded in the soul and then learning how to trust it that. The essential dynamic of life, death, and renewal shapes the pattern of apocalypse, but also represents the design of personal initiations through which the soul grows and within which the self within us becomes more conscious. As everything else seems to crack and dissolve and fall apart, the deep self moves closer to the surface and seeks to become known.

The archetypal dynamic of apocalypse involves the intensification of all that produces division and conflict in life; yet the archetype of the deep self is the inner wholeness that is secretly what we are being aimed at. The deep self is the intended personality, both the source of and the object of our longings and purpose in life. It is the true center as well as the core content of our lives; it is the indelible root from which our consciousness grows. Once awakened, the deep self exists as an inner wholeness and central guiding force that helps us swim in the right direction. The intended outcome is the living revelation of the uniqueness of each individual soul as an expression of the divine dream of life.

People often fear the moment of death not just as a point of oblivion, but as a moment of final judgment when the soul must be weighed and judged. Most creeds include a last judgment that comes at the end of life. Yet what will be found then can also be found now, as the essential judgment involves a defining encounter with the deep self that was seeking to be revealed all along. Much of the fear of death comes from an intuition that we will be revealed as having avoided encounters with the deep self within us. Since the dark times of apocalypse cause the last judgment to seem to be always at hand, the opportunity to awaken further to the presence of the self is also nearby. Whatever we might have to face in the end, we can also face up to right now. As the mystics have always said, what we find then is here now. Unfortunately, it often requires a felt sense that the end is near in order for us to become bold enough to make changes that were intuited and indicated all along. Even as we tread the spiritual waters, and dread the necessary changes, the deep self is trying to awaken and the divine has an interest in that awakening.

Swimming to the Divine

When the waters of the void are near, it is the living dream within that gives us buoyancy and makes the devotional swimming possible. When the real swimming starts, all arguments are with god. As a word, *god* has roots like any other aspect of language. It comes from the Gothic *ghuth* and the Indo-European *ghut* or *ghuto*, meaning "to implore." God is who or what we implore when all seems lost and there is nowhere else to turn. Seen the other way around, each soul is secretly pulled by something god-like, just as the divine hand was waiting once the old sage saw things more clearly and developed his way of swimming in the unknown. Swimming in the ocean of uncertainty involves learning to trust the vague glowing shape on the horizon of one's present knowledge. Then, it turns out that the divine is moving towards us as well.

There are endless ways to swim in the waters of spirit and catch glimpses of the divine. In the beginning of this emotional, spiritual swimming, accuracy counts less than a willingness to brave the waters of uncertainty. People are secretly pulled towards one god or another. Yet each needs a practice, a way of swimming inside life, in order to continue moving in a meaningful direction. Amidst the flood of changes and the threats of annihilation, a genuine art or practice helps to keep the fears, doubts, and the existential dread at bay. A genuine practice helps bring the glowing shape of the dream of life into view. Having a practice is like entering the unknown repeatedly and learning to swim in one's life.

Any practice that moves one closer to becoming oneself is a genuine way; but notice the natural division experienced by the first seer and seeker on the way. Markandeya had to look deep within and learn to center and settle himself. He also had to learn how the core of his soul could reconnect him to the dream of life. One way involves turning deep within while the other required an exertion of self-expression that moves him closer to the place of continuous creation. Like most things in this world practices can be seen to divide into two paths, one turning inward towards a silence at the center of things, while the other seeks to make the divine connections more visible and palpable. Each way connects to something divine and both are ways to find refuge in troubled times.

In ancient India a basic division was made between the Nay and the Yea of life. The path of the Nay involves those practices that remove a person from the tumult and commotion of the common world. On that path a person says no to this and nay to that as they clear a path to the still center of the self. The path of Yea goes the opposite way as the seeker says yes to whatever appears and bows before it. This is the devotional path, the way of the ecstatic and of those who produce art and music and all the outward elaborations of the inner creativity of life. It is not a simple division, usually not a clear cut choice. Some may follow one path to the seeming exclusion of the other; yet everyone must experience both the yea and the nay of life to some degree. Just like the two worlds, the two ways have need of each other and we are witnesses to both of them.

We each enter life under exact circumstances and in specific relationship to the dream of life, each caught exactly and accurately in the great spell of Maya. We are each a unique version of the original pilgrim and we each must find and form ways of awakening and that make sense within the natural orientation of our lives. A genuine practice combines the ground of uncertainty with intimations of something genuine and enduring in the soul of the seeker. Through a creative practice we play at the edge of illusion, touch the subtle threads of knowledge and feel the seat of the soul.

It is inevitable that we will experience both losing ourselves in specific illusions and also becoming disillusioned with the life as they find it. Being completely disillusioned is another one of life's common illusions. The metaphysical glass is always half-empty, or always half-full, as the illusions of life go both ways. The empty pours into the void and the void pours back into the world. And sometimes the veil between the two worlds becomes thin enough for us to see through. Over time, practice becomes a bridge that serves oneself as well as the world.

Markandeya had to consider that he lived a dream within a dream and that he existed within a questioning that doubted all that exists. He had tasted of the absence of things and knew in some inexplicable way that all and nothing were both nearby all the time and within him as well. And we, who come along so long after the dreaming up and fashioning of the world began, are the descendants of that pondering pilgrim. We are the latest wanderers in the dream of life and the most recent inheritors of the inevitable fall into the sea of doubt and oblivion. We awaken and we sleep inside the dream of the world and we cannot help but sometimes worry that we might wind up exiled from all of it and become lost in the great void nearby.

We may be daunted by the surfacing of all the dilemmas and troubles of this troubled world, but the deep self and soul within us already knows how we are intended to swim in the blessed turmoil of the waters of life. For humans exist to bring meaning to the surface of life and awareness to the dream of existence. The divine is at the edge of our awareness and vision, but it is also within us as the first seeker found when all seemed completely lost and forsaken. In order to find the dream of life again we must first find the way that the dream exists within our own souls.

Like Markandeya, we swim in the endless waters that loosely hold object and subject together. We exist as the object that fell out of the mouth of god and we become the unique and individual subjects trying to awaken further and swim our way back to the beauty of life. In learning the way that we are intended to be, we add to the dream of creation. For we are the lost element of the dream of life; the conscious witnesses to its existence, and the self-doubting agents of its renewal. When the world becomes dark and uncertain, mankind can act as the second creator, the conscious fish found in the ocean of unconsciousness and uncertainty.

The divine is at the edge of our awareness and vision, but it is also within us as the first seeker found when all seemed lost completely. In order to find the dream of life again, we must first find the way that the dream exists within our own souls. We may be daunted by the surfacing of all the dilemmas and trouble of this troubled world, but the deep self and soul within us already knows how we are intended to swim in the blessed turmoil of the waters of life. For humans exist to bring meaning to the surface of life and awareness to the dream of existence.

A Second Fall, A Second Calling

After his fall into the void, the first pilgrim resumed his path of devotion and learning the practices of being and doing in this world. Many years passed inside the dream of the earth before a similar fall happened. Inexplicably, the old sage slipped again and found himself falling out of the dream of life and from the mouth of god only to be deposited back in the endless darkness of the sea of oblivion. This time he adjusted more quickly and held more readily to the center and the dream within himself. In short order he spotted an island on the horizon and began to swim closer to it. As he approached, he could see a fig tree upon it and, standing beneath the tree, a luminous child cheerfully at play.

As the old sage pulled himself from the dark waters the youngster spoke and welcomed him by name, saying: "Do not be afraid my child, but come closer here to me." The holy man felt insulted by being called a child by a child. Child indeed! Who was more venerable and wise with age than the first pilgrim of this world? Did not the name Markandeya mean the "undying one?" Even the gods had come to refer to the enduring sage and seeker as the Long-lived One. It did not seem appropriate that a child should speak to a sage in that fashion.

"Who are you to call me a child?" asked the offended saint, forgetting all the ins and outs of mystery and the surprises of this wondrous world of illusion. The little one answered promptly, "I am your parent, the old mind and soul within that secretly sustains your life. I have a thousand heads. I am the cycle of the year that begins everything and the echo of the end that takes it all away again. I am the divine dreamer and the fount of wisdom. My name is birth and I am called death as well."

Markandeya suddenly understood that the ancient child before him was Vishnu showing him the contradictory aspects of evolution and dissolution, showing him the maya and magic of the deity that both creates and destroys, that sustains and annihilates. Suddenly, he felt a great sense of blessing at the privilege of being able to receive such a direct revelation. Then, just as suddenly as he appeared, the divine child disappeared. Before the old saint knew what was happening, the hand of Vishnu snatched him up and he was swallowed back again.

Inside the dreaming body of the divine, the sage felt a new level of gratitude and a new wave of wonder. This time, instead of taking up his wandering habits again, he sought a solitary place in which to settle and contemplate more thoroughly. After sitting quietly for a long time, he began to hear the breath of the dreaming god flowing out into the world and drawing back into the dream again. He realized that it was the life breath of the universe and that he was held in that breath even as he breathed within his own life.

The old holy man attended carefully to this awareness of the breath of the universe. He made an art of that attention to the divine breath and gave birth to the practice of "pranayama." *Pranayama* means to extend the breath and thereby extend the vital force of life. The old sage took up the essential practice of participating in the breath of creation and of helping to extend the unseen energy and vital force of life. For the entire world rides on the breath of the divine, shaping existence with its exhale and withdrawing energy from the forms of life with its inhale.

The old saint called the indrawn breath "ham" and the breath of exhalation he termed "sa." Taken together they make up the sound of the in and the out, the expiration and the inspiration, of the endless breath of the universe. The two syllables also intone the name *Hamsa*, which refers to a wild gander. Hamsa also turns out to be another title of Vishnu, who sometimes appears as a wild bird whose wings stir the air of the earth and the breath of the world. Vishnu's choice of an animal mount is no accident, for the wild gander can float easily on the surface of the ocean or suddenly lift its wide wings and begin a great migration, a grand pilgrimage to places at a great distance.

As emblem of the dual nature of creation, the wild bird wanders between the two worlds, at home in the celestial heights as well as on the waters that exist and flow on the surface of the earth. And we, like the old pilgrim, are also residents in two realms. We inherit the dream of the earth with its landscapes of pristine beauty and we feel the need to wander and wonder within it. We also long to be touched by the divine and awaken to the world behind this world. We follow the old knowers even when we know nothing of them. Whether conscious of it or not, our own breathing goes in and out—sings "ham" and "sa"—and contributes to the enduring breath of life.

As Markandeya listened to the song of the breath of life both within himself and in the universe, another secret of existence was revealed to him. He began to hear the phrasing of the eternal breath of existence the other way around. Instead of the original intention of "ham-sa," he began to hear "sa-ham." At first it seemed a mistake of some kind, another slipup that might disrupt the coherence and continuity that he had been building within himself for such a long time.

After a moment of uncertainty and insecurity, the old saint caught onto the little joke of existence. He recalled that "sa" and "ham" can also be translated as "this" and "I." When listened to both ways, as "ham-sa" and as "sa-ham," he could hear the underlying message of the breath of this world, saying continually: "ham-sa and sa-ham"—"I am this and this I am." The old pilgrim found himself singing the song of existence, the breath of life holding the two worlds together as they float on the endless ocean of the great void from which life keeps being created. As they used to say when people paid more careful attention to both the inner breath of life and the outer atmosphere that we all breathe together: "As above, so below; as within so without."

CHAPTER 9

THE TREE OF LIFE

Threads of genius and purpose are present in everyone, but may only become visible when something creative is attempted.

Cosmology may be the oldest art form as each tribal group, no matter how small in numbers, no matter how simple in technology, must have a story to explain the entire world. Ancient cosmologies often include an arrangement of core elements that combine to make up the world. Some cosmological designs consider four basic elements as the cornerstones of existence. Others imagine the basis of the world to be a combination of five elements with the fifth being the quintessence that holds the others together. Under the cosmological banner that states "As above so below," each person is seen as a microcosm of the elemental arrangement. Thus, there are five fingers and toes on either side and there are five openings and five senses in the human body.

Most cosmologies begin with fire, water, and earth as the core arrangement with additional elements imagined as mineral or stone, as air or ether, as wood or nature. Typically, fire is the initial element, the igniting force that sparks all of existence and that must be balanced by a large proportion of water. Life on earth exists within a great balancing act between fire and water as a primordial fire burns at the center of the earth and the blazing sun beams down from above. Too much water and the earth can be overwhelmed with floods; too much fire and the earth might be consumed in flames. It takes a great amount of water in its various states of liquid, moisture, and ice to balance the intensity of elemental fire on earth. Since fire can erupt just about anywhere, water must be spread all over the earth's surface.

Even more than water, fire was held by some to be the symbol of perpetual change because it can transform one substance into another without being a substance itself. Thus, Heraclitus stated: "This world, which is the same for all, no one of gods or men has made; but it was ever, is now, and ever shall be eternal fire." Like most of the pre-Socratic philosophers, Heraclitus began his considerations of life on earth with the elements of what we now call nature. When he spoke of god he did not mean the Greek pantheon that became mostly a logical arrangement of deities representing predetermined attributes. The old philosopher imagined the divine as a fire at the center of life, as a living flame in every soul, and as a spark in every material thing on earth. If we look back far enough, Western philosophers were intrigued with cosmology and could envision the divine flame of life as being central to each thing in this world.

Fire may be central, but it is also hidden like the inferno burning unseen at the center of the earth. Water is ubiquitous and unavoidable; it falls from the sky and erupts from springs in the ground; it flows in endless tides and runs in rivers and streams that travel almost everywhere. Fire, on the other hand, tends to hide inside things and only erupts under specific conditions. Once ignited, however, fire can go from warm to hot—from burning to out of control—quickly. And it can use almost anything for fuel. Fire is a problem in that way; it can provide warmth in cold climates and it can illuminate the darkness, but it can also become a raging beast that consumes everything in its path and threaten all that exists.

Like water itself, stories of great floods can be found on all continents. There are also tales of times when the earth became overheated and it was the element of fire that threatened to consume the entire planet. These days in which the atmosphere has become overheated and even the temperature of the oceans have begun warming up, it may be pertinent to consider what myths have to say about the effects of overheating and losing the balance between fire and water. An old folk myth told in South America describes a time when the elements on the earth fell severely out of balance and fire got out of hand. Instead of simply warming the world, fire came to dominate the other elements. For whatever reasons, a great fire was ignited and soon went out of control.

Icanchu's Drum

At first, things simply became warmer, causing ice caps to melt and parts of the earth to turn into deserts. Eventually, however, everything became overheated and the atmosphere went on fire. Soon, the great conflagration spread throughout the world and nothing anyone could do was able to stop it. The intensity of the flames reduced the singing green forests to cinders and even the mountains were melted down. The fire burned unabated night and day until all that remained of the verdant earth was a mass of ashes. That fire consumed everything that was alive at the time, leaving nothing standing or moving on the earth. There was just one thing that remained; there is always the one thing that manages to not be included even when it seems that everything has been consumed.

It happened that two beings, Icanchu and Chuna by name, had been visiting in the otherworld when the great conflagration reduced this world to ashes. The two companions had gone to the otherworld for some reason and they were mightily shocked when they returned to see that all that was left of the earth was an endless sea of ash. While looking out on the dark devastation left by the fire, they felt a great sense of homelessness. More than anything, they desired to return to their original homeland, but everywhere they looked, looked the same. They could not tell what was what or where they were; they had no idea which way to turn or where to go.

Suddenly, the trickster appeared before them and instructed them on how to find their place of origin. They were instructed to point their index fingers straight ahead while flying over the ash that covered the face of the earth. If their fingers began to tremble and then turn down of their own accord, they would be pointing to the place of their origins. It may be difficult to imagine this process of pointing and flying, of having bird wings and human fingers at the same time. Icanchu and Chuna were a pair of bird-beings; they could be birds on one hand and human beings on the other.

Suffice it to say that it was a long time ago, near the beginning of time, when stories tell of animals that could turn into humans and vice versa, when people could easily slip from one world to the other and come back again.

The old people believed that all humans were naturally that way, able to live in two worlds, and that maybe they were even required to do so at certain times. That was back in the time when animals were revered and to be "like an animal" indicated having additional powers, such as sensing danger or a storm coming, or having the ability to fly and effectively rise above problems and see them more clearly. Having been in the otherworld during the apocalyptic eruption of fire, Icanchu and Chuna were spared being incinerated. They were also spared having to witness the great loss of life. Now, they flew silently over the seemingly endless devastation.

As they flew, they extended their index fingers before them. They trusted the knowledge given to them by the trickster, for they knew that tricksters have to do with the magic of creation as well as with the tricks of destruction. They knew that this old world had many tricks up its sleeve as well as hidden resources that might only appear during times of great duress. Perhaps another trick remained in the mind of creation that could heal the earth and start things growing again.

As they traveled over the endless wasteland of ashes, their index fingers began to quiver and bend down towards the earth. Soon both fingers were firmly pointing straight down. Although the pile of ashes below them looked like every other place they had seen, the two travelers followed their fingers down and descended right into the ash. They felt that they might be near their old home, yet only ashes remained of all that they had known before. They were in the aftermath of creation, adrift in the ashes of existence.

Soon after they touched the face of the earth, the two remaining beings began to feel quite hungry. It was as if contact with the earth element stirred their instincts and ignited their appetites for food. Instinctively, they began to dig in the ashes in case something might remain that could serve as some kind of nutrition. After sorting through piles of ash, Icanchu only managed to unearth a single chunk of burnt wood. As a food item it was not very appealing, but while looking at the piece of charcoal, Icanchu felt a deep longing for trees. Once upon a time, the place of their origins had been like a garden resplendent with greenery and strong with many species of trees standing up in the light.

Icanchu imagined that the humble piece of charcoal must be the remainder of one of those tall trees that had once made their home a beautiful place. Suddenly the thought struck him that drums were also the remainders of trees. The people used to make drums from certain trees and use them for dances and for making ceremonies. First a tree would have to appear in someone's dream; that gave them permission for cutting it down and making drums from its trunk. A part of the tree would be chosen and shaped into a drum to be played for special occasions. Without thinking any further about it, Icanchu began to play that burnt out, leftover piece of wood as if it were a genuine drum.

Soon enough, Icanchu became infected by his own rhythm and began to dance. As long as he was dancing, he thought, he might as well sing. There was nothing to eat, nothing but ash to look at, and nothing else to do. Besides, dancing and playing gave him some small sense of courage. So right there in the midst of the ashes of creation, Icanchu began to sing and dance as he played upon his charcoal drum. He danced and played all day long while Chuna observed everything and seemed to meditate on the proceedings. At the end of the day, Icanchu became quite tired. There being nothing else to do, he simply lay down and fell into a deep sleep right in the ashes of the end of the day.

The Green Tendril of Life

When the light of dawn came and chased some of the smoky darkness from the world, Icanchu thought of his little drum and went to look for the piece of charcoal that had been the instrument for his dancing and singing. He was surprised to see a tender green shoot coming out of the blackened husk of his charcoal drum. Inspired by the greenness and freshness of the new tendril that stood out against the endless expanse of ash, Icanchu began to sing again. Throwing all caution to the wind, he danced with abandon around that shoot and sang and sang with all his heart. As he did so, the tendril seemed to grow as if being bathed in the song somehow nourished its tender life. Icanchu continued to sing and dance around the green shoot and it responded by growing larger and longer.

As Icanchu continued his singing and dancing, the tendril of life grew steadily and began to look like a slender tree. In no time at all, the trunk thickened and stood straight up and soon put forth long green branches that reached out in all four directions. There it stood in the middle of the expanse of ashes, the only vertical expression of life, the only green intention in the world, the only tree on the face of the earth.

Icanchu intensified his dance all the more when he saw that his song had awakened the life of the tree, which had grown from the little stem that had sprouted out of the charcoal from the ashes of the fire that had consumed most of the world. While dancing wildly around the tree, Icanchu's foot struck a stone buried loosely in the sea of ashes. He picked up the rock and without consideration suddenly threw it right at the amazing tree. It is hard to explain this impetuous action and seeming change of attitude, but when the dancer found another stone, he threw it at the tree as well.

After singing devotedly to the tree, dancing all around it, and taking great delight in the spreading of its branches, Icanchu began to chuck rocks at it from all directions. You might call it instinct, or foolishness, or another of those mistakes that happen in the vicinity of important trees. Perhaps the instinct for destruction is so closely tied to the creative impulse that when one returns to the world, the other has to become manifest as well. Creation and destruction can be seen as twin forces that are secretly connected like beginning and ending. In a creative situation it can be difficult to know which one will move the story of life along. For one reason or another Icanchu kept firing rocks at the firstborn tree. He tossed the stones with the same enthusiasm and abandon that he had devoted to dancing and singing to the tree. Throughout all of this, Chuna sat in silence, seeming to observe and perhaps witness everything that transpired.

What happened next could not have been readily foreseen. Each time Icanchu threw a stone it would hit a branch, and each time a branch was struck it would break off from the tree and fall onto the ash-covered earth. The strange thing was that each broken branch immediately took root in those ashes. Wherever they happened to fall, the branches would immediately begin to grow and soon multiply so that each branch quickly became another tree. Not only that, but each branch gave rise to a different species of tree and soon enough a properly diversified forest began to spread out and grow where there had been nothing but ashes before. There were countless species of trees and full-blown forests greenly growing and wildly lifting their branches up while sending roots deep into the old earth at the same time. It was as if the trees too were dancing in the ashes in the aftermath of the great fire. After the return of the forests the animals began to appear and eventually people came back to the world again.

Later, when people told the story of the renewal of life on earth, they talked about that green tendril and "revival root" that became the firstborn tree from the ashes of the former world. People called that tree the ancestor of all trees; they imagined it to be the original Tree of Life from the very beginning of time, which had come back from the ashes that appeared to be the end of everything on earth. That tree was so significant that they kept giving it names, as if singing its praises would help people remember how life can renew even when all seems lost. Some called it the Spirit Tree, saying that it was the same tree that shamans and healers first climbed when they sought a greater knowledge of this world and how to cure what ails it. They also called it the Medicine Tree because it brought back the good medicine of the forests that in turn brought back various species of animals.

According to the old myth, all the elements of the world reformed around the Tree of Life, which even now secretly stands at the middle of creation. Once the living tree came back from the ashes, the center became established again and the song of creation filled the world again. After, the people would gather once a year to remember and celebrate the time of renewal. They would tell the story of Icanchu and Chuna and the piece of charcoal from which the entire world came back. It used to be that way long ago; a story could turn into a ritual and a ceremony might invoke a new song or dance, giving rise to a tale that helped everyone remember what is most important about life on earth.

Each year, when certain trees began to grow heavy with ripening fruit, the people would gather for a renewal ceremony. Amidst the green branching of the trees laden with fruit, people would dance and sing as some also played drums. At the right moment in the celebration, people would throw little stones at the trees, aiming to knock down some of the ripened fruit. They would act out the dance of creation and destruction that was described in the story of the piece of charcoal that became a drum before it turned back into a tree.

While most of the people imitated the actions of Icanchu, dancing and singing and playing life back into the world, others would sit quietly nearby. They would silently contemplate the wonder of existence that allows the world to come back to life from its own ashes. Icanchu would be present again in all the dancing and singing and in the contrary but necessary action of throwing stones at the trees. And Chuna would be present as well in the silent practice necessarily performed by those who would observe and consciously witness all that happened and meditate upon it.

Ashes Time

This tale of fire and ashes is a folk myth that tries to say something about the mystery of this world and about the role people might play in the continuance of it. People have always worried about the continuance of life on earth and a tale like that of Icanchu and the charcoal drum looks directly at the possibility of a catastrophic environmental disaster. Since the tale arises from an ancient cosmological tradition, it views disaster, even worldwide conflagration, from a mythic perspective that transcends practical ideas and rational conceptions of what might happen if the world continues to overheat. In the same way that flood stories aim at something hidden in the human soul that can assist the natural world, this tale of fire and ashes aims at a deeper understanding of human imagination.

There is a suggestion that being in touch with the otherworld, or the world behind the world, might alter the damage that results from the elemental imbalance. There is a sense that the problems of this world might have to be solved by tapping roots that begin in the otherworld. Icanchu and Chuna do not become consumed by the all-consuming fire because they were in the otherworld; it is as if their connection to the Unseen protects them from what consumes everyone else. The idea here is not a simple escape through fantasy or denial of the seriousness of the dilemmas facing this world. Rather, the greater idea is that the roots of renewal are to be found in the deeper ground of living myth and genuine imagination that sustain our connections to the joy of life and the roots of creativity.

The danger now exists that nuclear proliferation combined with terrorism or simple foolishness might spark a conflagration that consumes the earth. At the same time, global warming threatens to melt the protective ice caps and ignite highly flammable gases that could set even the oceans on fire. Some may argue over the presence and importance of severe climate change; others simply deny the whole thing. Yet young people now grow up in an atmosphere that is increasingly polluted, amidst methods of communication that burn the airwaves night and day. As cultural conflicts flare up in all directions and everything moves faster and faster, it does seem that something might ignite a firestorm that begins to burn out of control. This era can be seen as a prolonged time of ashes, as natural disasters and man-made tragedies occur with increasing frequency and with deepening intensities.

Myth is not far back in time; like the otherworld, it is always nearby. Myth makes the events that people most fear in the future become present in the moment. Icanchu and Chuna bring a perspective from the world behind the world, the otherworld, where past, present, and future happen at once. Seen from the viewpoint of the eternal moment, what we most fear is already here. The issue is not simply that global warming might ignite the earth's atmosphere sometime in the future. Symbolically, we are already in the ashes, already knee deep in one of those periods when it seems that all the great hopes and dreams of life, as well as all the grand institutions of human society, are being reduced to cinders and ash.

The issue in the story is the issue in the present time in the sense that the conditions of overheating and burning up are already here. What becomes important in the time of ashes is that we find the courage to be fully present in the moment and not turn away from the devastation already underway. The courage to recognize the chaos and loss is the first act of necessary boldness, the willingness to witness what actually occurs. In the story, Chuna especially represents the practice of genuine observation and being a witness to the fire. There is boldness in this act, similar to the Old Woman of the World looking at the chaos of the black dog times and Markandeya staring into the abyss where all seems lost.

The two traveling companions look directly at the accumulation of ashes in the world, revealing the great longing for home. Of course, in stories "home" is often a code for the center. This old tale of the burning of the earth is aimed from the very beginning at finding the center again. Finding the center also means being present at the place of origins. For in the eternal territory of myth, the center is also the place of beginning and, therefore, the locale where everything can start over again. In the ashes of the world, in the aftermath of a war or the desolation after a natural disaster, what needs to be found is a center from which people can begin to make a world again. The end of one world can lead to the beginning of another, but only where people accept the full burden, grief, loss, and disorientation.

Witnessing the end of the world as we know it takes one kind of courage; starting the song of creation moving again takes another. A second kind of boldness is also needed to crack open the seeds of the center. While Chuna carries on the practice of witnessing from a deep place of awareness, Icanchu must act with the daring characteristic of creation. Icanchu has enough boldness to see a tree and a drum in the bit of charcoal. He had the imagination of an artist who always sees beyond the obvious, typically perceiving what is there but not there and what is trying to enter this world from the unseen. Art and creativity are found and become made at the juncture where the two worlds meet. Those intending to assist this old world to begin again will have to stand both in the ashes of all that went before as well as in the creative tension found in space between one world and the other.

The surprising story of re-creation in the midst of the ashes of time goes right to the center, where a dark remnant of all that previously stood up, breathed, and branched out waits to be found. The evergreen tendril of life hides within that seed of darkness. What is needed to quicken the seed into the cycle of renewal is something akin to the joy of life itself. Icanchu becomes the bold singer and ecstatic dancer who can activate the hidden seed of light and life by spontaneously expressing the life within his own soul. The wild presupposition suggested in myths the world over appears again: the spark of the divine that can assist creation and re-creation exists in each soul who enters the dance of life. Some seed ideas about the human and core symbols about the way of the world are so essential and important that they are sewn into folktales, fairy tales, and overarching myths as well.

The Dance of Life

Part of the message of re-creation tales is that those who would assist the renewal of nature and culture must find the creative spark within themselves. The characters in stories appear as primordial models of how to respond to disaster and critical moments, when life and death approach each other and the issue can go either way. The old woman in the cave begins weaving and a vision comes to her; old Noah has a dream and starts a huge, foolish project; Manu instinctively reaches out to another species; and Markandeya invents a form of swimming that brings god closer. When faced with a seemingly intractable obstacle or caught in a time of loss, we either boldly step into a bigger life or become a smaller version of ourselves.

Icanchu remembered that drums came from trees and that was enough of a vision to set him dancing and singing and resonating the sound of creation back into the world. The image of a drum reverberating with the rhythm of life is not accidental. Every known culture has drums of some kind even if they lack other instruments. The human heart has a drum beating in it, and when we find the right rhythm, we enter states of coherence that not only strengthen the heart, but also improve the functioning of other organs. The right rhythm preserves life and echoes all the way back to the original sound and primal eloquence of creation. Each heart secretly knows the dance that the soul would have us enact during our time on earth; but it often takes a great loss or fall from grace before we turn the way we were intended to go all along.

The image of dancing in order to bring back the wholeness of life is not accidental either. Dancing means finding ways of being and ways of doing that bring rhythm, meaning, and beauty to one's life. Dancing can also mean finding ceremonies and rituals that heal the wounds and losses of life. "Dance or die," say native people, who see all of life as a dance and all the genuine ways of being as forms of dancing with spirit or dancing the motions of the soul. When people feel lost in life they have lost their rhythm for life. In the midst of the ashes of whatever bridges have been burned or dreams that have come to nothing, it becomes necessary to find one's internal rhythm again.

Anyone who would truly dance must give themselves up to the dance. In giving oneself to the rhythm, a person becomes wholehearted. The dancer, at least momentarily, becomes a whole person. Then, wholeness speaks to wholeness as the dance of each life contributes to the great dance of life. Finding moments of wholeness helps to regenerate life from its source. Each soul harbors a garden where a true story dwells in seed form, waiting to be watered with attention and nourished with genuine emotion. The innate seeds produce the inner tree of our lives that grows as we grow, taking root where we live, trying to express why we live. Any genuine attention to the soul garden acts like an inner sun warming our lives and helping to ripen the inner fruits. The soul is supposed to ripen during its sojourn in the garden of earthly suffering and delight.

Until the soul begins to grow towards its own sense of fullness and awareness, it remains unripe and "green" in the wrong way. If we find a path of meaning in the world, the inner fruits ripen and become a resource and nourishment inside as well as a source of sweetness and reassurance to those we encounter on the way. If the fruits of the soul fail to ripen, they bear a bitter legacy that leaks into life. Should the inner pattern of the soul be strongly denied, the inner fruits become bitter and the rejected inner seeds spread conflict and division in the world. Life cannot be neutral for long, and bitterness and wisdom cannot dwell in the same place. Unless something ripens within and becomes a sweetness to be shared and enjoyed, a person will grow bitter with age. The inner bitterness of an unlived life tarnishes the subtle beauty of the world and it eats away at the roots of meaning.

We are indelibly and undeniably connected to trees. We need the oxygen they offer us and need them to transform the carbon dioxide we continually exude, whether we be arguing our fate or meditating quietly. We began essential exchanges with trees before birth and the first breath we took in this world secretly drew upon the trees. In the end we stand in our lives like an old tree. Tested by storms of confusion, weathered by internal climates, withered in some places, and hopefully bearing unique fruit, we stand like an old tree, rooted in imagination, leaning at life.

There is a third kind of boldness that is also necessary when the time comes to fully enter the dance of life. In order for the great dance to lead to moments of wholeness and re-creation, the contrary elements of life must be included. An essential meaning of *dance* is "to leap," and at times we have to boldly leap in ways that seem contrary to reason, logic, or common belief. Once he begins the great dance, Icanchu acts with an unhindered instinct for survival and a reckless abandon for what gives life its music, beauty, and surprise. Unexpectedly and even shockingly, the cosmic dancer attacks the source of life as well as chants invocations to it. Once the delicate thread of existence has been coaxed from the dark husk of lifelessness and begins to grow again, the singer and dancer turns to stone thrower. He who just sang the song of life to the tender tendrils of existence turns to throwing rocks and knocking branches off the stem of life.

It turns out that life breaks all the rules and does so all the time, but especially in moments of creation. There are times when reverence and respect, when care and consideration, are required to protect and strengthen the threads of life. And there are times when people must take the hard issues in hand and act with some abandon or else life can fail to take root and grow. Another kind of boldness appears when Icanchu finds a stone and instinctively throws it. Wasn't it the trickster who told the two survivors how to find the origins of their lives again? The trickster appears again when things need to go in a surprising direction if the full intensity of life is to return to the earth. Staying alive and helping the great diversity that informs and enlivens both the realms of nature and culture requires some knowledge of the tricks of existence.

Trickster Lends a Hand

Many creation stories involve tricksters right at the start. Some tales begin with a god who shapes a seemingly perfect world, yet something seems off. There is not enough laughter in it, or mistakes are treated as sins, or there is not enough diversity in the way that people dance or make love. Then the trickster comes along in the form of a raven, a coyote, or a knowing snake and makes people begin to do things backwards or see things the other way around. Icanchu finds a stone and has the urge to throw it. A strange bone in him aims it at the tree that has just grown before his eyes. Bam—a whole branch falls from the tree. It seems contrary and even perverse at first glance, yet the contrary action generates more life. Not only that, but the *contra naturum* gesture instigates a necessary diversity and multiplicity in the pulse and the productions of the re-creation of the world.

This surprising and inherent energy of radical diversity and contrariness in life continues to confound those who try to control things too much or insist on false reverence when life calls for wholehearted participation, reckless abandon, and foolish wisdom. Tricksters play essential roles in folk myths throughout the world. They throw dirt as well as toss rocks; they play with feces and throw it at people, even at god. They keep the dirt and the earth and the earthiness in the stories of life. They appear especially when the old order of the world needs to change; they are change agents and provocateurs and wise in wise-guy ways. They bring strange and unexpected pieces of wisdom that help to kick-start creation when it has collapsed or simply lapsed in its rhythm.

Icanchu accepts the instinct to throw stones just as he accepted the intuition to play the charcoal as a drum. He is consistent in his primordial responses to the world around him. He acts as artist and as trickster, as dancer and as a kind of odd inventor who experiments with whatever is at hand. It is as if creation also needs a kick start at times. Tricksters instinctively cross lines; they break rules and blur the common distinctions between right and wrong, between the sacred and the profane, and between one world and the other. In many native traditions, contrarians and tricksters would enter at crucial times in the most holy ceremonies. Their appearance breaks the spell of perfection and the rhythm of expectations. They might scare people a little or expose some shadow of pretense or self-importance. They might simply bend over and bare their bottoms in order to keep the backside of life more visible.

Fundamentalism can appear anywhere and people will repeatedly try to reduce the wonder and surprise of life to systems of belief and letters of the law even when the issue is the very vitality and complexity of the natural world. *Fundament* itself is an end word; the Latin word *fundus* means "bottom." What is fundamental is also connected to the rear end and to the backside of things. Any kind of Puritanism or fundamentalist approach to the issues of assisting with creation will make matters too rigid and will in the end get things ass backwards. Creation involves spontaneity and surprises that cannot be predicted or controlled. Insisting on "good behavior" or hard and fast rules, on dogmatic approaches or moral correctness, may keep people in line, but will not help creation and, in the end, will backfire.

In the proximity of the Tree of Life, all the opposites must meet and become mutually life-generating. The presence of the origin tree makes originality possible; when near it, life can go *contra naturum*, against a person's apparent nature, even against the typical ways of nature. It is the nature of great nature to change and the nature of creation to involve all possibilities. Those who make environmental concerns into a new form of puritanism remain distant from what truly preserves and regenerates life. Life on earth is not tame, and the balance of the elements occurs in the midst of a surprising dance, not in some kind of static arrest or steady state. The great dance that initiates the renewal of life must involve all the senses and the entire range of emotions and soulful emanations. The spark of life must at times be pulled from the smoldering ashes and be struck from the stones.

The Tree at the Center

The story of Icanchu's drum depicts the renewal of the earth from the ashes and it includes the rebirth of a living symbol. From the ashes of all that went before comes a symbol that in turn brings the world back from the brink of annihilation. When life on earth seems threatened and the usual centers cannot hold, it becomes time to take up the imagination and rhythms of real presence. One must become a branch of the kind of knowing that recalls the subtle ground of unity and draws upon the roots of the divine hidden amongst the ashes of the world.

The re-creation of the world had to involve all the elements and it had to be as inclusive as the original creation. In a sense, the two companions landed, not simply at the place of their origins, but at the very center of life where all the elements convene, where everything makes more sense—even nonsense. In seeking to find home again, the companions find the center where all the elements meet and the Tree of Life regenerates. The real home for earthlings turns out to be the center of everything; and the center turns out to be the beginning, the place where life began and can always begin again. The center becomes revealed as the place of renewal where the Tree of Life waits to be found and grow again.

An entire cosmology of elements is woven into this little tale of re-creation. After fire and water have gone out of balance in the extreme and the earth has been scorched and reduced to ashes, the elements of nature and mineral appear at the center and revivify life. Trees stand as a core symbol of the radical expression and exuberant diversity of creation. They come in a wide variety of forms, live longer than animals, and renew themselves from their predecessors. The return of life from the ashes is symbolized by the emergence of a little green tendril that eventually becomes the Tree of Life. At the same time, the diversity of life-forms that are necessary for creation ongoing must be instigated so the mineral element is thrown into the mix.

The strange little re-creation tale leads from the ashen remains of both nature and civilization to the tree hidden at the center of all life. The unifying tree has roots that plunge deep into the underworld and it has the capacity to reach up to the heavens. The original symbolism of the Tree of Life involved a mythical sense of a world axis, the "axis mundi" around which creation was created, the unified center where all dualities and oppositions come together. As center point, the tree remains eternally still; yet as the living, breathing Tree of Life, it presents a core image of constant change. It grows repeatedly from the same unseen roots, for it is rooted in the imagination of life and in the living Soul of the World. It is also rooted in the old mind and old soul of humankind, where it must be watered by dreams and longings and be nourished by songs and dances that make things whole if only for a moment. Each return to the tree at the center becomes a return to the origins of life and thus a renewal of the world.

The relationship between trees and people is an ancient one. Thus, things could start up again if that ancient and mysterious relationship were to become renewed and revitalized. The Tree of Life appears in almost all cultural heritages; it takes shape as the luminous Christmas tree that glows in the long nights of the darkest time of the year and it is the naked cross on which the Christian savior hangs. It is also the sacred tree to which Native American braves tie themselves during the Sundance ritual. It is the hollow center of the Navaho Reed of Life and the White Tree of Peace of the Northern tribes. It appears as the Tree of Ascent and Descent where the shamans seek the heights of spirit and the depths of soul. It is the Tree of Sacrifice and the Tree of Death, appearing at times as the "hanging tree." In the form of a bodhi tree it protects the Buddha and becomes the Tree of Enlightenment. It is the long-forgotten tree rooted at the center of paradise where it stands as the Tree of Unity.

The Tree of Life has always been there; standing in the midst of the archetypal pack of eternal symbols that keep arising into human awareness. In one sense, it is less real than any tree in a nearby garden or forest. In another sense, both a deeper and higher sense, the symbolic tree is more real than real. In that mythic sense, it is the original tree, the mother of all trees, the essence and source and sense of being rooted in life and central to existence. Centralizing symbols are needed to bring the mind and the heart to the doors of truth. Truth certainly appears differently to different people, but a genuine symbol speaks meaningfully to every seeker. A genuine symbol helps reveal what the seekers otherwise conceal from themselves.

Everyone at some point finds themselves in the ashes of life and longs for home. The real home turns out to be the center within each life and each return to that inner core not only calms us, heals us and makes us whole, but also adds some healing and wholeness to the world around us. When the end seems near, it becomes time to seek the center within and find ways to be central to the healing of the scorched and scarred earth around us. The great tragedies and dramas of life and the threat of it all ending try to return humanity to an awareness of the eternal presence of the divine waiting at the center of each life and all of life.

CHAPTER 10

THE GREAT WAY

At the center of your being you have the answer;
you know who you are and you know what you want.
Lao-tzu

There is an old idea that life on earth involves three necessary layers of human experience. The first layer of human interaction involves the common ground of exchange characterized by polite greetings, civil society, and practical social agreements. This is the territory of the status quo and the common expectations for keeping life moving along. On this surface layer simple exchanges occur, basic needs are met, and the deeper issues of life tend to be either avoided or denied. Here, life tends to go on and on unless something upsets the applecart or lifts the veil to reveal other layers and deeper issues calling for attention.

At the opposite extreme of life, the third layer, we can experience the deepest aspects of shared humanity in the form of universal elements such as beauty and love, peace, and mutual respect. At this layer of experience a mutual sense of sisterhood and brotherhood with everyone else prevails. The third layer reveals an underlying unity and genuine sense of the shared roots of humanity. It is from this deep level of understanding that people develop ideas and practices of compassion and altruism as well as a love of justice and a desire for finding and sustaining creative and peaceful forms of human community. When in touch with the third layer individuals experience both a sense of personal liberation and a desire to serve others in meaningful ways.

Early in life, each person receives at least one experience of the third layer of universal love and acceptance or else the soul will fail to connect fully to life. For some, the feeling of deep affinity may have to come from a small touch of love and understanding; others may fare better and find deep connections more often. However it may go in the beginning, each person will eventually have to seek additional experiences of love and beauty, of acceptance and understanding, or else become a lost soul. The life of the soul depends on at least occasional experiences of the third layer of universal oneness, as does the life of each human community.

All religions draw upon the intuition of the deep and abiding level of universal love and understanding, most governments claim to do so as well. People fall in love in order to fall to the underlying depths of healing and beauty found in the third layer of human experience that always remains nearby. Failing to find some ongoing connection to the underlying roots of passion, devotion, and understanding can cause people to lose their grip on life or else continue to live on the surface while feeling dead inside.

The third layer of life is the place of creativity and renewal that the soul longs to find and draw inspiration from. That level of human experience and expression is always close at hand; the problem is that in order to move from the surface layer to the deep ground of unity, we must pass through the second layer of life. If the first layer is mostly superficial and polite and the third layer involves universal acceptance, then it follows that the second layer contains all the ashes of life and the exiled feelings, all the wounds of the soul and the troubles of existence. The second layer includes all the injustices and betrayals of life, not just the wrong turns but also the roads of exile and the streets of desperation. The second layer burns with extreme emotions and fumes with resentments and angers that will not end. The second layer broods with negativity and fosters all the shadows and shady feelings of life. It festers with the sores of the soul and rankles with all the bigotries and treacheries of existence. On the second layer the black dog waits for the opportunity to pick up a loose thread and begin to pull the common level of human exchange into the haunts of chaos and confusion.

The first layer of life cannot contain the intensities of the human heart nor can it sustain the deeper connections of the human soul. Although most people aspire to be kind and polite and would like to simply get along with others, the first layer always erupts with unwanted emotions and unfinished business that tear at the fabric of civil society and that obscure the presence of the underlying unity of life. Civility alone cannot sustain the center of life or the best hopes of humanity. When the center has to be found again, people must traverse the deeply troubled and troubling second layer of life. In the dark times when the surface of life cracks more often and the holding institutions fail to protect and hold, the second layer, with all its disturbances and extremes, begins to erupt more often and the third layer of healing and unity can seem far away and impossible to find.

The Territory of Apocalypsis

The second layer of life is also the ground of apocalypsis, where things can polarize very quickly and any thought or feeling can suddenly be taken to the extreme. When in the second layer some feel pulled to the edge where people take things too literally and become rigid and ready to fight to the bitter end with anyone who dares to contradict what they believe or even offer another opinion. Others find themselves at the opposite extreme where their practical sense and boundaries dissolve as raw emotions and wild fantasies overtake them. When experiencing the second layer people can insist upon all kinds of unrealistic beliefs and subscribe to conspiracy theories that further erode the common ground of civil discourse. An intensification of the second layer leads to an increase of the politics of extremism and the policies of exclusion. When caught in the dynamics of apocalypsis and the extremes of the second layer, whole populations can come to believe things that are patently untrue but that somehow express all the unresolved fears, hatreds, and resentments that have festered under the surface level of life.

Under the pressure of radical change—and whenever it seems like the end is near—political parties and even the great religions can become the breeding grounds for extremists and fanatics of all kinds. The paradox of "religious terrorism" erupts from the second layer as people become caught in deep levels of psychic resentment and unexamined hatred that can become mixed with unconscious religious zeal. When times become desperate and there is no relief in sight, it can become more compelling to escape the individual ethical struggle of life and allow the collective fervors and fevers to swamp the fragile ground of the personal ego. Since religious paths often require denial of the ego and sacrifices of simple self-interest, religious groups can breed nihilistic fanatics while seemingly preaching noble goals. The weapons of warring states and of feuding religions are often sharpened on the inner despair of those who have nothing left to lose in this world and can only imagine finding the universal sense of love and acceptance by leaving it and/or destroying it.

This book began with a consideration of apocalypse as the first word of an extreme religious vision that has continued to shape the background for many of the ideas and images of the End. The issues of religious ideas and spiritual visions naturally come around again. The roots of *religion* include the Latin verb *religare*, meaning "to tie back" as with a ligament or a ligature that binds one thing to another. The religious instinct in people is archetypal and deeply ingrained and will not simply go away. We are tied to it and at times pulled back by it; we are all seeded with and aimed at something divine from the beginning. *Divine* means "of a god or of the gods" and we are each god-struck in some way and intended to be so. Even the title "atheist" has a bit of theism in it; all opposites remain connected at their roots.

The first layer of life can never satisfy the eternal longings and religious feelings that are threaded within each soul; if it could, life would be much simpler and people would settle for the obvious. Spiritual impulses are universal and arise from a core imagination of the divine that would lead each person to a state of awakening that includes a confirmation of their connection to transcendent and edifying feelings and truths. The entire journey of the soul seeks to find again the healing and unifying center from which it originally departed. All who wander out into the world secretly aim to return to the center where essential things wait to be found and be touched again.

Forget the modern obsessions with materialism and flashes of fame in the outer world. The deepest desires involve love and other divine things.

In the end, people live and die for a single touch of the divine—some will kill for it as well. The issue is not simply the presence of religious urges and spiritual visions, or even the fact that the original divine spark and seed of the soul moves closer when the surface of life rattles and cracks. The problem is that the underlying tension of the opposites and the historical conflicts that inhabit the second layer can move to the foreground. The problem is that the inner split in life and the dark night of the soul must be experienced on the way to the deeper levels where spiritual fulfillment and universal peace reside.

The Tree Behind the Tree

The territory of the third layer also includes the great symbols of unity and oneness that can give people a sense of collective harmony and unanimity. The Tree of Life remains one of the universal symbols of the deepest layer of experience and the living center that can unite everyone and everything to the healing and renewing roots of being. As a collective archetype of the psyche, it is a stem of imagination that resides in each individual soul. In the old roots of language, *tree* and *truth* are related—parts of the same branching family of words. Thus, all the branches of truth and meaning secretly grow from the same unseen roots and all spiritual and creative paths eventually lead to the same center and the ever-branching Tree of Unity. In this sense, everyone is on a pilgrimage to the same center, each soul seeking to find again the unifying place where even the opposites can be experienced as being connected.

As unifying symbol of the divine center of life, the holy tree can be found in most spiritual traditions and would seem to offer a way of connecting the roots of all religious systems; yet it rarely comes out that way. There is just one problem: in this world people tend to see the way to the center from the perspective of where they begin and tend to begin from places that are far apart and seemingly opposed on many levels. On the way to the deeper ground of unifying symbols a second layer of disagreement and persistent conflict frequently surfaces between religious groups and can threaten to put everyone and everything back into the ashes of life.

In many old stories the Tree of Life grows in the center of the garden of paradise. The human soul has tasted of the fruits of that essential abundance and longs to be in paradise again. The problem remains however, that paradise is a paradox that presents both the original unity that people long for and the original split that continues to divide the world. In the old bible stories the basic division was represented as the two essential trees standing in the garden known as Paradise. The Tree of Life stood at the center as the axis of eternity, secretly unifying the three layers of the world. When found at the center, the eternal stem was called the Tree of Unity as well as the Tree of Peace. Yet, the omnipresent tree could also appear in stark contrast as the Tree of the Knowledge of Good and Evil, which was also called the Tree of Division. The Tree of Unity and the Tree of Division both arise in the fruitful ground of paradise; they are essentially related even if sharply opposed. Thus, the enduring paradox found in the garden of origins exists in each human soul and must be encountered on all of the paths of true learning and spiritual seeking.

The issue is not whether to *believe* in the old religious stories; stories do not exist in order to inspire simple belief. Rather, stories exist in order to depict the living symbols and enduring archetypes that continue to operate in the deeper layers of human experience. The dynamics at play in Paradise can be seen as a religious version of the three layers of life. At first everything is just fine and there are no real problems. Things are very civil; the lions are lying down with the lambs and all the fruits are low hanging and ripe. The deeper issues are there, but they have not surfaced yet. In that sense, not much is really happening and the drama of existence is pleasantly on hold. Once the Tree of Knowledge has been pointed out, the real story begins. Leaving aside issues of whether it is a sin or a mistake that kicks things off, the trouble starts with the desire to know, with the longing to see what the gods see, with the need to perceive the deeper levels of life and have some understanding of what it all might mean.

The answer to the essential questions about life would seem to reside at the roots of the Tree of Life that stands at the center of it all. However, the story that began back at the beginning of time, and which continues to be the drama that we all play a part in, takes its shape at the base of the other tree. The search for meaningful forms of knowledge begins at the Tree of Division. For we first come to know by dividing things, by separating one thing from another, by distinguishing ourselves and deciding which way we are aimed to go in life. Knowledge begins with separation and most increases of knowledge require further separations as well as greater distinctions. All meaningful paths in this life lead to crossroads where choices must be made, where old patterns must be relinquished, where sometimes people must be left behind.

Though it keeps being forgotten, stories are intended to remind us that the search for knowledge and understanding was never intended to end at the same level where it began. The search for greater understanding began at the Tree of Division, but was intended all along to lead back to the Tree of Life at the center of it all. The point of all the longing and searching has always been to find again the holy living tree that unifies all that has become divided in the world and in ourselves. The tree of the knowledge of good and evil is a "starter-tree;" it is the necessary place of separation that starts the journey that leads to the long road of self-awareness and self-discovery. An old name for the winding and at times confusing path that leads from painful separation to healing unity was the difficult road to the center. The true ligaments of religion tie us to the roots and branches of the Tree of Unity found at the center and our spiritual aspirations and soulful longings would lead us all back to that holy stem.

The trouble remains that at the beginning of the spiritual adventure, everything seems to divide into opposing energies—such as good and bad, right and wrong—as the underlying split in life must be engaged. In this world of left and right and up and down, any attempt to reach the sacred garden of unity and abundance again will require a return through the areas of the soul that are most divided and rejected, that feel most abandoned and exiled within us. The problem remains that the Tree of Division, with all of its drama and trouble, with its extremes of desire and exile, with its confounding confusions and seemingly opposite truths, stands firmly in the second layer of paradise. It also stands in the way of finding a genuine path that might lead all the way back to the third layer of existence, where the Tree of Unity waits to be found again. The problem is that in order to touch the Tree of Unity again, we must also touch the original split in the world. No healing unless the original split is touched; no spiritual awakening unless the original tension of the opposites has been experienced.

It may be helpful to know that in the realm of myth and stories, the beginning of a tale sets up the dilemma to be struggled with. A story that begins with the Tree of Division is secretly aimed at the Tree of Unity. Near the Tree of Life even the opposites become unified; yet before the fruits of awakening can be found, the opposites will intensify. The Tree of the Knowledge of Good and Evil marks a place where the tension of the opposites must be entered and learned from. Good and evil, life and death, inner and outer, self and other, truth and falsehood—all become polarized before anything can fully ripen. Maturing the fruits of knowledge requires bearing the tension of the opposites that inhabit the inner life as well as the outer world. Any unity follows a season of tension, a period of exile where we each becomes caught in the thorny issues of life on earth. The Tree of the Knowledge of Good and Evil must be encountered repeatedly if the Tree of Life would be found again.

The Great Way

Many old stories refer to the "great way," the universal path that leads to the center that connects and clarifies all branches of truth and all ways of seeking. In ancient Sanskrit *marga* was the term for the great path, or universal way that transcends local traditions and historical systems of belief. The path of marga goes all the way to the source of knowing, all the way to the roots of being. It is the great way that opens to things universal and transcendent; it is the path we long to set foot on, the road of understanding that leads back to the Tree of Unity.

Since that unifying center exists in the depths of each soul, a person can have sudden moments when it all seems clear—when the underlying unity of life is sensed and felt. Such is the mystical insight that can appear as a sudden awakening reveals all that was hidden. It can also be seen as the accumulation of knowledge and understanding of a lifelong path that grows greater as the seeker grows deeper. Old mythic ideas suggest that once a person finds their way to the great way, they begin to see how all meaningful paths eventually head in the same direction. All true paths somehow wind their way to the center where everything began and the tree of profound unity connects everything at the roots.

The great way is the way our souls would have us go, just as the Tree of Unity is the place we long to reach. By definition each soul has a passport to the center and qualifies for access to the great way. The problem is that each soul must begin its search by stepping onto a local path. Everything must begin somewhere and the search for knowledge begins wherever we happen to be when we take our first steps on the great journey of life. We may intuit the aim of finding the place of universal unity, but we must begin with a limited, local version of the path of self-discovery and liberation. The local or lesser paths tend to involve fixed traditions and dogmatic ideas that separate one person from another, one nation from another, and one religion orientation from all others. These paths tend towards separation and exclusion, and they tend to bind people to fixed doctrines and narrow systems of belief that claim to be the only path to the divine center.

Desi is the Sanskrit word that designates a "region, province, or country;" it is also the term used to indicate the fixed attitudes and dogmatic tendencies of political and religious groups. For it is the nature of this world of time and space that traditions and belief systems take on local and historical characteristics. At the beginning of a spiritual path or a path of learning, basic distinctions and separation from general opinions are critical. The beginner needs something specific to commit to and a way of practice that allows him or her to leave familiar things behind. Finding agreement with like-minded people may be necessary in order to undertake the risk of growing, changing, and transforming one's life. Everyone must begin the search at a certain time and in a particular way, usually amongst those nearby who see the path in the same way. Farther along, things may appear quite differently.

Each spiritual and creative path tends to be great in its own way;

each may eventually lead a person close to the unifying center, but only if followed far enough. Once the true search is underway, a greater and greater surrender will be required or the path will fail to open wide enough to reveal hidden things. The center connects all the paths of desire, longing, and devotion; yet that cannot be known until a person suffers many detours and some dead ends. Often more than one path is needed in order for the soul to keep expanding. There is always the danger that a person will stop part way along the path and dig in. A long history already exists of inspired paths that, along the way, become more and more dogmatic and overly restrictive so that the way that seemed so elevated at the beginning becomes an obstacle to the great way.

Waking Up

Often enough it is the advanced students of a given path that become the source of the desire to reduce the original inspiration to a simple creed and a set of fixed doctrines and symbols. There is an old story of a little temple where some young disciples became intrigued with gambling. At night, after all the tasks were done and all the religious duties had been completed, the young seekers would gather and gamble in the dark. After all, this whole world is a great gamble and those who would truly change and grow must eventually gamble all that they know on something beyond their ken. Either intuiting that great gamble or simply in reaction to some narrowing of belief or exaggerated restricting of life energy, the novices had begun to play games of chance.

A certain advanced student took exception to this wicked practice of staying up at night and violating most of the rules and beliefs that had developed inside the temple walls. Feeling quite righteous and upset at the implied blasphemy, he went directly to the spiritual leader of the place and lodged a formal, if not meticulous complaint.

The master listened to the whole thing carefully, but did not become upset or insist on some punishment—not even a tightening of the rules. To the surprise of the advanced student, the spiritual teacher remarked that at least something was being accomplished since the initiates were staying up all night. Perhaps if they continued on that path they would learn why people remain awake and undertake vigils of attention and practices of contemplation that might bring them closer to the divine. The point made by the old teacher was quickly lost on the advanced student, who was feeling the power of having found a path and learned how to follow it. The problem was that he had not followed it far enough to see where it might actually lead. He was caught in the trap of being but part way along the way while thinking that he had arrived. There are revelations at the beginning of a path, but there are obstacles along the way and always the danger that the path narrows before it opens to the great way.

There are many ways of waking up; staying awake all night can be one of them. Meanwhile, a real path involves repeated risks and places where all that has been learned must be anted up for further growth. Often, those who have advanced to some degree become the most dogmatic about what to believe and how to act. Having reached some level of attainment and arrived near the head of the line, they prefer to protect their position and keep others in line behind them. Having found some understanding, they prefer to codify what they have learned rather than risk facing all that remains unknown. Usually that is a sign that they have stalled in their own progress and seek to mask their failings by controlling or condemning others. Any path can become dogmatic and rigid; it is easier to claim to have the truth than to continually gamble all one has in order to be closer to the roots of genuine being.

All genuine ways lead to the great way; yet the farther one stands from the unifying ground, the greater the differences between spiritual paths appear. The great religious battles and long-standing philosophical oppositions are sustained by those who have come but part way along the path they have chosen. Being at some distance from the unifying center, where things become clearer and clearer, they only see the differences and distinctions found in spiritual matters. Being insecure within themselves, they tend to claim great certainty regarding doctrines and dogmas. That which they proclaim the most keeps them stuck part way along a path that might eventually open wide and become much more inclusive of other ways of being and seeing. Meanwhile, there is no help for it; each must start somewhere and everyone stumbles along the way. Those that claim otherwise are hiding something or are doing something forbidden in the middle of the night.

Simply having an idea of the divine can cause people to feel superior and imagine that all who do not feel the same way are inferior. Those who see everything one way tend to believe that everyone must see things their way. It may be necessary to be single-minded when first undertaking a path of growth and learning. It is also a common mistake to confuse singularity of vision with wholeness of being. Too often people can hold a single belief or a single-minded vision of reality while projecting their inner conflicts and shady feelings onto others. Religious fanatics do that; secular leaders do it as well. Each has only a part of the picture, yet each claims to have the whole answer and the only way to proceed.

If the way to the center were easy to find—if it were capable of being captured in doctrines or were subject to human control—it would not be the genuine way. If the path that opens the heart and the mind could be found by simple belief, all the true believers would be opening the doors and windows of their hearts with gestures of true compassion. They would readily understand the common threads in the words "Jesus was right," "Moses led me along," and "Mohammed opened doors in my heart." When the great way opens even for a moment the path between mind and heart widens. The heart begins to find the thought of unity buried within it and the mind begins to see subtleties that were impossible to grasp just a minute before. Finding the great way requires a willingness to surrender again and again, not simply a zeal for bowing one's head in the same old way.

Two Mistakes Along the Way

There are two great mistakes that people usually make on the way to the great way. One mistake involves excluding others once a way has been found; the other mistake involves including everyone at the point where some subtle or esoteric issue requires careful learning before proceeding in a good way. Sometimes a path requires some exclusion before it can open in greater ways; other times, everyone who comes to the door must be welcomed with open arms no matter the way in which they might see things. Distinguishing between opening and closing the doors of spirit becomes a necessary practice along any meaningful path. Temples, cathedrals, and mosques can be indications that the divine is nearby; yet they can also become places of exclusion where even the divine cannot find a way in.

In this world where one thing can readily turn into another, the dream of making a sanctuary for spirit and refuge for those who truly seek it can easily become a nightmare of rules and restrictions that keep people from experiencing the presence of spirit. The instinct for building temples and churches can also create the danger of establishing fixed ideas and harboring blind beliefs. Setting everything in stone can lead to closing the inner doors where spirit tries to enter. Sometimes the temple is a valuable indication of the way to go and sometimes it is simply in the way. Sometimes a church is constructed in the middle of the way and its brick-by-brick dogmas become an obstacle to true learning and a blockage where an open mind and forgiving heart are needed.

Once a myth or a symbol becomes codified and is deemed orthodox, it can lose its capacity to deliver the flow of imagination and vitality that it originally possessed. That which was awe inspiring can become a "matter of belief," and soon it is only the fixed belief and letter of the law that matters. Truly seeing and simply believing can be two different things, especially when blind faith enters the picture. Those who follow blindly turn out to have little faith to begin with; genuine faith generates a willingness to face the unknown. "Orthodox" combines the Greek roots *orthos*, meaning "right, true or straight" and *doxa*, meaning "opinion" or "how to seem." In matters of the spirit there is always a danger that things become too straight and narrow so that a specific opinion regarding the divine becomes how it must be seen by everyone.

When the path of spirit becomes overly orthodox, other ways of approaching become nothing but heresy. Yet language, like spirit, likes to play with ideas and images. "Heresy" comes from a Latin root meaning "a school of thought or philosophical sect." The nearby Greek verb *hairesis* means "to take or to choose." A heretic is one who chooses a different opinion or takes a different path than that required by the keepers of the orthodox system. Some heretics may act out simple feelings of negation or rebellion; yet some depart from the orthodox path in order to open the doors and let the living spirit and divine breath enter where it has been denied by narrow beliefs and fixed ideas.

In this sense, each true seeker must become a heretic at some point along the way in order to escape any inner narrowness and move from the lesser path to the great way that leads beyond it. All the great spiritual leaders who become the models on which orthodox systems are built were in some way heretics and trailbreakers. Wasn't Jesus heretical in the temple of the money changers and in the eyes of the Pharisees? Didn't Mohammed break the mold of all that went before him? Didn't Joseph and Noah follow dreams? Didn't Buddha strike a new path and reform both Hindu and Jain practices? Those whose footprints in this world become revered and who are held in high esteem by many other seekers at one time walked the paths of learning in their own unique ways. All the ways that become orthodox and prescribed derive from those who followed spirit in their own way in order to find the great way again.

The great way keeps getting lost. Somewhere on the way to opening the deep levels that alone can nourish the individual soul and inspire the bonds of genuine community, something goes awry and everything gets thrown into the conflicts and confusions of the second layer of life. When religious stories lose the ability to tap the roots of imagination that gave birth to them, they tend to rigidify into fixed forms of belief that insist that they alone have access to the truth. Not only that, but they also tend to add fuel to the fires of conflict by claiming the right to dominate or destroy other religions and spiritual views. The language of peace and unity may remain in the official canons, but the actions will reveal the entrapment in exclusive or limited beliefs. Thus, we wind up with enduring religious battles such as Catholic against Protestant, Christians against Jews, Jews against Muslims, Shia against Sunni, orthodox against progressive; the Right against the Left; and so on and on.

The great path or marga would transcend differences in order to unify everyone, while the lesser paths tend to divide one against the other and even develop intense oppositions that bring out the most aggressive and egregious energies of the second layer of life. When the inner eyes of the soul fail to open wide enough, people can feel threatened by visions of the divine that are given to others. Not really knowing what they believe in, they shift to condemning the beliefs of others as being false and heretical or evil. Yet evil, like beauty and truth, tends to be in the eye of the beholder. On the paths to the divine the heart must open in order for the eye of the soul to see where the feet of spirit should go.

A Young Woman's Prayer

There is a story of a young woman who was on her way to meet the person she loved more than anyone else in the world. Her mind and heart became united as she walked along the path leading to where she would meet the one who ignited love and devotion in her. As it happened her path led her into a courtyard that some people used for saying prayers at particular times of day. On that day she entered the courtyard at the time when people stopped their worldly tasks in order to remember god and pray for a better life or a better world.

There was a certain man who routinely made his prayers in that courtyard. He was devoted to the articles of his faith and carefully followed the practice of praying to god at specific hours. It happened that on that day, the man of god had just begun the recitation of his prayers when the young woman entered the courtyard on her errand of love. There was a local rule against interrupting those who took the time to pray, but she walked right past the one kneeling in prayer and did not seem to notice him at all. However, the passing of the young woman distracted the holy man from his prayer; he became frustrated and unable to proceed in the usual manner.

Later, after meeting with her beloved, the young woman returned along the same route she had taken earlier in the day. As she crossed through the courtyard again the holy man was there and he interrupted her passage. He asked her pointedly, "Do you not know that it is against the precepts to interrupt a person who is praying to god? Are you unaware of the fact that people use this courtyard to pray and that in passing through here you interrupted my prayers? Do you not know that there are penalties for these transgressions?"

The young woman quickly apologized for interrupting the prayers of the holy man. Then she asked a question of her own: "What do you mean by prayer?" The holy man answered readily, "By prayer I mean my attempt to speak directly to god. Prayer is a spiritual conversation with the divine that should not be interrupted by the comings and goings of the secular world."

The young woman spoke again: "I have another question then. If you were talking directly with god at the time when I passed by, how come you noticed me while I, on my errand of love, never noticed you at all?" The great silence that subsequently spread like a carpet over the entire courtyard served as her answer.

It seems that when love is omitted prayers can be easily interrupted and even become misdirected. On the other hand, where love is involved every action can become a prayer to the beloved. It is not that love and religion must be at odds with each other, rather that wherever love and genuine devotion appear, there the divine will also be present. The self-proclaimed holy man preferred rules and prescribed attitudes to a genuine conversation with the divine. He forgot that the divine can enter anywhere and appear in any disguise. It is an easy mistake to make regardless of the spiritual path undertaken. Were he able to see beyond the local pattern and his own fixed belief, he might perceive how the young woman was carried by the prayer of love. Were he not so dedicated to a single-minded view, he would have glimpsed the presence of god in the devotional ways of the young woman.

Some might argue that the young woman was only on an errand of earthly love, that she was simply moved by some human form or bodily desire. Remember, a person must begin somewhere and giving one's heart fully can open ways of surrendering to greater and greater things. Lovers may think that they seek only each other, but the one who sets them seeking is never far from their loving. In the courtyard of life where people entreat the divine in many ways, the young woman was more devoted and more committed to something greater than herself. She was close to some presence that was inside as well as beyond her and could not be distracted from her errand. She was carried on the feet of spirit and there is no telling where such a divine errand might lead the devotee.

Once a person falls in the fields of love, all the rules are already broken; the lover becomes open and exalted in ways that transcend the local issues as well as the commonly held beliefs. Love, like genuine devotion, will find a way. Where duty becomes replaced with love, a greater and deeper faith will blossom forth. For the deepest meaning of "belief" refers to being loyal to what the heart already loves. As people used to say, "What the heart loves is the cure." The cure for healing the wounds and conflicts between faiths and systems of belief involves awakening to the unique ways that each heart carries devotion and love. When followed far enough, simple belief can transform into wisdom; raw passions can become a greater compassion that trusts what resides in one's heart and even in the hearts of others. Until the heart opens and the eyes begin to see there is always the danger of blindness and narrowness and the tendency to hold onto narrow ways of being.

An Elephant On the Way

Remember the tale of the blind men who encountered an elephant for the first time? This was new territory for them. They all gathered around what they could sense but could not see. It was clear that a living being stood before them; it was too big not to be sensed and they could smell its presence. Each instinctively reached out to touch what was before him and found a different part of the great being. In the Braille of their searching, each one felt some definitive and distinct qualities. One fellow held the trunk of the elephant and declared that the wondrous being before them was like a tube that had a capacity for spraying cooling waters like a fountain. For him the unseen presence was fountain-like and refreshing. Another, holding the elephant's tail, had to disagree strongly and insist that this was a "rope being" with a tendency to flail at anything that came near it.

Meanwhile, the one touching the great tusks had inner visions of carved statues and smooth body forms. Another leaned against a huge leg and described it as a pillar of a temple. Each held to what was near at hand and each developed a certitude based on what he happened to encounter and feel. Each named the presence and defined the situation on the basis of the initial experience. In becoming fixated upon a part of the unseen presence before them, they all failed to grasp the wholeness that it represented. They were each in touch with some element of a great presence, yet due to common blindness, the unity before them could not be discovered. The longer they each held to what they first felt, the deeper their need to be correct grew. Unless some greater knowledge entered the picture they might have argued forever, each of their views seemingly being substantiated by actual experience.

The animal presence holds all the conflicting believers together, yet they remain unaware of how the parts are connected. Strangely, the elephant cannot help much either, as it represents a different order of being. The elephant acts as an intermediary and representative of the otherworld; it connects the Unseen with the common realm. As such, it is a hint of a unity beyond ordinary sight; yet it can only offer seekers a partial sense of what stands near them all the time. It is only a little story and the great religions, political movements, and belief systems include elaborate and intricate forms of knowledge. Yet there is something to the notion of the blind leading the blind. There is something to the sadness that descends with the full realization that "in the kingdom of the blind, the one-eyed man can rule."

The common blindness involves confusing the parts with the whole and the paths provided by the various religious and societal ways with the true presence and the great way. The situation would be simply humorous and entertaining were it not that people develop religious intensities and fervors of belief that cause them to attack those who are holding a different part of the greater picture. How else to explain how spiritual seekers and religious devotees can convert to fanaticism, absolutism, and even terrorism?

Each way has a vision and an angle that can lead to the great way; yet each also can become stuck along the way. Those who insist upon one right and righteous way to travel to the unifying center have never actually dwelt there. For arriving at the center opens the eye of the soul and reveals that all the ways and paths lead to the same central place. The differences between certain paths and ways are real enough, but only appear mutually exclusive while one is still distant from the goal. Move closer to the inner unity and the differences and distinctions between outer paths diminish; reach the center for even a moment and glimpse the hidden unity behind all the conflicted opinions, battling beliefs, and fanatic attitudes. In the dark times it becomes easier to be caught in the second layer and begin to see things only in one way. When people insist upon seeing in one-sided and single-minded ways, everyone can become blind to the presence of the great way. Then more and more people become distant from the third layer where acceptance and compassion, where forgiveness and love, wait to be found.

East and West Must Meet

The underlying split in the world continually appears in the blind actions and beliefs of human cultures. When people want to play with fire and the tension of opposites, they develop the kind of animosities that can only occur between those who were once close. The Middle East continually erupts as one of the deepest trouble spots on the face of the earth and the underlying split goes all the way back to religious stories that both sides once shared. The historical roots and repeated troubles in the Middle East are complex and intricate like roots that have become twisted and enmeshed, no longer able to draw life and grow.

Many old stories place the Tree of Life and the garden of Paradise somewhere in the Middle East, often in old Persia. After all, *Persia* means "protected garden," and as such refers to the symbolic center where the water of life flows at the roots of the eternal tree. The Middle East can be seen as the center of historical conflicts as well as the ancient place where the division between the Tree of Life and the Tree of Knowledge first began. As if following the paradoxical nature of paradise, the Middle East has become a place where religious and political differences threaten to draw everyone into an endless battle or into a nuclear nightmare of apocalyptic proportions.

Some of those who take the old stories literally actually seek to create a world-destroying conflict in order to bring the garden of paradise back. Given the political intensities and the possibilities of nuclear attacks, the deeply rooted old problems have consequences that might endanger everyone. When seen against the backdrop of myth and old stories about the Garden of Eden and the Tree of Life, some things may become more illuminated.

The ancient tableland of Iraq and Iran can be seen as the dividing place as well as the troubled meeting ground of the Orient and the Occident. The troubles that erupt there become increasingly central to those in the far West as well as those in the Far East. Westerners may call the area the Near East; those in the East could readily call it the Near West. The Middle East is also the Middle West, the troubled and conflicted middle area that both separates and joins the earthly and cultural extremes of the Far East and the Western world.

Looking east from the Middle East leads to the Far East, but also to "Oriental views" of life. *Orient* refers to "facing East;" more exactly it depicts the moment of dawn breaking on the horizon at the beginning of a new day. The East is the "place of the rising sun;" the direction from which the sun first appears after its descent and long journey through the endless sea of the night. In mythic terms, the Orient is connected to the sense of an eternal dawn and to the myth of the eternal return of life from death, of light from darkness, and of the earth from the abyss at the edge of the world. Eastern worldviews tend to involve an "eternal return;" a recycling of life where death is an illusion and endless renewal is an expectation.

The magnetism of the East and of Eastern spirituality has long compelled people in the West, as if something rooted there might ground the restlessness of their Western ways. Western traditions involve the sense of turning to the East at critical times. In Christianity the rites of Easter celebrate the rising of the "Son of God" after a dark period of crucifixion and death. The savior rises like the sun from the tomb of the underworld. The rites of rebirth coincide with the arrival of spring when the whole earth becomes reborn from the dark and seemingly barren days of winter. The sense of spiritual renewal coincides with earth-oriented rituals such as the old tradition of dancing around a garlanded Maypole; the Tree of Life stands in barren form as the cross at the point of death, but also appears as the flowering, garlanded stem of life in the moment of renewal.

You can perceive a bow to the East in "Easter" and intuit the connection between dawn and rebirth. In the oldest stories, Dawn appears as a goddess who was considered the most beautiful and resplendent presence of all beings. One of her names was Eostre, which later became Easter. She was the beautiful daughter who returns from the deepest reaches of night and appears radiant in the East as she dispels the shroud of darkness that has overtaken the world. Often she was accompanied by a troop of rabbits, whose rapid reproductive cycles seems to mimic the rampant fertility of the earth as well as the procession of endless days produced by the fecundity of the eternal nights.

Another symbol connected to the goddess of the Eastern light was an egg that often appeared golden like the sun at its dawning. In ancient creation myths, life first appears as a golden egg floating on the endless ocean of night until something hidden within it stirs. The inner life grows outward until it cracks the shell of the egg and begins the separation of darkness and light that gives us the world as we know it. Life resides and sometimes hides in the unseen golden center of the earth-shaped egg until the time comes for it to burst forth again like the light of dawn that ever seems to arise in the East. The same image serves to depict the dawning of understanding that can occur inside a person who begins to awaken to the knowledge hidden within the soul.

The Sun Falling Down

Meanwhile, Western worldviews tend to turn away from the sense of an eternal dawn and focus upon the other extreme of the earth's horizon. Western culture tends to "follow the sun" and the sun tends to move from east to west. Eventually, the sun reaches the zenith of its rising arc and begins to decline and descend towards the darkening sea. This leaves the Western world looking at the end of the great arc of life and at the edge of darkness created when the sun goes down. The old word for the Western realm was the *occident*, which means "facing the falling sun," or "sun-falling-down place." In many stories the Land of the Dead resides in the West, where the sun sets and leaves everything in the dark, implying that all is lost. Western myths and worldviews tend to be oriented towards the far end of the arc of life, towards the shadowy remains of the day and the fall of the blood-red sun into the devouring mouth of the endless ocean of night.

Rather than an eternal return of the dawn of life through endless cycles of existence, Western myths and beliefs tend to fixate upon an actual and fiery end of everything. Western religious visions often stare right at the End as if compelled by the abyss that swallows the once-resplendent sun. Caught in the mythic backdrop of apocalypse and more recently thrown off center by theories of an accidental universe, the West tends to anticipate a fiery conclusion that ends the whole drama and settles all the conflicts and confusions with a terrible but cleansing conflagration. The West tends to count down and even count *on* the end of the world preceded by some celestial fireworks.

In the irony of existence and the paradox of creation, when the end seems near, the beginning is also nearby. As conflicts throughout the world intensify and even nature seems about to overheat, it may be important for the West to turn more consciously to the East in order to gain some respite from the myth of the eternal return. East and West represent opposite worldviews and the inherent tension between the beginning and the end. At certain times throughout the course of time, the opposing orientations of East and West become important to each other. This period of seemingly unending conflicts and great uncertainty may be the exact context for East and West—beginning and end—to discover each other again. Opposites must meet when the end seems near, not necessarily at the tree of conflicts, but much more fruitfully near the deeper roots of peace and unity.

When it seems that the world might end, how a person and how a culture view the world have a greater effect than usual. The potent mythological formula of the West takes a shape that pitches mankind onto the road of progress, but it also leans towards a one-time redemption that follows a final battle of good and evil. The extroverted, historical, and factual nature of the arrangement sets the stage for politically based "holy wars," as opposed to psychological and contemplative struggles within each soul. Eastern imaginations tend to take up the idea that eternity exists within each living soul and, turning inward in knowing ways, can lead to an awakening that transcends individual suffering. In awakening to the presence of the divine within, a person can reconnect to the cycles of eternity and the breath of the undying universe.

The East tends to present the individual against the background of eternity and even the backdrop of the void. The point becomes less the celebration of the unique character and more the realization of the eternal presence and mystery that surrounds the soul. This intuition has great value when considering the life of the planet and the continuance of the world. Meanwhile, the West champions ideas of the importance and dignity of individual life and the possibility of personal redemption from the dark night of the soul. The West has a gift for stories in which the value of the individual becomes celebrated and life finds its meaning through the unique struggles of a singular soul who will never appear again in this world. Such stories help to raise consciousness of the importance of each life being meaningful and valuable and worth living to its fullest extent.

At this time, Eastern practices like yoga and meditation find their way into most corners of the Western world, and Western notions of the uniqueness and importance of the individual life penetrate the East. Truth cannot be found in a single formula or a doctrine for it is a living thing that must be fashioned again and again from the roots of learning and the branches of experience. Each soul, each era, each culture must cultivate its own sense of life and its own symbols of truth. Yet the living tree at the center remains the symbolic axis that penetrates and connects all the branching thoughts and images that constitute the religions and philosophies of humankind. Each age must bring forth and shape symbols that combine the time-bound with the eternal. Each epoch must find again the river of life and ways to cross over to the garden of eternal imagination.

Ultimately, we take mythic steps to change historical conditions, reworking the ground of imagination to open things to the touch of the eternal again. When the opposites within the world become more revealed, the trick is not to contribute to the widening split—be it the nuclear division that makes it seem humanly possible to destroy the dawn and deliver an endless dusk or the opposing religious views that battle over theories of good and evil and obscure the Tree of Life. It is as if the whole world has entered a crossroads at the same time. The difficult road to the center waits to be found again; the lesser paths that begin in opposition to each other can still lead to the greater way that brings them closer together. Perhaps there can be an exchange of mythic imaginations that benefits each side so that the uniqueness of life becomes seen against the background of the eternal return, so that dawn and sundown—beginning and end—can become connected again.

It seems to have become the time for seeking the great way again, a time for giving up the arguments over the sources and causes of evil in favor of practices that ripen the inner fruits, heal the deep divisions, and awaken the genuine projects of the soul. When all seems headed for disaster, it may be the best time to practice ways of being able to hold East and West— beginning and end—together. Sometimes, East and West must meet; beginning and end must converse and exchange forms of knowledge that can lead back to the roots of knowing and reveal the ever-living tree behind all branches of wisdom: the unifying Tree of Life.

CHAPTER 11

THE LAST THREAD

Begin to weave and the divine will provide the thread.
Old Proverb

An old Native American story of the beginning of life on earth also describes the origins of ceremonies and rituals that first brought people together in ways that increased knowledge while making healing possible. It all started long ago—back when the heavens first became separated from the primal waters allowing the earth to form in between. Once there was some solid ground, the One Who Made the Earth fashioned the first people and placed them upon it. Like everyone who has arrived on earth since then, the first people found themselves living in a particular place that had specific conditions; that was where they had to begin their journey to find the way to the center.

As it turned out those early ancestors did not like the first place they lived in. They did not rest well there and they did not dream well either. Noticing how the restlessness and lack of sleep made the people more fearful and confused, the One Who Made the Earth advised them to take a journey and seek a location more suited to their needs. (This was back at the beginning, when everything was closer and the creator could speak to people quite directly). People have been wandering off ever since. All over the earth, people leave the place of their origins for a variety of reasons. Some have trouble sleeping; others just feel restless and compelled to wander. What happens at the beginning becomes an ongoing pattern;

people still feel the urge to wander and explore as much as they feel the instinct to settle down somewhere. The grass is always greener somewhere else and at the same time, there is no place like home.

Eventually, the first people found a place that seemed to suit them. They began to sleep deeply and soon were having big dreams. They rested well and began to dwell in that place in a good way. They learned the patterns and rhythms of that environment and tuned themselves to the nature of it. Eventually, they became attached to the new place; they grew roots there and called it their homeland. Things went well and people felt that all was good with the world—at least until something happened that changed everything. There is always something unforeseen, something that was bound to happen even if no one saw it coming.

Two of those first people became ill and, day by day, they became weaker and weaker. The other people did nothing to help them because it was the very beginning and they had no knowledge about sickness or pain. No one knew anything about healing. The One Who Made the Earth spoke to the people again, saying: "Why do you ignore those who are suffering amongst you? Why don't you do something to help them? Why don't you say some words over them?" But the people had no knowledge of healing or of curing ceremonies, so nothing happened and the sick ones became increasingly weaker as if life were draining right out of them.

Then it happened that four of the people left the village at the same time. They set off at dusk and as the darkness began to gather, each took up a position facing into the oncoming night. Once the dark had completely swallowed all the light, the One Who Made the Earth spoke to one of those people who was steadfastly facing the darkness. "Everything on this earth has the power to cause its own kind of sickness or make its own kind of trouble. That is the way it is on earth. But it also must be known that for each illness the earth has a cure; for each kind of trouble on this earth there is also a remedy to be found."

The person who first heard these words now had an understanding that knowledge was available on the earth and that healing was also a possibility. That was how the process of learning started; the possibility of healing began at the same time that the awareness of knowledge entered the world. Healing and knowledge began together and they remain connected in essential ways. To this day those two aspects of life travel together, so that knowing the nature of the illness is the first part of curing it; so that being willing to face the darkness and the unknown at the edge of awareness is the first step in learning anything.

The one who had received the knowledge about healing shared it with the others who had stared into the darkness. Once they understood that a cure was possible, those four people went out and faced the darkest parts of the night at the end of each day. The next night, the one who happened to be facing to the east suddenly began to chant a prayer and sing a song. On the following night, the one facing south began to drum and play a kind of lightning song. On the third night, the one standing and facing to the west began to chant a prayer. On the fourth night, the one who gazed to the north began to drum and play another lightning song.

People ask: Did those songs come to them from the outside world? Or did the songs arise from the darkness within them? The answer is: Yes. The songs and rhythms seemed to arise from inside, just as they arrived from outside. The One Who Made the Earth seemed to give them these healing songs in both of those ways as knowledge and rhythms came to them spontaneously. Even now, knowledge involves both the inner realm and the outer world, and genuine healing includes both as well.

When those four people were standing and facing the dark again, the One Who Made the Earth said: "Why don't you go to those sick people and sing for them and say words over them and help make them well?" So the four seekers of knowledge went back to the village. They brought the sick people right to the center of that first village and they invited everyone there to join them. In that way the sickness and trouble of some became central to all and healing became central to life.

Once the circle of people had gathered around the ones who were suffering, those who had gathered knowledge began to speak words over them. They began to drum and sing the songs that had come to them from the edges of darkness. They continued to sing and speak and play rhythms until the sick ones were restored and became able to join the dance of life again. Then everyone in the village joined in the dance as if some vitality had entered all of them—as if curing those who had fallen ill added to the health and well-being of everyone else.

This healing was a new kind of knowledge and after that, whenever anyone fell ill or lost their way, they would be brought to the center where everyone would gather around them. The trouble would be made clear and those who had knowledge would begin speaking and singing and playing while everyone else paid attention to the sick folks and to the way that healing entered and affected all who became involved. That was the beginning of healing ceremonies and the inception of useful knowledge that made it possible for everyone to come together and dispel that which could otherwise isolate some and eventually separate everyone.

This is an old story; the kind the elders would tell when times became dark again, when everything became obscure and threatening the way it was when illness first appeared and seemed to come out of nowhere. Of course, the elders did not mind the focus upon the darkness; after all, their sight was not what it used to be. More than that though, they liked the way genuine visions came from the darkest directions. The compelling dreams that are essential in the lives of young people come in the middle of the night and the visions of the elders tend to arise when they consciously face the things that have become most dark and troubling to everyone around them.

Becoming an elder involves learning to see in ways that go far beyond simple self-interest. In the old times, the elders would have to consider the effects of their decisions and actions on unseen generations. They had to look way past their own feelings like the four people who first stood facing the darkness in order to find knowledge. Imagine the current leaders in most places today trying to do that. The ancient notion of the elders had less to do with political power and social leadership and more to do with healing and deeper knowledge. It used to be considered that each genuine elder had some form of healing to contribute to this world. Elders were people who had survived the troubles of their own lives and had gathered some wisdom from facing the darkness within as well as what troubled other people in the outer world.

Since they knew that all people were bound to find themselves in trouble at some point and that darkness could overcome anyone at any time, they kept a fond eye out for the young folks who were always headed for trouble. They knew that young people had to find their dreams and had to enter enough darkness in order for the big dreams to form. The young ones were included when everyone gathered to face some trouble or try some healing methods. That way they might learn what kind of knowledge intrigued them and which paths in life might offer a way for them to begin their search for the great way. At that time it was clearer that in order for people to keep going in a good way the young people had to find their dreams and the old folks had to develop vision that could see into the darkness of the future.

Facing Darkness

In facing the darkness, the first people found some knowledge and learned about healing ways. They began to understand the old notion that suggests that we all should let the darkness season us. In facing whatever sickness or trouble appeared amongst others, they learned how to bring everyone together and make everyone stronger. Back at the beginning people were closer to each other and it was easier to see how the illness of one or two could secretly diminish the health of everyone.

The first people were "exemplary;" they set the example for how to deal with sickness and trouble. What they found at the beginning waits to be found again whenever things become dark and troubling. We are the inheritors of their knowledge and of the natural instincts for healing and surviving whatever troubles come along. The notion that anything in this world can cause sickness or trouble certainly still holds true. Some might say that it is truer now than at any other time. To be alive at the end of an era means to be caught in a growing darkness that troubles the sleep of almost everyone. The issues of resting well and having meaningful dreams have returned with a vengeance. The darkness around us seems to grow deeper each day and reactions of blind fear and terror seem to increase as well. Unwittingly, modern people may have arrived back at the place where the first people were when they recognized that something was quite wrong but had no idea how to initiate healing or handle the troubles.

In many old traditions, a sick or seriously troubled person would be brought to the center of the community. Often, a design would be traced on the ground—a circle, a mandala, or a tree—and it would represent the original design and implicate order of the cosmos. The person suffering the most would be placed there, in the midst of everyone, in the middle of everything, in the center of the cosmos. Of course, in the old understanding the center was also considered to be the beginning, the navel of existence from which all of life emerged and flowed. Bringing those who were on the edge of death, or even at their "wit's end," to the center could also bring them back to the origins of life.

Symbolically, the troubled soul would be brought back to the place where its invisible umbilical cord could be reconnected to the source of all life. Since the beginning harbors all potentials, the sick one could draw upon the potency of the beginning in order to start over again. Healing was not simply a medical situation, but also an opportunity for a greater renewal of life. All the troubles that eat away at people could be placed in the center, which was also the beginning and therefore the place of renewal. Often the words spoken to the troubled souls included creation stories— how things began when the earth first formed, back at the beginning before time began to wear people down. It was another way of knowledge and an attempt to bring the force of creation to those who felt life to be draining away from them.

This kind of treatment was used for all sorts of ailments including mental troubles, the loss of soul, depression, and the kind of trauma that plagues those who survive a war yet bring the battle of life and death back to their village. If the troubles eating away at one person could be shared by everyone, the pain and trauma could be more evenly distributed and be less overwhelming, and people would become less reluctant to bring the inner issues out into the light. Beyond that, gathering together for the purpose of healing could help everyone become less inclined to develop all the common ways of encouraging conflict and strife or else harboring feelings of resentment and revenge.

The Center is the Beginning

Unlike ideas that suggest that enlightenment might be found by imagining figures of light, the old stories and teaching tales prefer the kind of knowledge and quality of healing that comes from visiting the darkness. Notice how going to the edge and facing the darkest places can lead to both individual as well as collective awakenings. Ways to bring healing to the great conflicts and troubles that currently threaten the world might elude people unless we learn ways to face the darkness of the situation. There are similarities between running towards the roar, entering into the ashes, and accepting the presence of the black dog of chaos. All stories attempt some kind of healing or revelation of essential knowledge; all depend upon the presence of trouble and a willingness to enter the unknown.

Mythically, the center of one thing leads to the center of everything. Seen in this way, the illness of one person becomes the ailment through which all that ails a community can be addressed; the wound in one person can become the door through which everyone can find the center of life again. Thus, the afflicted one becomes the center of the community and the opportunity for everyone to commune with the origins of life. That is why people used to say that the afflicted are holy; they are one way through which holiness and healing keep trying to enter this world.

At the center, the original flow of energies, ideas, and images can return to life. If people connect to the origins, things might begin again. The center remains the source of unlived potentials, fresh starts, and second chances. Remember Icanchu who was able to stimulate life from the ashes by singing and dancing when it seemed that the entire world had been destroyed? The center contains all the potentials and potencies of life. The beginning involves the primordial sound that still reverberates and resonates throughout the earth.

The lightning of learning strikes where the darkness is deep. Despite their apparent simplicity, the old tales try to show the way to healing and surviving in this world. A time of increased darkness and apocalypse bring a greater danger of being devoured by huge energies rising from the depths that are being churned as time turns over and things turn around. On the other hand, things turn mythic again and healing and knowledge become available right where the darkness gathers. Facing the darkness can begin an about-face that brings the potentials of the beginning back into sight. We live in such in-between conditions, at a time when the betwixt and between quality of life becomes more revealed—a threshold time where endings and beginnings can change places rapidly.

Call it initiatory time, when some things must be left behind; call it revelatory time as many things become uncovered and revealed, when knowledge might be delivered directly as it was when the first seekers faced into the darkness. Those living in a particular time or era are not simply the denizens of history or the pawns of time, but are also the only possible recipients of the messages of eternity trying to slip into the world and sustain the eternal drama of life, death, and rebirth. The initiatory path opens whenever and wherever a person allows the intimations of the otherworld to enter and clarify what needs to be left behind and what needs to be revealed in order for life to be healed and made whole again, if only for a moment.

We live in initiatory times when each soul can feel more isolated amidst the dying breath of one world and the uncertainty that attends the forming of life's next design. It is not the lack of time that we as modern people suffer from, but a lack of connection to things timeless, mythic, and eternal. Like the moments of awakening to knowledge and healing experienced by the first people who willingly faced the darkness, the most real moments in life are timeless and mythic and open to the sacred. Seen with a mythic eye, each moment is potentially momentous, each instant capable of opening before us as the dream-world does each time we fall into the timeless realms of sleep. As the veil lifts on the wounded cycles of both nature and culture, the symbolic sense of re-viewing and revaluing life can lead to both new ideas and the return of genuine knowledge and earthly wisdom.

Myth offers a genuine sense of re-creation, a "recovery" process through which we rediscover the Real world with its metaphysical, mythical, and imaginal shapes. Myth is a vehicle of knowledge, a means of liberation from the "spells of the obvious," and a source of renewal for exhausted time. The ancient Irish had a mythic sense for how to weave the world back into fullness when the center went missing and all seemed about to fall apart and be doomed to darkness. Not too surprisingly, the old tale of renewal involved both the story of collective life and the individual story trying to awaken and unfold from within each individual.

The Secret Fifth

There were four main provinces in Ireland, but the old *word* for province literally meant "the fifth." Each mention of the word *province* would have a double meaning. On one hand, it was a reference to a particular area of the country; on the other, it was an oblique reference to something unseen, the "secret fifth." The fifth province was similar to the third layer of life, where universal truths could be learned and deep and abiding feelings of unity and oneness could be experienced. The fifth province was the unseen center, the place of tolerance and compassion, and the locus of reconciliation of all differences. It was the quintessence that held all other places together; the place for healing injustices, for forgiving offense and for touching the sacred roots of renewal.

The secret fifth was the most ancient place as well as the most immediate, ever-present ground of great spontaneity. It was hard to define, impossible to circumscribe, yet was always nearby. Time was radically altered there, so that a short time in terms of this world could be an eternity there. If something in the world had gone missing, it was sure to be found in the secret fifth province. And when the center of the world had gone missing, it too could be found where the fifth resided. It was one of the open secrets of life that the fifth represented the unifying center that is always being lost. It was where all the keys that fell into the dark wound up and where the lost key to forming a true community of awakened souls could be found.

When the dark times came, as they certainly did, when the center of life could not hold and chaos was loosed upon the realm, when disorientation became the common shape of life and the four directions seemed about to be blown to the wind, then the unifying fifth direction would have to be sought again. If the secret fifth could not be found at the center it had to be sought and found at the edges of the land, in the darkest places and along the misty cliffs where the otherworld plays hide-and-seek with those used to solid ground.

If people were willing to go towards the darkness, in the direction that seemed darkest to them, then each would find something of meaning and value. For the elements of the missing center were only to be rediscovered at the edges of life and in the margins where people suffer; where healing is most needed and knowledge can also be found. In facing the darkness, people would find a thread of meaning that could tie them to a specific work, a meaningful project that would carry them beyond their usual self, an art that could draw the Muses close, or a practice that could bring knowledge to places where ignorance prevailed and healing where the pain was greatest.

No one would have to trouble themselves over saving the world or coming up with the right idea or righteous way for everyone to go. But each person would find a thread of meaning and purpose that could tie them to the world while also drawing upon the unseen threads of the eternal world behind the world. If people would pull the unique thread of their own life from the edge of darkness and back to the center, the secret fifth would be reconstituted and be present in the middle of life again. Since the center is also the beginning trying to begin again, everything could start over. From the ends of all the threads that try to draw people onto the paths of meaning and purpose the great way could be found again and the beginning could be made anew.

Amidst the current unraveling and flood of radical changes and the conflicts threatening to tear the earth apart, there can be no shortage of meaningful tasks, healing adventures, and worthwhile projects. Each of us can find gainful employment nearby—whether it is in the margins of culture or amidst the mysteries and profundities of nature—if we are willing to face some darkness and be in the right trouble. In the willingness to face the troubles of life and lend a hand to creation we might discover the "seeing instruments" that allow us to develop genuine foresight and valuable insights. Seen in this way, the effort of each person initiates a reversal of the unraveling begun by the black dog of chaos. Each imitates to one degree or another the Old Woman of the World who boldly faces the mess of things and bends down to pick up a thread from all the chaos and confusion that has entered the world and begins weaving the living garment of the world all over again.

In this way, there is no need to know what plan is best or whom everyone must follow, for the new design will appear from the creative darkness all around us. From the eloquence of the beginning, the original sound and song of life will be heard again as it continues to murmur and sigh, to resonate and hum and whisper its many-tongued, living language that continues to articulate the shapes and forms and dreams of creation ongoing.

ACKNOWLEDGEMENTS

The seeds of this book were planted when young people repeatedly asked me if the world might come to an end soon. In the course of making the book, the seeds were watered and tended by many people who have provided encouragement and inspiration. Especially, I want to express my gratitude to the stalwarts at Mosaic, Jacob Lakatua and Peter Fedofsky, who wear many hats and gracefully juggle many tasks; to Anthony Crispino, Jack Kornfield, Luis Rodriguez and Lou Dangles for continuous support; to Rick Simonson, Lisa Thompson and Molly Blumenstein for creative input and editing.

Stories

Index

and anxiety, 27
and awakening, 44
and death, 166
and safety, 26
facing, 163
meaning of, 43
of apocalypse, 17
Final judgment, 4
Fire
as symbol, 173
Fish
as symbol, 145
Fundamentalism, 8, 10, 16, 27, 28, 33, 62, 82, 117
and economics, 36
meaning of, 186
Garden of Eden, 59, 119, 209
Genius, 21, 97, 101, 143
Gifts, 90
and second adventure, 91
inner, 98
Gnosis, 90
God
meaning of, 166
Golden Age, 59
Hamsa, 170
Healing, 117, 189, 191, 192, 206, 214, 223
and change, 97
and knowledge, 215
and otherworld, 221
and soul, 193
Heart, 122–124, 201
Heraclitus, 173
Heresy
meaning of, 202
Hero's Journey, 57
Hidden gold, 85
Hidden third, 30, 33
Hidden thread, 38
History, 106
Icanchu, 174, 220
Ideologies, 11, 28, 30, 31, 36

Illusion, 164, 168
meaning of, 158
Imagination, 2, 33, 44, 61, 75, 77, 78, 93, 107, 109, 113, 115, 125, 143, 153, 161, 184, 194
and creation, 82, 83
and loss, 35
and soul, 66
and stories, 24
and tension of the opposites, 34
collective, 129
crisis of, 65
hidden, 34
loss of, 37, 124
mythic, 16, 17–18
roots of, 76
Individual
creative, 33
meaning of, 32
Initiation, 38, 92, 221
thread of, 95
Isis, 132
Ja-ni, 15
Jesus, 5
Job, 10
John of Patmos, 4, 16
and end times, 7
Judgment
final, 39, 165
Kairos, 71–72
moments, 72, 74, 92
Kali
meaning of, 160
Kali Yuga, 160–161
Knowledge, 36, 49, 70, 107, 113, 136, 158, 162, 213, 214
and folk myths, 127
and healing, 215
as gift, 120
darker, 53, 91
genuine, 50
of the soul, 66
transcendent, 119

ABOUT MOSAIC

Mosaic Multicultural Foundation is a 501(c)3 nonprofit organization, a network of artists, social activists, and community builders. Mosaic formed to create cross-cultural alliances, mentoring relationships, and social connections that encourage greater understanding between diverse peoples, elders and youth, and those of various cultural and spiritual backgrounds.

Mosaic means putting essential pieces together; forming a whole from separate, divided, even estranged parts. The process of finding, fitting, and weaving together divergent, yet necessary pieces involves making new social fabrics from existing ethnic, spiritual, psychological, and political threads.

Mosaic events draw inspiration from the traditions of many cultures and incorporate knowledge learned in the trenches of contemporary community work. Efforts at problem solving rely on locating the genius of the situation, as the unique spirit of each individual becomes a key to understanding issues and fitting the pieces of community together in new ways.

Mosaic's nationwide youth and mentoring projects help veterans return from war, assist addicts in recovery, and inspire youth to find their way in life. Current projects involve homeless and at-risk youth, high school and college students, combat veterans, tribal communities, as well as those in detention and on probation. The practice of mentoring offers the oldest, most natural, and most effective method for awakening genius in youth, creating mentors, and developing elders.

GreenFire Press and **Mosaic Audio** are imprints of Mosaic Multicultural Foundation that serve to foster cultural literacy, mythic education, and multicultural community development. Proceeds from sales of books and recordings directly benefit Mosaic's work with at-risk youth, refugees, and intercultural projects.

For more information or to order additional titles contact Mosaic:
4218 1/2 SW Alaska, Suite H Seattle, WA 98126
(206)935-3665, toll free (800)233-6984
www.mosaicvoices.org ~ info@mosaicvoices.org

Books by Michael Meade

Fate and Destiny: The Two Agreements of the Soul

The Water of Life: Initiation and the Tempering of the Soul

Mosaic Audio Recordings by Michael Meade

Alchemy of Fire: Libido and the Divine Spark

Branches of Mentoring

The Ends of Time, the Roots of Eternity

Entering Mythic Territory: Healing and the Bestowing Self

The Eye of the Pupil, the Heart of the Disciple

Fate and Destiny: The Two Agreements in Life

The Great Dance: Finding One's Way in Troubled Times

Holding the Thread of Life: A Human Response to the Unraveling of the World

Inner Wisdom: The Eternal Youth and the Wise Old Sage

The Light Inside Dark Times

Initiation and the Soul: The Sacred and the Profane

Poetics of Peace: Peace and the Salt of the Earth

Poetics of Peace: Vital Voices in Troubled Times, with Alice Walker, Luis Rodriguez, Jack Kornfield, Orland Bishop

The Soul of Change

Books edited by Michael Meade

Crossroads: The Quest For Contemporary Rites of Passage, edited by Louise Carus Mahdi, Nancy Geyer Christopher, and Michael Meade

The Rag and Bone Shop of the Heart: A Poetry Anthology, edited by Robert Bly, James Hillman, and Michael Meade

Books including contributions by Michael Meade

Rites and Symbols of Initiation, Mircea Eliade

Teachers of Myth, Maren Tonder Hansen

All purchases from Mosaic Audio and GreenFire Press support work with at-risk youth, refugees, and intercultural projects.

For more information or to order additional titles contact Mosaic:
4218 1/2 SW Alaska, Suite H Seattle, WA 98126
(206)935-3665, toll free (800)233-6984
www.mosaicvoices.org ~ info@mosaicvoices.org